LAUNCH INTO
INTERIOR DESIGN

a beginner's guide to the industry

Jenny Kennedy

Kennedy Literary Agency

ISBN: 978-1-7776548-1-8

Cover design by: Annie Spratt on Unsplash
Library of Congress Control Number: 2018675309
Printed in the United States of America

CONTENTS

DEDICATION

To my parents, who never fail to support their family and are the very definition of 'dedication'. Thank you is not adequate but perhaps it is enough.

To my children, dream without limitations and find magic in each day. You are my greatest joy and blessing. My inspiration.

To the people who believe in me, you know who you are. You have kept the wheels from falling off this crazy train a time or two. I learned what unconditional love means because of you.

To my Bella, who interrupted me a million times while writing this book but whose company I miss dearly every single day.

INTRODUCTION

As a child, I had many dreams about what I would be when I grew up. They ranged from architect, veterinarian, archaeologist, travel agent and interior designer. I would have been the female combination of an animal-loving "Indiana Jones." I would roam the world collecting art and artifacts to bring back and decorate my fabulous loft apartment. When it came time to choose a career path, I did not see this description anywhere on the list of college or university courses. Frankly, I think I was intimidated by having to choose only one. Instead, I decided to go into banking, which seemed secure, and I already had a job offer.

After three children, two career changes and twelve years, I was ready to try my hand in a business where I could be creative and satisfy some of my dreams. I did not see many opportunities for Ms. Indiana Jones. Still, I could capitalize on the home staging trend that was taking off.

That was my start in interior design. I took a course on home staging. I attended a business class to teach me about managing my company, marketing strategies and problem-solving. I started my home-based business with my heart in my throat and my dreams in my hand.

In the past sixteen years, I developed a successful staging and design business that lead to a full-time design position with a well-known design centre in my area. I discovered a passion for digging into my clients' projects to find the perfect color, window coverings and décor. I found my most outstanding talent was intuitively learning my client's needs and then tailoring the consultation towards meeting them. My services included color consultation, staging homes for sale in the real estate market, custom blind sales, drapery design, and later flooring, counter-top and tile selection. I offered home decor that I sourced, which quickly became a favorite element of my career. I wrote design articles for my local newspaper. I built my reputation until I was doing ten to twelve consultations a week.

What I found was while I was learning new skills with my home staging company, I could "see" the finished result in my mind's eye, something that my clients could not. That is when I knew I had the unique ability to put a plan into place for them with confidence, knowing the result would be fabulous! When a client loved the suggestion I had made? Those consultations were the most fun, and often, the most satisfying for every-one. Over the years, I gained knowledge in various elements of design. But who wants to wait years to know all the practical hands-on techniques?

Being fresh out of school, or even just thinking of becoming an interior designer, means you are eager and willing to learn. "Launch into Interior Design" will provide you with some of my tried-and-true methods in running a successful interior design business. All of which give you more experience in your back pocket as you break into this fascinating and creative field.

With the information I provide, you will have a solid under-standing of design fundamentals. Your focus can be on gaining clients and developing your creative abilities without the train-ing wheels.

This book aims to give you knowledge that typically comes with experience before you end up learning the hard way on a project. As you read through, take notes or highlight any how-to's you may want to refer to or incorporate into your own busi-ness.

In the first chapter, we focus on your personality as an inter-ior designer, the aspects of working with the client and initial consultations, collaborating with contractors and suppliers, and the equipment you will need.

The order of the remaining chapters is crucial. They show

you the order of selection from flooring and cabinetry to paint and simplifies the process with solid reasoning. By following the guide, the subsequent design element selection process becomes more straight forward. However, the order of product selection does not mean the order of installation. Those are two different things.

My goal is to help develop your design business to understand your customers' needs better and have a memorable and successful outcome on every project. The confidence you create and the energy you project becomes electrifying to your clients. Their trust in your judgment comes easier.

I am so excited to take you through the steps and share my insights!

Thank you for investing your time, energy and money in this book, but also for investing in yourself. I hope you find the information here invaluable to your own business from my sixteen years of eye-opening, headshaking, heart-warming, heart-thumping, breath-taking, gut-wrenching, humbling and exciting experiences.

Jenny Kennedy

CHAPTER ONE - INITIAL SET-UP

In This Chapter, You Will Learn...

- About different types of designers and where you fall
- How our ego can show our strengths and weaknesses
- Payment and policies
- Equipment you will need.
- How the client ticks and the initial consultation questionnaire
- About in-home consultations
- Meeting contractors, suppliers and salespeople

This chapter will get you thinking about how you will operate as a designer and how your style may meet some clients' needs more than others. It helps you correlate your strengths with the client's best interests for smooth interaction.

This chapter also gives you the information you need to understand a thorough consultation process and determine a course of action that is precise and pleasing. Essentially, this chapter is about you!

The Designer In You

Starting a career as an Interior Designer can be intimidating. We rely heavily on the ability to "sell" our creative skills. Not just to potential clients, but employers as well. Some of us come to interior design with diplomas and accreditation—others with practical hands-on knowledge and the ability to learn on the fly. I was the latter of the two.

My confidence did not happen overnight. The more I talked with potential clients and made connections through networking and trade events, the more I understood how to apply my skills and knowledge. Thankfully, I was successful enough to develop a positive reputation. I got referrals to my clients' friends and family.

Opportunities can come when you least expect them! I found myself offered a position with a large design company in my area after three years of operating my company. While it meant giving up my business to take the job, it also meant that I would have constant exposure to design clients and a tremendous amount of experience.

Listening to my client's struggles with their home's function or how they were just ready for a change, I discovered what caused them confusion. It was the information they were receiving from outside sources. The best friends, neighbors and even other trade professionals made a great list of examples of what not to do and what they should do. Still, quite often, they did not consider the client's preferences. The design of a person's home is as unique as the individuals living there, and their space should reflect that.

This chapter is about understanding yourself as a designer, how you navigate decisions and discovering your strengths. Getting an idea of where your challenges are is equally important because you then know where to improve and when to look for outside guidance for help.

Types Of Designers

Quite often, my client started the consultation, lost and confused. After going through the process I developed, they were smiling and relieved to head in the right direction. I will admit, being a keen listener and intuitive to clients' needs and wants is a unique skill that has served me well. I also discovered not everyone has the same approach.

In my experience, there are two types of interior designers. That is not to say that each of us is not unique with our flair for doing things. But with two kinds of designers comes two categories of clients, and each is more suited for the other. It goes without judgement, as it's about who is better suited to fit a client's needs.

Designer One:

Is confident, assured, powerful mental "eye" and can quickly visualize a design for their client after a short time. After gathering the critical information, this designer can tell the customer how the project will look, the steps and the time frame for completion. I like to call them the "tell you what to do" designers. This designer is happiest when they can pull from multiple sources and selections to bring a vision board together for their client's approval. They are mostly working on their own with a little direction after the original consultation.

In turn, the client who utilizes this kind of designer does not have the time to focus on their design project. They could also be so unsure of themselves, unable to visualize any part of the project. They heavily rely on their design professional to pull it all together for them. Overly anxious homeowners get reassurance by someone else "calling the shots," so to speak. Those without the time to decorate look for a designer to make quick and concise decisions with their instructions. That is where that confidence comes into play.

The upside of this situation is designers can get their creative juices flowing if they are working within the allotted budget. They must be careful to have their client sign off on all decisions and be very clear about where the responsibility lies if the client not like something once purchased or installed. These designers can fall prey to expensive problems if their client believes they did not choose or approve the item or design. I have seen this happen.

Designer Two:

Easy going, creative, empathetic, cooperative and can easily communicate their client's needs back to them. This designer listens closely to the client's desires and asks many questions designed to get a good feel of their personality. They have a strong mental ability to "see" the project in their head. This designer can quickly see where their clients have been struggling, make quick suggestions to get them off on the right foot and create a plan that includes them in the decision-making process. Designer Two helps their client visualize the project for themselves and give their input as ideas begin to flow.

The client who often fits better with this style of designer is one who loves the idea of designing their own home and wants some extra expertise. Sometimes they just need a little direction, such as a paint color consultation, or they just want reassurance as they make decisions through their renovation. Clients are more likely to meet in stores and with suppliers to go over products and colors with their designers. Often, a designer can develop a strong relationship with their clients and generate a positive stream of referral business.

The interior designer and the homeowners are working closely together in the selection and design process. More ideas flow, and the client will truly get to feel as though they *own* the process. Clients can be more dependent on their designer for every decision that they have to make. They must carefully maneuver this situation to ensure that the designer is compensated for their time while still caring for their client's needs.

Designers are often asked, "What would you do if it were you?" Designer One is more likely to give direction without pause. Designer Two is more likely to ask questions, discover their client's tastes and then offer different alternatives that will appeal to them.

The client/designer relationship is always a little bit of each situation. However, knowing which you are more comfortable with will find you gravitating towards a specific comfort zone. There is a client for every designer and a designer for every client. Sometimes a designer will recognize that they are not quite the right fit or visa versa. Rather than take it personally, offer the client a referral to someone who would compliment them better. Believe me, if you are not the right person, they will not have hard feelings over it. The more professional you are, and the quicker you release any disappointment over it, the more positive the energy between everyone involved.

The Ego

The ego is a delicate subject. The word ego usually has such a negative connotation to it. It is the ego that criticizes others' confidence, talent or projects. It also stems from a fear that our abilities will not measure up to our competition or our client's expectations. I have witnessed some rather ugly ego-based behaviour from fellow designers. It sours their credibility with colleagues and clients alike.

It also promotes a rather unprofessional reputation, which is the opposite of what our goal should be.

Confidence is the ability to believe in ourselves and creates an element of thriving in our personal and professional lives. Our ego, rather than the former version, is how we identify ourselves. "This is who I am." Confidence is knowing ourselves and what we are capable of. However, when we let our ego run wild, we find ourselves bragging, bossing people around, losing sight of empathy. In general, we can come across as overbearing. We have all done it at some point in our lives. Some have grabbed hold of that persona and run with it.

I have met my share of designers and watched their interactions with people. Some successful designers are self-assured and don't question themselves. However, I believe the most promising are the designers who not only keep their ego in check but are humble and easy-going too. Do not get me wrong; there is a time and place where a person must be firm on what they expect and deliver strong communication. There is more progress when everyone is respectful, considerate and polite.

Being genuinely interested in all the people you are working with pays off. Solid relationships with your tradespeople, suppliers, clients and colleagues mean you have a team at your disposal. You have the support you need when the doody hits the fan — because it will.

If you glare, become sarcastic, and take your frustrations out on people, not only will they not perform well, but they will not be supporting you when you need it the most. Reacting with a poor attitude when your client gives you an adverse reaction to your ideas, the client will immediately shut down. Things can become problematic very quickly. You can lose their business without hearing from them again. It is not their job to cater to your emotions.

Having confidence is being compassionate, knowledgeable, interested, assured, creative, eager, desirable, energetic, understanding, cheerful, happy, approachable, curious and proud.

Being ego-driven is distant, cocky, snobby, confrontational, unapproachable, two-faced, easily upset, unrealistic, persistent, lack of understanding, overwhelmed, intolerant, chauvinistic, and prideful.

Again, we can be all these things at different points of our lives or in varying degrees. Still, a successful professional is not out to eat people for lunch and win at any cost. They want to take people with them, find ways to build connections and give more than they take.

Your client's personality may lean more in one direction or the other as well. You may decide to work with them no matter what or choose to pass on the project, knowing that they may be too difficult to work with. In looking at our behavior and that of our clients, we can recognize some potentially sticky situations and steer ourselves in a more positive direction. Our journey is to have a happy, healthy career, after all, and anything less than that aspiration will pull you from your goal. Keep your intentions in the forefront of your mind with every interaction. And keep your ego in check.

Strengths And Challenges

I love helping people. That is my main intention whenever I start with a client. It is not necessarily my skill as a designer that I believe in the most. I will endeavor to find the most innovative products and solutions within their budget that I can. I know that I am exceptional at relating to people. I am a great listener and have developed almost a sixth sense of interpreting what a client likes, dislikes or might consider.

I selected paint colors with a woman hoping to update her home a little but was nervous about integrating livelier colors. After looking over her furniture, art and other elements, I decided it was worth trying a color that she was not expecting. I selected a color called "Azores" from Benjamin Moore, a lovely medium toned sea blue with a slight green undertone. When I looked at my client for her reaction, she looked wide-eyed back and forth between me and the paint chip.

"What made you select that color?" She squinted at me.

I was not quite sure about her reaction. I thought perhaps she did not like it, and a re-selection was needed. I looked at the sample and back at her. "I felt it might have been something you liked."

Her expression did not change. She kept looking at me with a puzzled expression, and I was starting to get uncomfortable. *Did I really mess up here?*

"But why did you pick *that* color?" She asked again.

"I don't know specifically. It was just an impulse." I am sure I shrugged. I am sure I looked concerned and likely more confused than she was. I could only wait for her to clarify why she was questioning me.

"I have no idea how you did that." She said. "I can't believe it! You really didn't choose that color for another reason?"

I just shook my head.

"I am from the Azores Islands!"

It fell into place, and I was just as surprised as she was. Of course, she painted the color in her home, and I walked away realizing that there was a little more going on than just picking things out for people. An instinct or intuition pulled me in the direction of the perfect color that suited my client on a personal level. I was just as amazed as she was that this *coincidence* had just occurred. It taught me to trust myself more, to go with my gut and be playful with ideas. Sometimes, you just need to try out the impulse and see where it takes you.

With time, you will develop these skills too. The more you follow your instincts and pay attention to your client's reaction, the sooner you will feel confident in your selections.

I realized a vital component of successfully navigating design projects was my ability to empathize with my clients. I could dig into their preferences and go with my instincts based on my expertise and the information they gave me.

When I was not so successful, I rushed, did not trust myself, and was distracted. There were the odd times where I just did not jive with the client. Everything that I seemed to suggest frustrated them further, or I could not read their reaction. When I realized the client needed someone who would just tell them an overall concept and then let the designer handle the project. It is my strength to know that I lean more towards Designer Two because I enjoy working with my clients and helping them make empowered decisions. Once I knew this about myself, I released any feelings of disappointment, confusion or failure when I did not exactly hit it off with someone.

To determine your strengths and challenges, write out your responses to these questions. Let's start with finding your strengths. Dig into your answers to see where you shine.

What activities make you feel the most creative?

What activities make you the happiest?

What do people tell you that you are good at?
What skills do you feel you excel in?
What appeals to you about a career in interior
design?
What do you love about working with people?
What makes you feel confident in yourself?

Now let's investigate where we may have some challenges. Do not be afraid of your answers. It is just a way of knowing where you can focus some continued learning or feel more comfortable referring to other professionals for help.

What does appeal to you about a career in interior
design?
What do people tell you that you struggle with?
What is your reaction when someone does not like what
you created/suggested/made?
What do you not love about working with people?
What is your recaction when organizing multiple tasks?
What skills do you feel you need improvement on?
What designer describes you more? Designer One or
Two? Why?
Do you operate from confidence or ego?
Describe what it means for you to operate from each.

After writing your responses, how are you feeling? Do you feel like you have a clearer picture of how you will apply your marvellous self to your career? Hopefully, it has shown you where you have the most confidence or perhaps some ego issues going on. Now you can find ways to highlight your strengths and redirect yourself through challenges. Every encounter is a chance to learn and evolve our skills. Stay open to new concepts, genuinely hearing the input you are receiving and trusting your gut instincts. Having a strong ability to filter what sounds viable or utter rubbish (with a smile on your face) will get you a lot farther, especially in your design career.

Your Style

Finding the unique style that sets you apart from other designers is part of the fun! What you will incorporate into your brand, your designs and even exclude determines your professional stamp. How does a new designer choose this for themselves? Research baby!

Design magazines are a great place to start. Flipping through the pages, we are eager to see what new trends are happening, the colors used, and the furnishings featured. As designers, we are predisposed to assess a room and determine what it needs or what to eliminate.

Out of fairness, no one was the fly on the wall to see the designer's process with her clients or what they chose. It is a unique creation each time. We can appreciate the little elements and thought that went into every corner of the room.

Magazines are not our only influence. We see television shows, social media accounts, competitors' advertisements, show homes, home-shows and trade events. Some of our favorite famous designers show up on all these creative marketing platforms. Those of us who have completed course work have studied specific genres and eras, some of which we have loved and others we outright despised. With each decade, we evolve into fresh new looks or tweak a genre from the past, and if it is popular enough, a whole new trend takes off. But it is all subjective. Everyone's taste is so specific to each person, including our own.

It is fascinating to soak all the current trends in and be inspired by it all. So, where does your style develop? Where do you apply your creative abilities?

What makes us talented as designers are not that we have better taste than everyone else. Well, in some cases, yes, it is true!

But those folks are usually not the ones who care about getting a design consultation anyhow.

You need a style of your own; not in terms of *this is what all my designs look like*. Instead, all your clients will have your specific brand applied to their experience with you while achieving a personal space that is still their own.

A talented designer, in my books, is one who can put their own taste aside and work with their client's preferences while creating a unique and genuine design tailored specifically for them. It's one that can work with any style their client may have. Overcoming the space's challenges and showcasing the clients' personalities in their home is the makings of greatness. Especially when the couple does not see eye to eye!

Of course, your ability to determine what works or looks good in their home comes down to style and taste, where sometimes you need to use your own to guide folks along. This is where your branding comes in.

Knowing what will suit their home's age and style is vital—including the type of furniture or the kind of art they select. Understanding their reaction to specific colors or patterns is essential. There are many associations with color to consider, trust me. Why you love something does not mean a thing unless the client loves it too. In my experience, I found that once I worked through a series of questions with the client, I had a better feel of who they were and what direction to go. What I like and how I like to live in my home means squat to anyone else...though I have had a lot of people say, "I would love to see what your house looks like!"

It does take some originality, creative problem solving, and a little retail therapy to bring a room together. Clients who can do this for themselves do. Those who have some idea of what they like but need direction or flat out do not have the time to do the work often seek out professional advice.

One look does not work in every house. One style does not work for every person.

If you are always giving the same advice, the same design,

the same *feel*, then your work as a designer will become pigeon-holed into a dead-end street. One day, people will want something less generic and more personalized, and you will find your business dwindling. A cookie-cutter approach will only work until everyone has had a taste of that kind of cookie.

To avoid that scenario, I recommend getting into design studios to see the selection of wallpaper, fabric, furnishings and decor items. Get a feel of what your clients are likely being influenced by and see what excites you. Understanding what items complement each other and suit a specific theme creates a mental catalog that you can pull from when that look happens to fit a client. Absorb the atmosphere of little out of the way shops, use other businesses and professionals to inspire you. Go ahead and strike up conversations about the manufacturing of items, if they are organic or locally sourced. Look at all kinds of price ranges and qualities. Dig for the gold mine of selection available to you.

Clients want to come shopping with you, and nothing impresses them more than when you say, "I know the perfect place to take you! You will love it!" Especially when you have so many hidden spots to choose from and find something to suit almost every customers' desire.

Allow your client's ideas and love of colors, even that are contrary to your own, without judgment. Hear them out. Let their creative juices get involved for a more organic experience. Then the magic happens! You can weave their ideas with your originality in ways they had never thought of, and with a flare, you can be pleasantly surprised as well.

We will go into more detail in the coming chapters. At this point, I want you to consider what your most significant fashion and design influences are. What creative talent are you eager to bring to the table?

Write down a list of your favorite stores. Write down a list of stores and businesses that you intend to investigate. Determine if there is a theme and look for genre gaps. Investigate companies that can fill in the gap and make a list of those. Now, write down what makes them stand out to you.

Next, it is time to write down what elements your business brand will have and what it will not. Perhaps you refuse to use Bohemian crochet wall hangings, or you always use a feature of navy blue. Maybe you are more inclined towards holistic clientele and will never design anything remotely western or country. The more you define who you are as a designer, the better you can direct yourself to your target market.

Payment And Policies

As a designer, clients are asking for your expertise. Essentially you are there to help your customer achieve their goals. The trick is to know how much of your skills are required to accomplish them and the customer's expectations.

We will go into the actual consultation process; however, you must have the right documents ready to go before your appointment with the client. You need to know in advance what services you offer, what you do not, what you will be charging, how you will be charging and what your policies are.

I started with consultation services that often entailed a minimum of one hour at an hourly rate. Then there were the times that I was on a lengthy project, and I had to consider a lump sum fee for a set period. Only you can decide how you want to develop your business and how to be compensated. The best way to determine this is to know what other designers charge in your area. Secondly, consider all the questions that a customer may have around compensation, as well as the loopholes you could find yourself in. Third, be fair but do not sell yourself short. You are the expert, after all.

Once you have gathered the information you need and have set your pricing schedule, it is time to start writing a contract agreement. Document the expectations of both you as the designer and them as a paying customer. Customers do not always understand that three phone calls a day should be compensatable time. For example, I had a client who had me come for a color consultation at their business. Everything went well, and the results were lovely. They paid their consultation fee for the appropriate amount of time and even referred me to other clients. But after that, instead of having me consult in person on the next project, they would just call me up for free advice over the phone.

In this case, I had gained a fair amount of referral business from this client, and I decided that was a fair trade without mentioning anything to them. However, some love to get free advice and take advantage of your skills. I have had those situations too. It is a tough conversation to have later when you have not given them a document that details how you expect payment. Had I done this, to begin with, I would have included telephone consultations at a lower fee than those conducted on-site.

Another thing to consider is add-ons. Add-ons are extra projects outside of the scope of the original project. They can be an excellent opportunity for you and that of your trades. It can also be a bit of a hairy experience if your customer expects additional work under the original fee you agreed upon. Ensure that your agreement has a statement covering additional work and new charges. The more professional and prepared you are with your documents, the more you are taken seriously. It gives you a written document to fall back on if there is any confusion with your client.

If you find yourself in a unique situation not covered in your policies and payment schedule, be prepared to negotiate fairly with your client. You can amend the documents later. You may have to give them outright what they want because they caught a loophole you did not see. Maybe you forgot to include mileage in the job when they live outside of your general trade area. Perhaps they want to return a special-order item that cannot be returned to the store and did not include return policies in your agreement.

Having policies and procedures in place shows your clients

that you are a detail-oriented, trustworthy professional.

Equipment

Your excellent taste and wonderful personality are not the only things you will need for interior design. You will need to invest in some hardware and equipment to get the ball rolling.

Whether you are working from home or have a studio, you will need to set yourself up a proper workspace. Having a professional space will inspire you to get your work done and help keep you organized. Especially when you have more than one project on the go! Having a comfortable chair, a desk, shelving, file cabinets, and storage is vital. Trust me, you will likely end up with various hand samples, and you will need a place to keep them organized.

A lot of correspondence will be done by email, possibly video conferences and with photography. The handy smartphone will save you a lot of work when you document samples for your client. Still, the quality could be questionable if you are taking room scene photos that you intend to use for marketing down the road. Getting yourself a device or camera that is capable of a wide-angle shot is vital. There are many projects where I did not have photos simply because I did not have the right equipment with me, and the images from my phone were too grainy to use.

Here is a list of items you will need:
Measuring Tape (that shows the numeral measurements in 1/8ths if you aren't confident without them)
Laser Measurer
Portfolio: one that holds business cards, graph paper, pens/pencils
Laptop or Personal Computer (designated for your company)
Color Printer/Scanner

Digital Camera
Scrapbook Tape (Double sided craft tape)
Graph Paper
File Folders
Black Sharpies
Draft pencils
White erasers
Scale ruler(s)
File Cabinet
Shelving
Business Cards
Post-It Notes
Schedule (Physical or in your Phone)
Smart Phone
Design Software (optional)- Minutes Matter
Books: "The Design Directory of Window Treatments" and "The Design Directory of Bedding
both by Jackie Von Tobel

Consider a hard hat, safety glasses and steel-toed footwear. Some construction sites are very strict about their safety regulations and require you to be appropriately "geared up." Some will provide a hard hat for you, but it could be something you need on more than one occasion. Besides, you can select your own and look very fashionable on-site!

I will explain some of these items in more detail in the coming chapters, but it goes without saying, be prepared! The more organized you are on the job site, the more focused you can be, and the clients will appreciate your efficiency. Fumbling about does not inspire a lot of confidence if you know what I mean.

The Client

Without the client, there would be no job. The design aspect is likely the more straightforward part because there are tried-and-true results. The client is one of the significant unknown variables. Their ideas can seem like they came out of nowhere. They can be tense, stressed, confused, disorganized and in the middle of a crisis. They could be in various building stages, renovating, painting, organizing or moving and have sought you out to assist them with their chaos. Because let's face it, all aspects of building or renovating are upheaval from the client's daily routine. Not very many people thrive in that environment.

That is not to say that our clients are not remarkable people. When you first meet, they can be the sweetest person you have ever met. But when something goes sideways, they lash out at the most convenient target. Others can seem rather tense and lacking expression but are just uncomfortable having strangers in their house. You do not know their situation when you are walking in, but it helps to keep a friendly, open mind no matter what.

I have developed lasting relationships with many clients over the years. I have had them follow me through different companies when I offered various services and even received job offers. I also had some uncomfortable encounters where the wife was changing things whether her husband liked it or not...and he clearly did not. I tiptoed through the house, whispering my suggestions and quickly getting the heck out of there. I have jokingly said, "Hey, I am not responsible for your divorce." In some cases, it was not that much of a joke.

I have watched husband and wife teams closely to realize she is the one giving and getting the information, and he is dead silent. When I raised an eyebrow to get his opinion, I got told, "Yup, looks good." or "Whatever she wants." It made me laugh, and then I would respond, "That's okay. I know you will have a *for-real* conversation in the car where I can't hear you." It always gets a chuckle, and I just do my best to tell them why I have made the suggestions I did and then let them determine what suits them best. I am not there to put anyone on the spot or make them feel like heck for their opinion. It is their house, after all.

Having great people skills comes in very handy as you enter your clients' personal space and essentially pick it apart. You must be intelligent and classy enough to offer positive critiques without offending. You must also stealthily maneuver the best friend, neighbor, mother, mother-in-law or sister that happens to show up to the consultation with your client. Even trades-people offer advice based on some narrow views of how some-body should do it. Never mind the amount of information, some of it very false, that a person gets on the Internet. No wonder your customers come to us confused and a little gun shy!

They do not want to get it wrong, and with every opinion they get, they are told what to do or not based on the person giving it. Not very often is an idea given with the homeowner's pref-erences in mind. That is why I prefer to work closely with my clients, as I have said. It empowers them to join in the process and understand the reasoning behind the choices being made. It is imperative to highlight the reason behind the selections when working with businesses, or non-profit organizations, with sev-eral decision-makers. Or the person you are dealing with must take the information back to their board.

Any decorating or renovation project is an emotional experi-ence for a homeowner. They are excited, but they are also anxious, stressed, concerned about money and sometimes im-patient. There are many dreams tied up into the outcome. Once demolition begins, there is a complete disruption to their daily routine. Knowing that your clients are emotionally involved helps you to prepare for the odd emotional reaction. Under-standing how they tick, what may be more of a challenge for them and how their lives will be affected during the process will help you appease them. There are many skills needed in the in-terior design field, more than just a great eye for style.

Having a pathway through the decision-making process helps the client understand what they need to do, the outcome, and why the plan works. When they do hit a moment of doubt or concern, you will be able to remind them why you came to that decision together.

The Initial Consultation

The initial consultation takes place after the potential client has made an appointment with you. Maybe you are meeting them at your design studio or a retail establishment. Sometimes you are meeting for the first time at their home. Either way, having some tips and questions to get the process underway will give you some confidence going into the meeting.

Where do we even start? We smile, shake hands and introduce ourselves. The client tells us who referred them or how they discovered you and what made them decide to seek out your services. (Important information for marketing, by the way!) But then what? Where do you get started?

Many designers end up working in retail establishments that sell flooring and tile, blinds and drapery, paint and color or home furnishings. Whether you are operating an independent interior design company, a firm or working within a retail/consulting business, it will automatically steer your conversation in a specific direction.

I have done both. I had my own company and worked for independent companies that sold decorative goods. I learned to analyze my clients' needs quickly when they came into the store. What was smart was when I could tell they would be interested in more services or products than what they originally came in for. Even working trade shows has given me a quick strategy to get the information and gain enough interest to seek me out.

No matter what the situation is, knowing what questions to ask and what order, is crucial to sealing the deal. An in-store consultation is different than one held in the home too. Once you are in the house, your chances of winning a job increase significantly. You can develop a hands-on understanding of what the client wants and why. The *why* is a large component to a successful outcome.

When I first meet, let's say a couple, I ask myself: *What has brought them here today? What do they need to do? What are they struggling with?* It can be as complicated as renovating an existing house, building a new one or as simple as making some cosmetic changes. Whether they just need an hour of my time or two years of construction, they get treated the same. You never know when one small project turns into a larger one down the road. From my personal experience, it has happened many times. Again, check your ego if you feel like these smaller jobs are beneath you and do not qualify for your time.

As they answer my questions, I watch their reactions, body language, which tends to do the talking, how close they stand to each other and their facial expressions. I can pick up whether the couple is excited about the project or they just had a flood in their basement and are under a certain amount of stress. I can tell if there is some tension between them over the process. I can tell if they are organized or completely unsure where to start. As they talk about their home, I will ask what parts of the house they like to spend their time in, whether that is together or apart, and what functions they need each room to have. Does the couple have a family, and what age are their kids? That makes a difference too.

Sometimes I will ask what they do for a living. You would be surprised to know that someone's profession can explain a lot about how they like their home life to be. Someone with a desk job in a cubicle is more likely to have more fun and colorful space at home. In contrast, someone with a very stressful, hectic job, say a teacher, for example, may prefer to have a calm and serene space where they can relax their busy brains. Painting red in the house of a doctor or nurse is not likely going to impress them. Nor is "hospital scrubs" green, for that matter.

I like to know the location of their house. Is it in the city? The countryside? Do they have a lot of trees in the yard? How old is the home, and what style is it likely to be? Are the changes being made to update and work with the existing feel or to modernize it completely? Knowing the house's age can tell you what past trends you could be working with, such as stippled ceilings, hardwood floors, challenges with the construction of the walls etc. Will you run into any historical society restrictions? There are many factors to think of, but there is a trick to keeping it all straight.

Do you see how getting the project's specifics can play a massive part in the timeline, scope of the project and limitations you could be dealing with? It makes sense that you would not start off advising on what colors to paint when you have no idea what the client likes or what they already have on the walls. You must get the right information, in the correct order, to properly advise your client. It also helps sort their thoughts out too.

The Questionnaire

Here is a list of questions that I use to understand my client's project fully. Keep in mind that some additional questions may need to be asked depending on the situation. Shopping for flooring is different from someone who is just painting. Some questions will relate to in-store consultations more than in-home, but all are relevant.

Please tell me about your project.

What is your goal?

Do you have any photos of the home or what you are hoping for?

Is this project an interior/exterior or both?

How much of the house will this entail?

What can I help you with?

Are you planning to sell, or are you doing this for yourselves?

When are you hoping to get started?

How much of the work are you planning to do your self?

Where is the home located?

How old is the home?

How many people live in the home?
Do you have pets &/or children?
What way do the living room, kitchen, bedroom windows face?
How much light do you like/dislike in your bedroom(s)?
When was the last time it was painted/had new flooring/ new window treatments/decorated? What color/type of flooring/style of window treatments do you have now?
What color are your cabinets and baseboards?
Do you plan to paint them/replace the cabinets and/or baseboards?
Are you changing countertops and backsplash?
Are you keeping or changing existing tiles?
Will you be keeping or replacing existing furni-ture?
Are there any brands you wish to use?
What do you love about your home?
What are you struggling with within your home? What design or style appeals to you the most?
What do you love when it comes to color/style lighting/ space?
What do you dislike when it comes to color/style lighting/ space?

As you can see, I ask a lot of questions—open-ended questions, preferably. I save the yes/no questions for when we have narrowed a selection down, and I just want the client's reaction to, say, a color or specific sample. These questions can lead to more, but once you have an idea of where to start and get into the habit of asking them, you will always have a way to steer back to what you need to know. Ensure that you document important information like dates, hired contractors, who referred them to you, the marketing tools that worked and the brands they would prefer to use. This information gets stored in their customer file along with any copies of drawings or photos they may have brought with them.

To give you an idea of what information I am looking for, I

will provide you with the reasoning behind some of the questions.

Having the customer describe what they are looking to get done in their home seems kind of obvious. And the start date too. Their answers can determine whether this project is within your ability to achieve based on your skillset and comfort zone and whether you can work within their timeframe. Knowing what they are planning to complete themselves, such as painting, removing existing flooring or baseboards, will also determine which trades you will need. You will also know what quotes to get. Clients often change their minds or have a change in their schedule and are suddenly unable/willing to complete the work they thought. It helps to have a spare contractor or business in your back pocket that fits these unexpected jobs into their schedule quickly.

There are many reasons why a homeowner wants to make changes to their living space. Downsizing, upsizing, jealous of the neighbor... or maybe getting ready to sell their property.

Understanding who the changes need to appeal to is also essential. There are many avenues one can take in interior design, all of them stemming from personal taste. Selling a home must become a marketing strategy to appeal to the highest number of buyers possible while still showing off the home's originality. It must be memorable after all. The mistake is when the homeowner wants to decorate with their own taste in mind rather than who they are selling to. That pumpkin orange may be their favorite color. Only a certain percentage of people are going to agree with them. It will be your job to work with your client to market their home to what most people are looking for, and that is when knowing the current design trends come in handy.

As I mentioned previously, the house's area can tell you the style and approximate age of the buildings in that subdivision. Planning an ultra-modern flat top build in a historical neighborhood may not only raise some eyebrows but also tricky to get a building permit approved. If the home is in the countryside, there is more privacy and determines how your customers approach window coverings or landscape design. Knowing you have neighbors close by changes things a little when you streak from the bedroom to the laundry room for your clothes in the dryer!

The number of people living in the house and their ages will tell you vital information on your suggestions' practicality. How likely will the floor get scratched? Are their seniors or people with special needs to consider? Are they going to have trouble operating the blinds? How washable do they need the paint to be? (For me, that goes without saying, but it matters when it comes to sheen) It can tell you what kinds of activities are happening in the living room area, backyard, or all the bedrooms' function. Pets are hard on houses, especially larger ones. Recommending hardwood floors may not be a good idea with a heavier active dog. It is an excellent habit to note everyone's names, including the cat and dog. It makes a good impression on the client!

It matters which way the windows face to determine how much light and the direction it enters the room. It plays a vital role in how light or dark you plan a room, what the function will be, how much light is required and the tone of light cast into the home. In my neck of the woods, North never gets direct sunlight and casts a blue hue. East and West have direct light in the morning and evening, respectively. At the same time, Southern exposure gives the best, all through the day yellow light. South is excellent for kitchens and family rooms, not so outstanding for night shift workers who need to sleep through the day. The tone of light will alter that of the paint colors. Knowing that in advance can save a lot of money, time, and frustration when the paint's subtle undertones just became a significant overtone.

My parents had white walls for over thirty years before my mom got fed up and decided to paint with deeper colors. Trust me, they were not wild by any stretch, but moving from white to a medium tone was a very drastic change to them. It took some getting used to, and once the painting was complete, they loved it. Understanding what a customer has been used to and now why they want to change it can give you an understanding of what to avoid, what may come as a shock or where their comfort zone may be. Paying close attention to the client's expressions as they describe their home can lead you in the right direction.

Who wants to go through the time and money to redecorate their home and come out with the same thing? No one that I have come across. Though people often lean towards what they know, you may have to nudge them to be a little braver on their selections to avoid that very issue. Being a designer, you can visualize the outcome of their choice where they cannot. If they could, they would not need your help, would they?

There will likely be elements of the house that are staying as is. Cabinets are a costly item to replace, and baseboards are reusable. Are they painted or wood? Is the customer opposed to painting wood? The funny thing is men are most often going to object to that idea where women are all for it. And because flooring and cabinets are the starting point for selection in a design, it is smart to nail down what changes, if any, will be made to them. Baseboards are tricky because they run throughout the house, and they must look good with every flooring type and paint color. Selecting the trim and baseboard color first will save you time.

If you are making changes to cabinets, it only makes sense that new countertops and tile will follow. Likely, if the changes are mostly cosmetic, you will be doing them in the bathroom(s) as well. After the cabinets and flooring selection, the counters and backsplashes are next. They need to be cohesive with the cabinetry. If the client wants contrast, you must decide if it will be in just the tile, the counter, or both. Do they want laminate, quartz or granite countertops? Is there a tile style that they have been eying that may be tricky to coordinate with the countertops?

Even if you are not at the selection stage as you ask these questions, it gets the creative juices flowing. Keep taking down notes on what the client is saying they like and do not like. Relying on your memory can backfire when you are working on more than one project at a time. If you end up with an assistant or other trades who need your notes, then there is a way to find that info without making you run around getting it for everyone.

Without getting too redundant, the client's furniture can say a lot about the directions you can go in or can not. If they are replacing furniture, a brief discussion about what they are hoping to get will give you some fresh ideas for them. It can also show off your skills when designing around three different antique family heirlooms that your client is insisting must stay.

Brands can tell you a lot about a person. Suppose someone is more likely to throw out furniture than to reupholster it or to always look for a sale over quality. In that case, you know whether to head for custom craftsmanship or a box store when you are shopping for them. Sometimes people just do not know the difference and will look to you for your expert advice.

Be careful about your advice if you do not know what you are talking about. Educate yourself on different types of flooring, fabric, blinds, paint, types of wood… use the knowledge and skills of professionals in as many areas as you can. If you are considerate, consider compensating them for an hour of their precious time too. The advice you give, if inaccurate, could get you in hot water and, at the very least, create some confusion or misunderstandings. At worse, it could get you sued or fired off the job.

Educating yourself is an essential investment of time and worth every minute.

Finally, when it comes to getting the client's opinion of their home in the current state, they may have no idea what they like. If they have been spinning their tires, they may be perplexed between what will look good in their home and what appeals to them. When I find a client stumbling over the answers of what they do like, I will begin asking what they do not like. They answer rather quickly if they hate purple and would never decorate with Navajo patterns. Let them talk and read their facial expressions. Look over any pictures they may have brought and have them describe what appeals to them.

It is key that you keep your poker face on throughout this process. Grimacing, making negative comments or turning up your nose can backfire because the client reads you just as much as you are reading them. They want someone who will not judge them for their lifestyle, personality or the state their house is in. You do not know if they were taking care of a sick loved one or trying to finish school while working a full-time job. You do not know if Great Gran painted the house purple and the client has just moved in after she passed away. Be sensitive to your client and respect their feelings. Keep a pleasant expression on your face, and your mind open. Show that you are understanding and compassionate even if you are not sure there is a sensitive situation you could be working around.

Helping people identify the positive attributes in their home will make the discussion about the challenges go a little easier. Finding a positive spin on any critiques you may have will lessen any defensive responses the client may have. It is a very personal experience for them with a lot of emotional attachments. It is the difference between designers who come off as know-it-alls and those with a genuine desire to help people while finding creative solutions… and having fun doing it!

On-Site Consultations

If the first consultation took place at your office or workplace, the next step would be the on-site consultation. Even if this is the first consultation, you will want to consider a few more steps to the process.

You will need your measuring tape or laser, camera or smartphone, a portfolio with graph paper, business cards, pencil, pen and eraser. You will want to draw out a rough floor plan and if the client has them available, request a copy of the blueprint. Print the blueprint to scale should they email it to you. You can do this at your local print shop with a little notice. If you have paint swatches, it is prudent to bring them, even if you just leave them in the car for now. Of course, if you are selling blinds or drapery, you will have likely discussed what products to bring with you as well.

Now, after the pleasantries are over, right off the bat, I ask for a tour. I ask the questionnaire questions while taking notes and drawing the rough floor plan if it is relevant. I am taking note of which direction the windows face, how many trees or overhangs they have in front of them and whether they have window treatments. Do the customers like to keep the window treatments open or closed primarily? I am looking at the state of repair the house is currently in to see what kinds of prep or construction will need completing according to the project. I am also looking if they have squared off or rounded corners on the drywall. Is it perhaps plaster? Where can I start and stop color changes comfortably without having a glaring or awkward color change?

Flow is crucial because we experience our home by walking through it from room to room. Is the experience pleasant as you travel, or is there a jolt as you go from one space to another? How can you create flow through the home while still allowing for a fresh approach?

If the client is considering new floors, there are several factors to check for. How thick is the current product? Was it installed over any pre-existing flooring such as sheet vinyl? Can sections of their home handle heavy products like tile or hardwood? Lift the heat registers in each room as required. You should see any layers of flooring or determine the thickness of the existing flooring and subfloor. If the house is in a demolition stage, be careful not to step into open register vents... it hurts from personal experience!

I am determining what kind of light fixtures there are and their location. Are they going to provide enough light in darker areas such as staircases and hallways? What type of light bulbs are they using? Just like the natural light casts a hue on paint colors, the light bulbs will too. I have been known to climb into a bathtub and draw the curtain closed to determine how much light the vanity light projects into the shower area. It is a little outside the box, but well, it gets me the information I need and gives my client a laugh.

I like to document the elements that will be staying, sometimes by taking pictures. It also helps to photograph any tricky areas like staircases and railings that connect with other trim or molding. Installers will need to know if there are any troublesome areas because they will charge differently for them. If carpet installation is in the basement, will they have trouble bringing it through the stairwell, or will they need to pull/push it through a window? Is there a window that can work for that? Will the clients need area rugs, floor protectors in their furniture legs, or have a problem with slipping?

While the clients describe their home and answer my questions, I'm getting a feel of the place. I'm starting to visualize furniture layouts, possible color schemes, what may require more work than initially thought and where we can save on the budget. It is also essential to know if the clients have any health conditions aggravated by dust or fumes. Even exposure to light or lack of it are all vital pieces of information. Will allergies play a factor in the type of flooring you select? You do not want your clients to have an asthma attack or migraine due to oil-based paints. Even painting dark colors when someone is suffering from seasonal depression is a concern.

While walking through, I am also aware of odors that could indicate pet stains, mold or mildew. Are there water stains anywhere on the ceilings? Do they have skylights, and are any of the seals broken, causing leaks? Are their window coverings adequate to protect furnishings from sun damage?

Do they keep the house clean or kind of unkempt? If you design a beautiful open concept with white walls and hardwood floors, are your clients going to go nuts trying to maintain it when they can see every mess or spot of dirt?

There are so many factors to consider, but you will understand what will work the best for them as you work through the questions and develop a conversation. Once you get into the swing of consultations, it will not seem like you are trying to re-member every question, however, it may be a good idea to have a questionnaire on hand. Getting the details right in this initial consultation will keep you organized as you work through prod-uct gathering and selection. It will help you organize the correct tradespeople and get accurate quotes for the client.

You may choose to offer the client a consultation folder that includes: recommendations for paint, decor, furnishings, a re-ceipt for their consult (if this is a one-time appointment) and your business card. You can include swatches if you have them to spare. If the project is ongoing and requires quotes, give them a reasonable idea of when to expect it. Set up the next appoint-ment and highlight the cost of your services. Have the clients sign your agreement with a deposit to officially hire you for their project. You may not be the only one offering proposals on the job, so you will have to navigate each consultation as needed.

It is exciting to make money doing something you love. Even better? You will get to help the client design their home into a beautiful expression of their hopes and dreams. That is where the fun is really at!

Meeting Contractors And Salespeople

You can design the most fabulous house with all the trim-mings, but if you do not have the right trades or contractors to pull it off, it stays in the dreaming stage. Your design business's success is linked directly to the quality and professionalism of the trade referrals you develop. Don't hire your handy brother to install custom cabinetry or install new blinds because it can cause you more problems than seeking proper professionals. Not that you do not have acquaintances that fit that description. You want the best available, who genuinely know what they are doing and will guarantee their work.

Staking your reputation on giving your friends or relatives work out of kindness is simply not professional of you. Your clients trust your judgment but will still likely hold separate meetings with tradespeople to get quotes and decide whether they want to use their services. You want clean, respectable, polite and organized tradespeople to represent your business and theirs well. You will be creating your team of professionals who refer opportunities to each other. Having a solid crew will put your client more at ease and keep them from eagle eying every movement the workers make while in their house. But they will still be watching!

As a side note, you want to be very clear about how tradespeople behave while on site. Trades should not be smoking, using substances including vaping or drugs, or creating an unsafe working environment. Be clear about how they are to clean up the work site each day and contain dust and debris as they work. Share your client's health issues, if any, with them, so they have a maintenance plan in place to lower any risk of exposure.

So how do you find these fantastic people? Why go directly to the sources who can refer you to the best trades!

That means you want to go to top-quality suppliers and get their recommendations for contractors, installers and painters. You can bet that the businesses which operate based on their reputation for expertise will know others who are doing the same. Again, if you are selling blinds and drapery, you will need a workroom and trained installers. If you are offering color consultations, you will need at least two to three top-notch painters in your pocket. Suppose you need flooring, cabinets, countertops and tile, but are not selling them. In that case, you need to work with a retail establishment with a solid reputation. They will handle the installation for you and can offer warranties on their work.

When warrantying their work, ask your trades, retail companies and suppliers to provide a copy of their warranty as well as any policies they give their installers. Understanding what they expect of themselves, the people they hire or refer, and seeing how that lines up with your client's expectations, can avoid plenty of misunderstandings or discord later. There is less opportunity for surprises. It shows you that everyone has the bases covered, and you have a better chance at a smoother outcome for your project.

You can work out a referral program or designer discount with the businesses you refer to in some cases. It could be a discount on a product, or it could be a gift card for referrals. It's up to you how, if at all, you want to pass the deal along to your client. Getting discounts gives you an opportunity for additional income on the project. Getting creative with compensation and cost savings is expected in the industry. Be fair and transparent because you do not want to appear to be benefiting by over-ordering products or overcharging on items the customer could have found themselves for less.

Trust me... they will be comparing prices and researching on their own. The following sections are some tips when you are looking for your trades and suppliers.

Flooring Stores

There will be lots of stores to choose from when it comes to flooring. Some flooring stores are a complete design showroom with multiple types of products available. If you need an all-inclusive destination, start researching companies that offer many services. Flooring experts that have been in the business for a while, preferably with installation experience as well, are the people you want to align with. You want them to answer your questions regarding the pros/cons of their flooring products. Including sustainability and environmentally friendly options, suitable recommendations for your project and what installation may entail. They should be able to do a professional measure and discuss all issues that will need attention. They will be able to quote you once the client approves the product.

You want to ensure that their installers meet your criteria and are the proper fit for the job. View photos of completed projects, check out their Google reviews and read through both the review and their responses. (Keep in mind that there are Internet trolls out there who purposely trash a company.) Look at their website. Does this company feel like a good representation of your brand? Do they have a broad selection in the current trends plus tried-and-true samples in top brands? Do they have in-stock items to help with those fast-paced jobs? Are they happy and approachable when you arrive with your clients? Are you able to borrow samples?

Avoid places that are overly pushy for sales, intrude on your conversations with your client past professional customer service or who outright ignore you. Customer service has tremendous value. While your clients are likely to be price-conscious, they demand good service. Otherwise, they would be shopping themselves and not likely needing you. By taking them to the stores that provide a stylish, knowledgeable and friendly environment, you are gaining their trust and your reputation.

General Contractors

A top-quality general contractor can be challenging to find. Everyone who has a hammer has called themselves a contractor for the sake of getting a discount in a store. So how do you find the real pros? Where is this mystical beast who you can trust wholeheartedly with your client's house? You could ask the salespeople at the flooring and paint stores. They will often be working with people that they know are genuinely good at what they do. They will know the companies who are cutting corners and are out for a quick buck too. When you visit the local design and home shows, make sure you see past the pretty booths. Stop and check out the contracting company's booths as well. These businesses could do projects from small renovations to large scale rebuilds.

You want to have two to three contractors to call on, depending on the project's size. Some will not be interested in a small bathroom remodel. Others will be eager for those projects because they do not have employees. Again, you want to get references both from the contractor but also from the people recommending them. A cold call to one of their previous customers with a positive review is worth way more than finding out the reference you called is their mother.

How long have they been in business? Are they bonded? What skills do they have, and what are they not able to do? Do they show up on time, ready for the day, in clean attire and freshly showered? Are they accurate with their estimates and installation of products? How do they handle overage/shortages? Are they organized and neat? How are their people skills? How many employees do they have, and do they all have the same work ethic? Are they covered by business insurance and have the proper licensing? Do they have experience with permits? Are they good listeners and offer solid advice to you? Do you have comfortable conversations about what needs completing? When changes happen, are you able to quickly resolve any problems? Essentially, can you work as a team with this person?

The general contractor can handle a large portion of the project. No one is an expert at everything, though. Just because they *can* do it does not mean you will get the perfect result you were hoping for. For instance, tiling is a difficult project. You want someone who does tiling every day, with a solid reputation, rather than the person who occasionally does it. You also want a certified electrician and plumber to handle those jobs if your contractor does not have those tickets. It is not like having your dad come over to fix the dishwasher. It is your reputation and your client's trust at stake.

Electricians/Plumbers/ Drywallers Etc.

Doing your research on these trades will come down to finding reputable companies that have a long-standing track record in the trading area. Again, asking your trusted people who they use and can recommend is a solid start. You want to find trades that are priced fairly for excellent work. The highest price does not guarantee you a good job any more than the lowest. Sometimes it is necessary to ask for up to three quotes to work with.

I caution you on low-ballers. These companies are out to win the job at any cost, usually yours. You will not be guaranteed to get good craftsmanship. The quote may not include necessary items that create an expense later, which exceeds the quotes you originally got from other companies. You want to have a clearly defined and detailed quote to work with. A reputable company is trusted to uphold their quote and complete the project within the timeline promised.

Drywalling is a tough job and very labour-intensive. Not many can do it well, and it wears a body out. When it comes to construction, a good framer provides the bones for the drywaller to work with. Good drywall gives the mudder/taper a better chance of smoothing out the seams. All of these give the painter a better chance of adequately coating the surface with a perfect result. You can see how every trade, laborer or contractor needs to be on point at every stage.

Painters

Believe it or not, not just anyone can give you a professional paint job. From experience, I had seen many people in this profession who decided to become a painter when their other industry or line of work failed. There is so much more to it than picking up a brush. I highly recommend you go to the top brand paint stores and ask them for their painter recommendations. Some stores will even have a list.

Quality painters will be clean, personable, knowledgeable, trustworthy, insured, transparent and priced well. When they quote you, they will tell you the number of coats they are completing, the exact products used and an estimated length of time to complete the project. They may need to rent scaffolding, hire additional help or complete extra quotes depending on each job's specifics. Ensure that they include touch-ups in the details of their quote, along with what other costs of moving furniture etc., back afterward.

Once you have established a relationship with a few painters, you know you will get a top-quality finish.

Unfortunately, there are some unscrupulous painters out there. You will make your recommendations for paint colors in the brand of paint you have chosen with your clients, and some have been known to match the color in a different brand. The problem with this is the tones are often not right unless hand-matched, but worse, the sheens and quality of paint are not up to snuff. I am a confessed paint snob. You can have everything look beautiful once finished until a client washes the wall; it turns into a nightmare with low-quality paint.

Warning: some painters charge for a top-quality brand but pour the lower quality brand into the other brand's buckets. It makes it appear like you are getting the product you specified, when in fact, you paid top dollar for low-quality paint. It is dirty! It puts more money in their pocket, and your client has no idea what is happening when they try to wash or touch up their paint, and something is wrong.

You must prime bare drywall. You need two coats of quality paint on the walls to get the proper adhesion and wear on the paint job. I know of new homes that got one coat of tinted primer and one coat of paint. This practice does not meet new home warranty standards. Still, no one is overseeing this process to ensure quality. It *does not* give you the proper coating on the walls for durability. I will go over paint quality more in Chapter Four, but knowing these tricks of the trade, you can now ensure that you are not only hiring the right painting company but getting the color and quality you specified on the job.

Furnishings/Decor/Art

Isn't this the fun part? Getting out there, digging into our favorite stores and finding new ones? I loved exploring workrooms, shops and businesses that got my creative juices flowing. It was, and still is, one of my favorite things to do. Even when I was between projects, I would head out and just do a little snooping at the latest goods.

It helps to be friendly with the staff. Not just for product knowledge and happy chit chat when you arrive, but to also have someone keen to show you the newest items from their latest shipments. Ask the staff to contact you when the product arrives so you do not have to guess when it is shipped, and you get to be the first to see their goodies. Suppose you are looking for specific items, colors or fabrics. In that case, they may have even done some personal shopping for you with their suppliers. They were perhaps bringing in items with you in mind. Some small or family-run décor stores are only too happy to have guaranteed sales with designers.

New products are always arriving at stores, so it is a good idea to do "the rounds" at least every month or so. Get familiar with the brands each store carries and what they may be dropping. If they are dropping a product line, ask the staff for their reasons if you have a client looking for an item that they can no longer get, or worse, have ordered a discontinued item. It is not fun having to scramble to reselect an item because it is no longer available or back-ordered.

Remember when I said it was essential to know about any allergies your client may have? Well, knowing the details of the fabrics you choose helps you avoid them. Understanding the types of art that a customer prefers or avoids will tell you what to show them. Having developed an in-depth understanding of your client, you can use your "feel" while shopping for the perfect items. You can also describe what you are hoping to find to the different suppliers so they can narrow down the search for you.

Do not be afraid to find some favorite online shops and artisans to shop from. There are many exceptional, handcrafted items, unknown artists and sculptors out there. Now more than ever, more people can showcase their talent market themselves without a brick-and-mortar shop. There is no better way to get a unique and unexpected look for your client than to shop for unknown talent. If you can become known for your sleuth skills at tracking these magical items, trust me, you will be highly coveted.

If you have a storefront or the budget to travel, going to international trade shows for home furnishings and interior design is not only thrilling but highly beneficial! They keep you inspired, informed, current and relevant with trends. You can share your enthusiasm through your social media and marketing. It bleeds into your projects, and your clients catch the wave with you. Look into trade shows across the country, or even try to visit manufacturers when possible. The more information you can get firsthand, the better you understand the functionality and quality of the items you are suggesting. You can use the supplier's sales information as educational marketing techniques of your own.

There is a lot of groundwork to be done before starting your design business. The good news? In the beginning, you will have the time to do it. While you are developing your skills and reputation, this is the perfect time to build your dream team. Do not be afraid to ask questions or need more information from the experts you have found. Do not act like a pro in areas where you are a novice, but do not be afraid to educate yourself until you are a pro! Get to the point where you can sufficiently handle questions during the consultation process and then refer to experts for more information when you need it. You will gain more respect in saying, "I don't have that answer for you now, but I will ask for you." It is a sign of strength.

One day, after you have asked your questions and gained more experience, you will be the expert and will not have to rely on others quite as much. There will always be something you do not know and the opportunity to learn, though, I will say. Stay open to information, open-minded and humble enough to accept it from others.

In The Next Chapter...

You now understand who you are as a designer, approaching the client, how to handle the consultation and build your team. We venture into the specifics around each element of a design project. If the client is only doing certain aspects like replacing the carpet, baseboards and paint, follow the order to start the selection process. If you break from these steps, you may end up making a costly mistake or wasting precious time. Otherwise, it is relatively easy to follow along. As you will see, the logic of why you build first, from the flooring and cabinetry to finally the paint, will become apparent.

CHAPTER TWO - THE FOUNDATION

Here Is What You Will Learn...

- Cabinetry selection and tips
- Flooring selection and tips
- Countertops & backsplash selection and tips
- Doors, baseboards & masonry tips
- Lighting selection and tips

The first time I landed a major long-term project was when I was doing consultations for a paint and design center in my city. I was used to walking customers through their projects both in the store and in customer's homes. Still, those consultations were usually two hours tops. Most of the clients were capable of doing the work themselves. They just needed a little direction and some fresh ideas.

This consultation started in the store the same as any other. I introduced myself and began asking what the project was and what stage it was at. The woman was pleasant while she described they were renovating their entire house and that she was struggling with selecting new windows. She had been getting advice from several sources, I could tell. She had pamphlets on new windows, shingles, siding colors and some photos of what she liked. As she talked, it was apparent that she was very unsure what direction to go. Her head was spinning on where to start.

Part of what was giving her pause is that she had a designer recommend red-colored windows. Not the trim around the windows, the fibreglass components of the windows themselves. My client is quite artsy and Italian, I was to discover later, and she did love the idea of having something different. She was just not sure of her decision. She had not ordered the windows yet.

I could tell from her expression that she was more concerned about the idea than she was excited.

"Do you *love* these windows?" I asked. Windows is typically a costly investment, and I could tell that these windows would be above typical expense.

"Well…. I do not know. What do you think?"

"These windows are a very definite statement about your house. If you choose them, you will be working with this color both inside and outside your home. They are also going to be expensive." I am always careful not to put an overly negative spin on my advice as I want the customer to understand the pros and cons. I just offer perspectives they perhaps had not considered yet. "If you love these windows, then we work with them. But if you are not sure, then you may not appreciate them for the long term and will regret the money you spent."

I spent the rest of the meeting going over two options for siding, depending on her window selection. We went our separate ways, and each of us was happy that there seemed to be more options for her to choose from.

I did not realize was that she was the wife of my boss's doctor and a family friend. I treated her as I did all my clients and made an impact. They spoke to my boss and specifically requested my help for the rest of their project. A little bit of genuine interest in helping them, our hitting it off, and some of my common-sense steps gained me a two-year deal as well as a new friend. These customers do not come along every day, but it was a joy to see their home come together.

As designers, we look forward to designing!

Getting to dig into the design aspect finally is delicious. Like building the house itself, you must start in the right order to create a solid design from the bottom up. The framing does not happen before the foundation is poured. The paint can't be painted until the drywall is fully prepped and primed. And the paint color can only be chosen once you have all the other elements selected. Trust me, people try to start with paint because they feel it is the most comfortable place to begin, but it is backwards.

The house is the spine, the foundation and the framing essential to how the entire house holds up. The wiring and plumbing are the nerves and organ systems, and both are required to allow the home to function. As we go through these step-by-step guides, we are also developing the body that holds your whole design together.

It is a little like, "this bone is connected to the funny bone," but truthfully, that is precisely how we must approach it. If the spine is out, then the rest of the body is misaligned as well. And sometimes, you must work with a few quirks like crooked walls. I think you get the idea.

As you go through each design element, you will see that I go entirely in-depth. You can get a lot of this information from a salesperson in their respective industry, so you may question why you need to know this.

The answer is: it makes you a pro. You are the trusted advisor and helps you counsel your client. It saves you time and hassle by choosing samples you can work with instead of looking good but won't install or function correctly for your client.

Let's get started!

Cabinetry

The most considerable expense when furnishing a house is going to be the cabinetry. Costs vary depending on the amount of detail involved and whether you select solid wood or a composite. As with anything, there is always a pro and con to what you choose. Having a firm idea of what different types and styles of cabinets can cost will help you direct your suggestions based on the budget. You need to know what kind of maintenance your client is up for, along with how much storage they require.

The cabinets are the first element of style that is going into the home. After the questionnaire, you should have a firm idea of the direction you are going. This first step leads you in a specific direction.

Because it is the largest expense, selecting the cabinets first is a must. Why? Think about what items the homeowner is likely to replace first in the home. They will paint again before they do anything else. They may replace the light fixtures or window treatments but guaranteed, there will be a great deal of time and "wear and tear" before they go through the expense of cabinetry again. Every future change they make to the house will likely be with the original cabinetry and the flooring in place.

To begin, if you do not have experience with cabinet design, specifically kitchens, then having a reliable supplier in your pocket is essential. You can turn to them with the questions you have and create a plan for you. Spend some time learning ways that you can save money on cabinet projects or what add-ons can cost. That way, while you are listening to your client describe their dream kitchen with all the bells and whistles, you can mentally add up a price range for them.

They can also discuss little elements like correcting newly exposed, unstained wood after replacing the countertops and how to resolve them.

In the idea stage, it is an important wake-up call to inform the client that if they are hoping for a sixty-thousand-dollar kitchen with a twenty-thousand-dollar budget. Having a realistic expectation will save a lot of time in estimating and quoting stage.

First off, are the cabinets going to be replaced, refinished or painted? The most expensive being replacement, then refinishing, then painting.

Replacement

Replacement of cabinets allows for additional drawers with pullouts, organizers and more functional storage space. Re-organizing the shelving can give the homeowner more access based on their routines. If they are not replacing the flooring, the design must stay in the previous cabinets' original dimensions. You must ensure that the new format will not expose the sub-floor. The existing flooring may have cabinetry installed on top, such as with hardwood. More often, the flooring butts up to the toe kick.

Replacing the cabinets gives you access to new styles in the door fronts. One less expensive option is to replace only the door fronts and have the cabinet bases refinished to match. Maybe there will be glass features added, under cabinet lighting and height added, so the uppers reach the ceiling. Usually, the client has gotten tired of dark wood or their inexpensive Melamine cabinets. They must dislike the style or function of their cabinets to get to the point of replacing them.

Get your client talking about what they have been struggling with. Does the location of the sink, fridge and stove make sense for them? Is the "triangle" functional?

The points of the triangle represent the fridge, stove and sink. The farther apart they are, or the more elongated one side of the triangle if you were to connect the three dots, the less functional the kitchen is.

What do they love/hate about the existing cabinets, and why they want to change them? Take note of any special needs that make specific tasks difficult. Are they going to need wheelchair access in the future? Is there a visual impairment? Do they cook with their partner or kids? Are they a neat "freak" or possibly legitimately obsessive-compulsive? What style do they have, and what are they more likely to enjoy now?

There is always a way to work in *some* of the more expensive accessories, staying closer to the original budget. Maybe the corner feature door can have a glass front with display shelves rather than all of them. (Keep in mind that you must keep all the shelves very neat with glass doors. You see everything!) Maybe the pots and pans drawers pull out because your client will have trouble with them stored on shelves, but not all the cabinets are turned into drawers. Look for solutions with some compromise when necessary.

The kitchen may be the entire renovation project, with a larger budget towards the cabinets. Knowing how custom the cabinets will be will determine which kitchen design studio you pull out of your pocket. Some companies are more skilled at sleek and modern designs. Others will specialize in cabinets with all the corbels and intricate woodworking designs. You will need suppliers for every taste.

Tip: Usually, with the replacement of cabinets, the toe kicks are done to match. It becomes more relevant when let's say in the case of a flood; the flooring needs replacing and you need to instruct either the cabinet company or the flooring installer to handle the toe kicks.

Refinishing

Refinishing cabinets is usually when a client has solid wood to work with. Often, the project starts with the client hoping to touch up the worn areas around the knobs and handles, especially if they are trying to update the hardware. The difficulty lies in the protective finish. The new clear coat will be a different sheen than the existing aged one, even when fully cured. Another thing to keep in mind is the clear coat applications in their various forms. Back in the day, more chemicals were in the clear coats, and oil-based coatings were standard.

Nowadays, we have environmental regulations that require all coatings to meet or exceed them. Current clear coats may not adhere to previous ones. Previous coatings may have been sprayed, either with an oil-based urethane or lacquer. Unless the new clear coat is sprayed, any other sundries would likely leave noticeable streak marks.

First, who is going to refinish the cabinets? The homeowner or a professional? What equipment or skill does the homeowner have? What time of year are they hoping to complete their project? I highly recommend that anyone wishing to complete their cabinets before a significant family dinner or event ensures their cabinets have 30 days to cure. Shelving should not have bulky items like dishes or pots and pans placed on freshly painted or stained surfaces. A full cure takes thirty days, and in closed spaces like that, the substrate will stay tacky longer. That means that those items will pull the paint off or leave marks on their freshly painted surface!

To completely re-stain the cabinets, they need sanding down to the bare wood. You want to go from rougher grit sandpaper like an 80 to remove the topcoats and then move to a 120 grit for removing the stain, so the surface is smooth. Do NOT polish the wood with sandpaper too much. It will not take the stain the same.

The sides of the cabinet bases are often a veneer, and with it being so thin, a person cannot sand them. You will go through the wood to the composite underneath. You are more likely to need to use a new veneer and stain it to match the door fronts. With that in mind, wood has its own tone, and older, previously stained wood will take a stain color differently than new. Veneers take stains entirely differently because they are so thin and can darken more than intended.

Before a person begins staining everything, they are better to do a test spot in an inconspicuous area, say the back of a cabinet door and on a spare piece of veneer. Suppose it is challenging to get the stain to match on both. In that case, you will need a custom stain created for one of the surfaces, so the color is the same, but the type or thickness of the stain helps get the depth to match between the different surfaces. It would take the skills of someone who has extensive knowledge of stain matching. It is an excellent idea to inquire about these services at a paint store, such as Benjamin Moore. I did stain matches for many years, and I know how finicky they can be to work with.

There are other products out there, other faux finishing techniques such as antiquing with gel stain or even chalk paint, that can work on refinishing cabinets. In those circumstances, I would highly recommend you find people who have a lot of experience in refinishing with them before you offer that idea to the customer. DO NOT offer to do the work yourself unless you can guarantee your work and precisely understand what you are doing. Do your research on the products and the steps involved. It may not be worth the risk.

After sanding and removing all the previous stain or paint, remove all the dust to ensure that the wood is clean. Sometimes a little wood filler is needed to repair any damage but use a stainable or paintable filler. Otherwise, the waxy substance will prevent absorption or adhesion.

When it comes to the clear coat stage, understand that this protects the surface from debris, cleaning solutions and water damage. Spraying a clear coat gives the smoothest finish, but it takes the right spray equipment, knowledge of the proper spray tip size and how to clean them correctly afterward. If they are not having them sprayed, you want to use a high-quality fine flat paint brush, about 2 1/2" for the flat areas and a smaller 1/2"- 1" angled one for the smaller details. Or they can also use a high-quality lint-free mohair roller. Do not use foam rollers as they tend to bubble the product and leave a mess in the finish.

Several thin, even coats of the clear coat are the ticket. Give proper time between coats for the product to dry, or you will reactivate the previous coat if you start too soon. Thin, even coats give you a harder finish, whereas thicker coats cannot cure well and remain soft.

Please note that it is illegal to spray lacquer in any site without an enclosed spray booth in some areas. Huge fines can be handed out, not to mention the horrible effects on people's health. Any trades on site must be following protocols and safety laws, and it will be your responsibility to watch for these types of situations if you are overseeing the project. You will likely have found professionals who would never do anything like that, but sometimes you learn the hard way.

Having the cabinets professionally refinished may see the whole kitchen blocked off in a protective plastic room to spray the base cabinets. Usually, they take the doors to their shop to lay them flat for coating. These are easy to mark up, and the pros want to make sure that they get the right curing time before transporting them back to the homeowner's house.

Painting Cabinets

Yup, the least expensive fix there is. Is it easy? No. It takes a labor of love and a test of a stable relationship to get through painting the cabinets. Sometimes one partner is less enthused about painting wood than the other. Still, when they see the cost of replacing the cabinets, they usually concede.

Like many previous steps, the sundries' quality or the skill with a sprayer is the difference between success and a big old mess. So is the quality of the paint, primer and doing the right steps in prep. Yes, I have more experience in the paint world than hanging light fixtures. But I can say this, our finished surfaces are the first thing to wear, and when you cut corners and costs, it usually bites you in the butt later. Sometimes not that much later.

Again, the homeowner can be doing this project themselves or completed professionally. The pros will likely do much of the same process on-site and in their shop as they do with a stain project, but it will not take as long. Instead of sanding all the previous cabinets' coatings, they can be scuff sanded with 120-grit sandpaper, then move to a 180 grit for finishing. Regardless of whether they are melamine or solid wood. The idea is just to mar the surface enough for the primer to grab onto. All the dust then needs to be removed from the surface, including the work area, to prevent it from contaminating the paint. (That goes for walls too!)

If a client wants to get rid of the wood grain look, a paintable filler can be used and sanded. It takes several thin, even applications...and some patience. I once had clients do this process themselves and painstakingly refinished their cabinets over a month. Their original quote to replace and add on to their cabinets was forty-thousand dollars. When they finished, they spent six-hundred dollars in paint supplies and two-thousand dollars for extra shelving and lights to bring the uppers to the ceiling. That is a huge difference!

Oil-based primer. You need this because it bites through and holds to the existing surface while providing a good bond with the coming topcoats. Yes, it is smelly. Be careful with your client's health issues should they have any. Get the windows open to ventilate but preferably not on too windy of a day. It can blow debris onto your wet surfaces and mess with dry times. After one good coat of primer, you are free to use either oil or latex-based paints for the topcoats. It is imperative to sand between coats with a fine 180 grit sandpaper to remove any small lines or tiny bubbles. Two coats of top-quality cabinet or latex paint give the proper thickness for durability and color retention.

The lovely thing about painting existing cabinets, besides the savings, is you can be more playful. The uppers can be a different tone or color all together than the base. The island can be a fun feature with a pop of color because painting is a relatively quick and easy change later. Therefore, you see so many fun ideas in magazines and displays!

When you select the color and tones for the cabinets, keep a couple of things in mind. First, the location of the kitchen. Which direction do the windows face, how many are there and how much light comes through them? It determines the amount of natural light they will have in a work area. If it is not much, you will want to go lighter with the cabinets or compensate with artificial light. Perhaps keep the uppers a light color and the lower cabinets a deeper tone when the light is poor.

How much light a client wants or needs is a decision they

need to make for themselves, with a little direction from you.

My mother is visually impaired. I grew up feeling like I could not see without the kitchen brightly lit to see what I was doing, even though my eyesight was fine. You would think my mom would need the same amount of light. However, with her condition, the bright light causes her migraines, and she would prefer enough light to see but not so bright to strain her eyes.

It is an excellent example of understanding your client's needs in their home and working closely with them to create both function and design.

Cleaning is another task to consider. Will the customer go nuts if they can see every spec of dirt on their light cabinets? Do they *want* to see it because then they can clean it? Darker cabinets show fingerprints more, as do high gloss or semi-gloss sheens, which will also highlight imperfections or the woodgrain. People often choose a satin or pearl finish so that the cabinets are easy to wipe but hide imperfections a little more.

Those same considerations apply to the flooring selection.

Flooring

Flooring travels through the house and is the first item that creates a flow from one room to another. Some homes have the same flooring throughout the same level or even all levels. Natural breaks occur at stairwells, kitchens, bathrooms and bedrooms. However, a good design will still have the flooring coordinate with each other for flow.

You need to know what flooring is staying and which is to be replaced. Is there tile flooring that is remaining in bathrooms, the kitchen or entrances? Flooring heights play a considerable role in what flooring selections are most appropriate or require additional subfloor installation. As the homeowners and family travel through their house, flooring changes should be as smooth as possible to avoid "toe stubbers" at the transitions. It means one floor isn't higher than the other, or the transition covers the height difference. You can direct them towards or away from certain products based on their flooring goals.

There is always the durability and how the homeowners live to keep in mind. They may love the idea and look of hardwood until their golden retriever chases a ball across the room and scratches the finish. Others may hate the idea of faux products like vinyl plank or laminate and are more prepared for the care and maintenance of hardwood. For some, allergies prevent them from having carpets or require them to install wool rather than synthetic fibers. Environmentalists may want to see the impact on Mother Earth and will only install organic products. Time to do some research with your flooring experts!

Keep a couple of things in mind.

Firstly, when it comes to hard surfaces, every flooring type can be scratched or damaged, depending on the situation. A little rock in a shoe, a pet's nails or a child with a jackknife... you can only recommend the best flooring possible with that caveat in mind. Preparing your client is smart; buying a couple of extra boxes is smarter!

Secondly, all hard surfaces need the chance to acclimate to the environment they are about to be installed in. They need to adjust to the house's moisture and temperature, even more so in the wintertime. Hardwood always needs to acclimate no matter the season. Others need the chance to warm up from the cold properly...and not just the outer boxes on the pallet. Spreading all the boxes out helps each to acclimate.

Let's go over the available products with their pros and cons.

Hardwood/ Engineered Hardwood

Hardwood has a beautiful warmth and vibrancy to it that is simply not matched in any other product. It adds significant value to a home if it is in good shape. All hardwood floors need to be maintained with the proper cleaning solutions and accessories. Still, there is something more that is vital to the longevity of a hardwood floor. Humidity.

A home MUST have a humidifier and a dehumidifier, depending on your area's average humidity levels. Wood is a natural product that absorbs water, which causes it to expand, and without it, it contracts. In simple terms, it moves a lot and needs to have the humidity levels averaged and kept in a range between 30-50% to remain stable. It must be installed according to the manufacturer's specifications and given the proper time to acclimate to the client's home before installation. Watch exterior temperatures for installation as well. Minus forty degrees Celsius (and Fahrenheit) outside means the house will be frigid by entrances and have the furnace turned up. Those variables are too much for the flooring, and installation needs to be postponed.

Solid hardwood is typically 3/4" thick and is using valuable top-quality wood all the way through. It means that there is more wood to react to variances in moisture or dryness. A person can refinish it any number of times as it has plenty of wood to work with. The most expensive option, hardwood sheens can vary from a satin finish to a high gloss. Most people think of a high gloss floor when they picture a solid hardwood floor. Again, any disturbance to the surface is evident in a high sheen, including the topcoat's poor application, imperfections in the wood itself, or simple footprints.

Engineered hardwood is a hybrid hardwood of sorts. You still get a hardwood floor with the top layer or veneer, and those vary from a very thin veneer to a thicker one depending on the brand and quality. The thinner the veneer, the less expensive it will be but will never have the option of refinishing the floor. The thicker the veneer, the more it will cost; however, you may get one or two chances to refinish it. Various layers of counter glued top-quality plywood is used to create overall thickness. Counter glued layers mean the plywood is glued with the grain running in one direction. The next board glued, running in the opposite direction. When the boards react to the humidity or lack of it, they are pulling or pushing against each other unable to expand or contract as a solid hardwood could.

Engineered hardwood is more stable and typically less expensive than solid hardwood... especially in environments that see extremes in seasons. Of course, the more exotic the wood or the design elements, the higher the price of even engineered flooring will be.

As we mentioned with the cabinets, you can opt to refinish them. Still, it will create a drastic interference in a client's home to do it, never mind the expense and finding someone capable of the job. It is often less expensive to replace the hardwood than to go through the hassle of refinishing it. That doesn't sound very good for anyone with an environmental inclination, but it is the truth. And some folks just cannot bring themselves to do that to a hardwood floor, so it is important to have that discussion with your client.

Laminate

This flooring has had a lousy reputation...let me rephrase that. Laminate used to have a bad reputation. It is a wood particle composite product with a wood grain laminated image to mimic hardwood. Laminates from the past were less susceptible to scratches and the wear and tear of hardwood. But oh, were they ever troublesome if any water came into contact with them. Sitting water or floods would warp or ripple the laminate in no time flat. They needed replacing entirely unless the homeowner had enough spare boxes kicking around to repair the damaged area. One of these laminates may even be the reason that your client is in the middle of a renovation.

Laminates today have evolved. They had to to compete in the vinyl flooring world. There are water-resistant laminates with tightly compacted composites that prevent water from absorbing when there is a spill or sitting water. But to a degree. If you come home to a flooded basement, I suspect that the flooring will need replacing for insurance purposes. The imagery has also improved with many styles to choose from, such as rustic with chatter marks and knots, country cottage with white-washed effects and traditional hardwood looks. It means that even though they are more scratch-resistant, they hide more on a surface that already has rustic or a relaxed style.

I recommend a water-resistant laminate when the budget or intended maintenance does not fit with hardwood. Laminates still provide warmth, texture, natural wood tones and character to the home. Laminates use a click system instead of nailing and gluing, with the installation itself being more affordable. An underlay vapor barrier is needed, which is typically a poly foam. A thicker acoustic underlay can help buffer sound transfer from the house's upper levels to the lower.

Laminates are also a good option when taking out thicker flooring. It comes in thicknesses ranging from about 8mm to 12mm. In some cases, they can butt up to existing or new tile flooring without adding subfloor, therefore saving more expense. And trust me, the client will be all about saving more money when they can.

As with all click system products, they have to be installed correctly for them to function properly. Seems simple right? There are many DIY types out there, or even some installers, who treat flooring like anything else. "Hey, I'm handy! I can figure it out."

Click systems are a floating floor, which means they are not attached to the subfloor anywhere. It operates as a single unit in the home. If the walls are out of square, the sub-floor is uneven, or the house moves a lot, the flooring is trying to maneuver with any movement. First, it just will not work in a home that has a very uneven surface to install on without levelling it first. Secondly, if the flooring is installed too tight to the wall, then when the house moves, the flooring is locked into place and will buckle. If the flooring is installed too far out from the wall, the floor can shift and show gaps or even have a problem staying locked together.

A laminate floor will click together on the long side of the board in a tongue and groove, then butt up together at the ends, simply put. The flooring must be fully engaged for it to remain "clicked." A professional installation is always a good idea. Still, at the very least, some professional advice and following the instructions included in the flooring box should get them off on the right foot.

Click Or Loose-Lay Vinyl Plank

Maybe your client has heard of vinyl plank flooring; perhaps they have not. Unless your clients have been doing some research or chatting with the neighbors who just installed it, they may not be aware of it. You do not have to be a flooring expert, but it is good to understand so you can adequately make suggestions to them.

Vinyl plank comes in two styles. Click vinyl, which interlocks as a tongue and groove and is a floating floor-like laminate. Loose-lay vinyl plank adheres to the subfloor either in a perimeter glue or a full glue-down application. I will go more into each one of them in a moment. I want to talk about vinyl itself first.

What is vinyl in the first place? It is essentially plastic. Why is that a popular flooring option? It is scratch-resistant, long-lasting, waterproof, and typically very budget-friendly. They clean easily, with the right solvents, so a build-up does not occur. When it comes to being recyclable, of course, they can be, but you do not want to buy a vinyl floor made with recycled plastics. In this instance, virgin vinyl is the only way to go. Recycled plastics can have chemicals that do not translate well into a quality flooring product.

Off-gassing is a severe problem because it introduces chemicals and odors into the home. For those who have health issues, this is even worse. How does off-gassing occur? Usually, when the product is heated when it is in direct sunlight or by a heat register. Inexpensive plastic blinds or fabrics can have this effect as well.

In short, cheaper is not always better.

We need to talk about the wear layer. It is the protective layer placed over the laminated image on the vinyl flooring. It is there to protect from sun damage and regular wear and tear to the floor. You will hear this terminology a lot when visiting the flooring stores. It is measured in *milliliters* because it is like a poured clear coating. You will see *millimeters* for the thickness of the flooring as a whole.

Wear layers can range between 8 to 22ml, and I have to say, I would not purchase one below 12ml and rated for residential use. 20 to 22ml is rated for residential AND commercial use, which means a homeowner will get the thickest wear layer and more endurance for their buck. You will notice wear layers in the descriptions for laminate as well. The better the wear layer, and the thicker the overall flooring, the higher the price; however, as the adage goes, "You get what you pay for."

Loose-Lay Vinyl Plank

Loose-lay vinyl plank is usually 5mm thick, very pliable, and can work for any area of the house. Well, do not apply this in an outdoor setting or where cars park. It will fail under those circumstances! This vinyl can be glued both at just the room's perimeter or as a full glue spread. In some cases, if the room is quite large, run an additional strip of glue down the middle of the room. The glue plus the weight of the product keeps it in place. It does not interlock like a click system but instead butts tightly together with rectified edges on all four sides. If installed correctly, and it is a quality product, then there will not be any gapping.

Some lesser quality loose-lay vinyl will shrink and expand in extreme temperature changes to the point where the planks have larger gaps. The glue used is typically a heat-release product, so, in some situations, direct sunlight from large windows can release the adhesive. In those instances, you want sufficient window coverings to filter light in the room. Or, if that is not an option, do not suggest this type of flooring. Good quality loose-lay flooring gets acclimated in the manufacturing stages. Any shrinkage or expansion will be minimal and quickly self-correct after resolving extreme temperatures.

Loose lay 5mm vinyl is optimal for situations where the sub-floor is not even, in poor condition, or if the house moves a lot.

For example, a historical home may have uneven floors from the house settling over the years. If the homeowner is not pre-pared to lift the house and rebuild the foundation, then you may want to replace the flooring with this flexible option. It would need fully glued to respond and move with the variance in the roller coaster subfloor in that setting.

While this product's thickness and flexibility will hide small imperfections, you still want to have the substrate properly prepped and levelled as much as possible. Skipping steps is usu-ally where the failures happen. It may disguise small dips or bumps to the eye, but you will indeed feel it when you walk on it in those areas.

There are other thicknesses of vinyl plank flooring available. 2 and 3mm thick products are for full glue-down applications only and meant for commercial projects. They have zero for-giveness in hiding imperfections in the subfloor or concrete. They genuinely do not have any cushion to them. Many flooring stores and home builders use this product in new construction or renovations because they are an inexpensive option. They also have wear layers that range from 8 to 20 ml for durability on the surface. However, I have an issue selling this in a customer's home unless we need to apply it over existing hardwoods with-out adding more flooring height. I believe that flooring should provide comfort as well as making sense for the client's home.

Click Vinyl

Installation can vary in a click vinyl with a tongue and

groove system. There are a few different click systems out there, and it is a good idea to inform yourself when shopping. A 2G locking system means that it clicks together on each plank's two long sides, where a 5G locking system clicks together on the sides and the ends. The Unilin locking system is also a high-quality locking system on all four sides of the plank. It is essential because you have more of the board locked in place. With the improper installation of a 2G locking system, the plank can slide apart at the butt ends, creating gaps. Knowing what system a product has may help you in your decision-making with the client.

Click vinyl plank comes in various thicknesses ranging from 5mm to 8mm. Some have the attached pad or underlay already. Those that come without it still require the underlay, which will be at an additional charge on the estimate. Keep that cost in mind when you are making comparisons. Some have a cork back, and others a foam. Both are mold and mildew-resistant. Both are great options for soundproofing. I like the cork backing only for a little better cushioning.

Another difference in vinyl click is that some are solid vinyl plank, which will be warmer on the feet. Others have a stone core for stability, which means the plank is even less bendable, and it can be cooler on bare feet. There is a time and place for each kind, but it is something to look for and know the options rather than just picking flooring for the color or style.

It can be a very durable and appealing option when selecting flooring. There is a reason that it has become so popular in the industry. When you consider a less expensive, thinner vinyl click, the click system itself may not give sturdy support. The wrong move during installation, or having a weak area in the subfloor, and the clicking mechanism can snap. I am not inclined to offer the cheapest product out there for the sake of pinching pennies. I can assure you that replacing the flooring within a couple of years will not be money well spent.

Spend well once.

While you are shopping, you will notice that some vinyl

click flooring has various seam designs available. A micro-bevelled edge has little distinction between the boards. It can look like a sheet good, except that the boards' variances will still give a subtle plank appearance when properly installed. A bevelled edge has a slight groove on the plank's side to create more of a cut look. This style has more distinction of a hardwood plank with clear lines. A painted bevelled edge is another term for this; however, you may notice some edges have contrasting colors that stand out more. Make sure you know which your client would prefer because it is a very personal decision.

Some installers prefer one type of flooring over the other. They may have had bad experiences with a specific type of flooring. Many factors come into play. The difference is installing the right flooring for the house and getting a professional installer capable of completing the job. Many installers insist on telling the customer what to buy, and trusting their opinion, narrow their selection without knowing why. The installer is there to assist in successfully installing a product, not critiquing the flooring selected. If a product is indeed problematic, the installer notifies you. Then speak to the store so they can talk to the manufacturer. Give the homeowner the information and discuss their options once you have a solution.

It is not about disguising an issue. Do not get me wrong. I have known a contractor or two who voiced their opinions out of turn, and it caused the homeowner to feel insecure about their purchase. Worrying phone calls start coming in where you start looking into potential problems that have not even happened yet, and in some cases, deal with unnecessary returns. It is another reason it is so important to have trusted professionals working with you. You know that any issues that happen to come up are dealt with in a less dramatic or problematic fashion.

Suppose you are worried about the repeat in pattern from a manufactured product vs natural. In that case, there is about four to six picture "films" designed for the vinyl or laminates. Not every box will have the same variance, though. Hence, to catch repeat boards, it is important to install from two or three boxes to achieve a more random installation across the floor.

Sheet Vinyl

Sheet vinyl, also known as linoleum, is a twelve-foot-wide vinyl flooring that rolls out with fewer "seams" as vinyl plank products. It was used quite heavily in years gone by, and the trend is less popular now. Indeed, older clientele may be more interested in linoleum for projects like holiday trailers and modular homes.

As with all types of flooring, there is a good, better, best range of linoleum. The less it costs, the thinner it tends to be and can be less flexible. The thicker it is, the more cushion it has. But, it costs more.

This product can be installed over pre-existing linoleum, but only if the seams are intact and the flooring is in relatively good shape. A skim coat is needed to fill any patterning that could telegraph through the new flooring. Still, it is also required to give the new glue a good surface for adhesion. Years of cleaning products build up a residue that acts as a barrier to adhesives. Telegraphing describes when you can see the old patterns or shapes indented in the new flooring.

My relatives helped my grandmother with a new flooring project. They happened to install new sheet vinyl over the old one without skim coating it. The original flooring had a lovely, checkered pattern with little flowers in the center. The new pattern was more of a stone look. Within a year, odd squares started to appear through the design of the new flooring. Voila...telegraphing!

The most popular designs in sheet vinyl tend to be in brick or stone patterns. Manufacturers have started coming out with trendy tile designs like damask, fun colors, and geometric shapes in recent years. They can be a fun option to consider in a laundry room or entrance.

Installation in large areas is not a fun process, and this type of flooring is the least favorite of installers. Before specifying sheet vinyl on a project, ensure that you have an installer willing to work with it. The stiffness of the product combined with the twelve-foot width makes it difficult to maneuver and work with.

My personal preference is to go to this idea last. You do not see many linoleum installations in the magazines anymore. It does not feel like an inspired approach to a fresh design—just my opinion.

Tile/Tile Products

Ah, the beauty of newly installed tile in bold and creative new designs, nothing like it! The opportunity for texture, variance in patterns, and tile layouts are endless. Tile is in entrances, kitchens, bathrooms, laundry rooms, backsplashes, tub surrounds, and steam showers. It can be a feature around a fireplace and hearth too. From frescoes to ledgestone and everything in between, tile is an excellent step into texture and style.

Tile is not so easy to install and is also the most expensive flooring for labor costs. To begin with, it's heavy! It is not always easy to cut. It must have a level surface and the tile installed according to the proper applications. Paying for a professional tile installation is well worth the money, though. Thick grout, uneven tile setting, improperly spaced or cut tile can all look like a dog's breakfast. Tile setters who are mostly handling tile projects for a living are often way more skilled than the general contractor who can do a bit of everything. Be very sure about a person's skill set before you have them do any large tile projects for you. Floor tile set unevenly creates "toe stubbers" or lippage. Meaning an edge or a corner of the tile is higher than the one set beside it: a definite tripping hazard and an eyesore.

Every type of tile gets designated by the manufacturer. A person can use floor tile on walls, but not wall tile on floors. Glass tile is not recommended for floors as it will easily fracture and break. Some tile is not suitable for wet areas such as showers.

This information is found on the supplier's sample board or on-line. If you have difficulty getting the information, your flooring/tile store can do some research to get it for you.

There are different types of tiles to consider for your project. Some will be better suited, and others less so.

A porcelain tile is more expensive and fired all the way through for extreme durability. Some porcelain tiles are designated for exterior projects, but not all of them. Ceramic tile is only fired on the tile's surface, so less expensive and is not as durable. If it is not labelled, inspect the tile sample's edge and look for a difference in tone and texture. If it is uniform throughout the thickness of the tile, then it is likely porcelain. If it has more of a jawbreaker look with a layer, then it is ceramic.

Natural stone will need to be sealed on occasion to protect it from dirt and dampness. Travertine, marble, and slate are well known for natural beauty but create distinctly different looks in the home. Not only will the expense of the tile itself be a consideration, but the maintenance and sheen will be as well. Honed travertine is smooth and polished for a more elegant look, whereas tumbled has rough edges and more pits for the grout to find its way into.

A rectified edge is a precise cut to the tile, again adding some expense, and allows you to leave very little space between the tiles. It is the way to reduce the amount of grout to clean or the grout lines' appearance. Bevelled edges in tile allow the grout to stand out, and this is where you may see more grout color options coming into play.

The most significant functional element to consider when picking out tile for flooring is SAFETY. How slippery is the tile you are considering? Where is it going? Is there going to be a chance of water sitting on the surface? Are the clients more likely to have an accident, such as older adults or those with some physical limitations? You can have the most beautiful rectified and polished porcelain tile with a Calcutta marble pattern planned for a client's bathroom. Still, unless they wear water shoes into the shower, there could be a lot of falls.

Carpet

There was a time where carpet rather than solid hardwood was a sign of wealth, which is why we found so much hardwood underneath it in historic homes. Its popularity comes from being a budget-friendly option, cushioning, warmth on the feet, and buffering sound. It is the least expensive flooring to install, especially on staircases and comes mostly in twelve-foot widths, but some are available in fifteen.

There are many options when it comes to carpet too. A cut pile can be shorter or longer, and you will hear them described as plush or even shag with the longest strands. Cutting the top of the fiber loop after being woven through the backing is called a cut pile.

A cut loop pile means that some of the loops are cut, and others are left, creating various patterns and textures. You typically see this in shorter stranded carpeting.

The loop pile is another found in professional buildings, formal areas, and places where there is a lot of furniture or heavy traffic. They tend to be tightly woven and have a short pile. Thicker looped carpets are often referred to as Berber and were quite popular in the last twenty-five years.

One thing to note about Berber: It developed a bad reputation for running or zippering if a snag developed. Pulling the snag would unravel the weave due to how the fiber is threaded through the backing. The better Berber carpets of today are now singularly looped so that if a snag occurs and does pull out, it is that single loop and is not a continuous thread.

Carpet quality can vary, and many consumers make the mistake of shopping based on a low-price tag. The more fibers per square inch, the denser the carpet is. It makes sense that the better the density, the better the carpet's quality, and that it would cost more. The less fiber per inch, the less dense it is, the less cushion you have, and the quicker the fibers wear.

I have felt what a standard "builder's grade" carpet is. Not only could I see the backing, but I could easily feel it with my fingers when I probed a little. You can easily see the sheen from the carpet backing when wrapped around the stair nose and as you stand back from it. Now I can understand what folks do when they are in a pinch, but I was not about to settle for that to even suggest it to my client.

To test a carpet's density, you should run your hand on the surface of the rug and then probe to the back of the sample as if you were playing the piano. Was it easy to feel the backing? Or difficult? Do the fibers move without much resistance, or are they standing up to your inspection? Sometimes manufacturers will put the "pounds per inch" on the sample's back, but that happens less frequently now. Your older clientele may be more versed in those terms, but that is less and less common too.

What the fibers are made of is an integral part of the decision-making process. To regular customers walking off the street, they mostly shop on price, color, and feel. In that order. But to people concerned about stain resistance, allergies, and how long the carpet will last have way more questions.

Polyester fiber can be dyed easily, which is why you will find many polyesters or poly blends in carpeting. Polyester is soft and durable as well. Nylon, however, does not dye and must be manufactured with color. That makes it extraordinarily stain-resistant and durable. It is stiffer than polyester, standing up to the dents from furniture legs better, though it is not as soft to the touch. You will often find poly/nylon blends in carpeting, which gives you the best of both worlds. Of course, each manufacturer has its terminology for stain protection in their carpets. Some are proprietary, and others use the familiar Scotchgard brand. Truthfully, most carpets have some stain protection.

The softest rugs will have a percentage of silk in them. They are pricey and of good quality, but oh man, are they divine on the feet! People who suffer from foot problems or arthritis may enjoy the comfort this carpet provides. I cannot help myself when I feel the silk carpet samples. I must touch them and have trouble stopping!

Wool carpets are the most expensive; however, they are also the hardiest. They can be dyed and are hypoallergenic. People who prefer wool will be the type who wants to make a lasting investment in their flooring.

I have known some who were replacing their wool carpets simply to change the color. The rug itself was still in perfect condition.

They range in softness as some are surprisingly touchable and others are rougher, but the only way to tell is to feel them. When cleaning wool rugs, they need professionals, and your warranties may only be in place with proof of maintenance.

Let's talk about underlay. You would not think this was a big deal, that it is just a pad under the carpet for comfort. It is what protects the wear and tear of the rug itself while it is giving comfort. It is measured in pounds per inch and comprises densely packed foam pieces of different qualities ranging from 6lb to 10lb. A good average to stick to is 8lb underlay, and here is why.

The 8lb underlay gives the most comfort and protection. Going less may interfere with your warranty, and your carpet will not last as long. Going to a 10lb underlay is very firm and is better suited for the heavy impact on stairs. Carpet manufacturer's warranties will specify a minimum underlay to go under their carpets, which you get from your salesperson.

Tip: Less scrupulous flooring stores are known to win a quote with what you think is an apple-to-apple comparison. What they are doing is installing a thinner, cheaper underlay instead of what was originally quoted and purchased. Once out of sight, no one is there to check it against what the consumer thought they were getting, right? Know who you are buying from, the standards and quality they provide and that they are trustworthy.

Carpets are most often found in bedrooms and basements these days. Of course, it can go anywhere in the house, but I would not recommend it in the bathrooms. Oh yes, I have seen it, and you may see it too!

Installing it means that rolls of precut "fabric" are about to be pieced together in the home, and the rug needs rolled out to accomplish it. That means it may roll out with the roll ends contacting the wall as they go and scratching the paint. I will get to the paint in a moment. They have developed a soft backing for carpeting to avoid damage to the walls and make it easier on the installer's hands. You can ask for this when the salesperson is showing you samples.

The question always arises, is it better to paint before the flooring is installed or after? The flooring installers will want you to paint first; the painters will want the flooring installed. Neither wants the other trade to cause damage to their product.

So, where does that leave us? Well, again, who is painting? A professional painter will not risk any scratches or damage to the flooring. You may want to consider whether they will need ladders or scaffolding on your newly installed hardwood. Then it may be prudent to paint first. Knowing that carpeting is going to roll and potentially scratch the paint. Either wait to paint or at least get the primer and first coat finished. Then the painter can come back for any repairs and the last coat.

The flooring installers should be as careful as possible; however, they should also be documenting the state of the walls and railings before installation and after. So they have some comparison to determine what they are responsible for fixing.

There have been clients who decided that the flooring installer caused all the damage to the wall and insisted the whole thing be repainted. When in fact, it was pre-existing damage. It may even be prudent for you to document any issues before the trades going into the house, so you are on top of these situations before they happen.

All flooring types have appealing and less attractive aspects. Still, with a little knowledge under your belt, you will be able to marry the best of them together for a beautiful outcome!

Countertops And Backsplash

I love the thought of walking into my kitchen in the morning, still wearing my robe, and drinking my tea at the island, just taking in my relaxing space. Having beautiful countertops to make my favorite food or set out dishes for a family get-together is part of that fantasy.

When we begin to focus on countertops and backsplash, we tend to gravitate towards the kitchen and then consider the bathrooms throughout the house. Depending on the budget, bathrooms can become a "later on" project, but in some cases, it may make more sense to do the bathrooms at the same time. There are many types of countertops with all their colors and patterns to pick from. Once again, there are many factors to consider regarding what is more suitable for the homeowner and their project. I had more than one client come to me swimming in ideas and random samples, trying to make sense of it all and what would be the best choice.

I learned a little trick that I used quite often. Every time a client had been overwhelmed with what to pick, I did this every time, and I found myself teaching them as we went.

It is easy to stare a set of samples down until you believe everything looks fine. They get installed, and then one day, you are standing there brushing your teeth, you bend over to spit, and bam... something does not quite look right when you see the counter with the flooring. Why does this get noticed in those moments? Because while focusing on other items, your gaze is softened.

When I am helping a client through tile selection, I go through a process. I explain the color theory of how colors interact while also organizing the samples a little. Usually, this initial process would eliminate one or two options right off the bat. Again, I do not tell people what to see; instead, I showed them what could happen if specific colors were in the same room or how busy or straightforward a tile may be.

I began a process that was a little like going to the eye doctor. I wanted their first reaction, "I like it!" or "I do not like it!" I did not give them time to get their thinking caps on, as I showed them different samples. I knew which pieces to gravitate towards because of their responses to both the questions I asked and their reactions. It has narrowed down a lot of samples to just a few very quickly.

I would place one or two of the remaining flooring options on the floor by my design table. Then I put the countertop options on the table, but at the edge, so it did not leave my table showing. If they brought a cabinet sample, I would lean this on the table leg or place it on the flooring. It mimics a cabinet, counter, and flooring scenario. I try to organize the samples to represent how the light will be hitting it and eliminate any outside influencing elements, like the showroom flooring.

I asked my client to stand on the flooring at the table edge and look down past the counter sample to the tips of their toes. I did not want them to focus on the samples just yet, just their shoes. To just look softly and allow their impression to come through. I asked them if they liked the effect of the patterns together, if there were any unexpected or unpleasant tones showing up or if they liked them. Once they answered it, I would shift to a different sample and carry on until we narrowed it down.

Keep in mind that the lighting in a store or design studio will be completely different from the home. You always want to make the final selections in the house with their lighting. You also want to be careful if the client intends to change the light fixtures, especially if they move them because it can create different tones than initially planned.

It is a good idea to have an Option A "look," or collection of samples, and Option B. That way, if the client does take them home and does not like a set of samples, they have another option to go by. Ideally, you will be present for the on-site selection, and if nothing is working, your keen eye will pick up on what direction to go. If you can, go shopping with your clients to prevent them from bringing home the whole store.

If the client wants the island featured with a different paint color or wood tone from the main cabinets, consider a feature countertop for the island. Again, be cautious about the idea that you can put more expensive quartz on the island and save dollars with less expensive quartz for the main cabinets. You must look at the per slab price and whether that economically makes sense for the budget. Another thought would be to use a beautiful quartz or butcher block on the island and then go to a lesser expensive countertop for the main. Sure, it is ideal to have the same surface on all the countertops; however, sometimes, we must be inventive and work with the budget or space.

Let's visit the types of countertops available, and then we will discuss backsplash.

Laminate Countertops

No, this is not the same as the flooring laminate. It is the least expensive option for countertops. It consists of a plastic, photography, and transparent coat layer pressed to a thin particle composite board and sold in thin sheets. Many images mimic quartz or granite but are not limited to stone looks. They have had leaf designs, faux paint finishes and come in any color under the sun. The top clear coat layer can also be glossy, matte, pebbled for texture, or even slightly metallic. Most times, there will be one pattern with a few sheen options to pick from, so be careful to show your client all the sheens available.

With all countertops, the edge profile has different options. The standard is a squared-off edge, but there are rounded and bevelled options available too. Of course, you can opt to have a wooden nosing stained to match the cabinets if the laminate

There is the consideration of wear and tear when you are planning this element. A square edge profile means the laminate is cut into a thin strip and adhered to the surface, creating a seam where it butts together. It has the potential of eventually lifting and catching on clothing. The edge profile is the most likely area to wear, especially by sinks or heavily used work areas. Some prefer the rounded profile, or shape, even though the cost may be slightly higher.

As most kitchen cabinets do not run on one wall, the laminate will "turn" with the cabinets on different walls. In the instance of an "L" shaped kitchen, there will be a seam, and there is no getting away from it. It is crucial to ensure that your client knows the seam placement, especially if you have someone who is extraordinarily detail-oriented.

The other thing to consider with this change of direction is the pattern of the laminate. A sheet-good must be cut to fit. When the design has a heavy line running through the entire piece, it can make the counter look like it runs in a separate direction when cut and the second piece installed. Specific marble or natural stone designs may be better on larger islands that do not change direction.

When it comes to picking complementary backsplash, I have found laminates to be a bit easier in lining up sheens and getting tones to marry well together...especially when it comes to whites. White is never white. A manufactured product like laminate is quite different in sheen and undertone than quartz or granite, and selecting backsplash tile can be a little more limited.

Granite

Granite countertops are genuinely a solid natural stone product. Its beautifully polished surface is a magnificent work of art. No piece can be duplicated. It is so unique that a store sample will not give you the most accurate depiction of what the full slab will look like. That is why it is better to see the slab yard in person, preferably with your clients. Handpick the slabs for installation.

I have an appreciation of what mother nature can do. The suppliers see people like me coming a mile away because slabs with more elaborate color, veining, and patterns will come at a premium price. The more commonplace the slab, the less it will cost.

Granite and quartz need to be cleaned with a special counter-top cleaner to properly restore the counter's sheen and prevent dulling and build-up. Some homeowners want as little high-end maintenance as possible and may balk at having a different product for every surface in their house. Knowing what kind of clients you have on your hands will help you educate them to have realistic expectations.

You would think that only doing the kitchen and dropping the bathrooms from the quote will save more money. Granite and quartz countertops come in precut slabs, and you must buy the entire slab for your project. You utilize more of the product by keeping the bathrooms on the quote, depending on the kitchen's size, as you will be charged for the number of slabs needed, not by the square footage. You would have required the same number of slabs to do the kitchen, but with waste, waste that would have been enough for the bathroom project.

People often ask for these countertops' square foot price; however, each slab is priced individually, they are only ever an average. You will not know the cost until you get the quote. There is usually a price range indicated on the samples at the store to give you some idea of what price range you are working with.

Quartz

Often showcased in magazines, It is no surprise why it is a

favorite of designers and homeowners alike. Quartz has quickly become one of the most popular choices when it comes to countertops.

Some mimic Carrara marble; others have little chunks of glass or sparkles or a pebbled look. The solid colors are popular choices with white to black and many natural-toned colors in between. Some quartz options with resin variations can make it appear a little like a riverbed or a galaxy. It is the benefit of a manufactured product with the beauty of unique quartz material.

Quartz is made up of natural ground down quartz crystal stones into a fine powder. Color and designs are added and then processed into the finished slabs. It is a manufactured natural product. The quartz quality comes down to what percentage of quartz is used compared to fillers, and that, my friends, is the question.

You will not likely get that information when you are shopping. As with most items you buy, North American products are manufactured under strict environmental, safety, and health regulations. Quality control and warranties give the consumer reassurance when they are spending their hard-earned money.

In foreign countries, they can skip steps or use lesser quality components in the manufacturing process, and you would never know. Their prices are so enticing because they can give you a more budget-friendly option. Still, you also do not have the warranties to assure the performance is there. Yes, that means that North American quartz products are a higher price point but so is the quality. Your job as a designer is to give your client all the information to make an informed decision.

To get rid of fingerprints, grime, and smears on quartz, you need the proper cleaners. Even with clean gloves, some white quartz samples are very prone to stubborn fingerprints. The installers cannot put the quartz in without getting fingerprints all over the slab that are almost impossible to remove. And when a homeowner spends thousands of dollars on something, they expect it to be pristine when they first see it and not be problematic.

I will caution you to ask the supplier lots of questions about installing the quartz you have selected. If there are any known problems with that brand or color and what the recommended maintenance should be.

Do not get me wrong; quartz is a gorgeous and hardy surface for countertops. For the most part, it is stain-resistant and should hold up to standard household wear and tear. One client was on a stool getting a jug off a top shelf in her kitchen. It was not that heavy, but it slipped from her hands, hit the edge of her quartz countertop, and shattered. After she finished cleaning the jug up, she saw that it had hit the edge just right and chipped the countertop.

Dropping a hammer or being reckless will likely lead to damage, which is why installers or other trades should *never* put their tools on a quartz countertop.

I know of another customer who poured a cleaning solution into a separate plastic container then got called away. When she returned, the cleaner had eaten through the plastic container and was pooling on her quartz. After cleaning it up, she saw that the cleaner had roughed up her quartz, essentially acid etching the surface.

Carelessness can lead to expensive damages no matter what the surface. Only the supplier can tell you if a repair is possible, but it will have to be replaced or lived with in most cases.

Pricing is calculated the same way as granite. The fancier the slab, the more money it will be, and every sample is individual. They are priced as builder's grade, standard, premium, extra premium, and exotic, starting from the lowest price to the highest. Each supplier will use their unique terminology. You cannot compare a North American manufacturer to a builder's grade in a foreign one. Suppose your client wants a quote in more than one sample. In that case, an apple-to-apple comparison can only happen from two different suppliers in the same brand and color.

Butcher Block

This style takes the cutting board and enlarges it to fit an entire island or complete set of countertops. Butcher block adds a sense of natural warmth into a kitchen when the other surfaces are painted or tiled. It speaks to a reclaimed or modern farmhouse feel with its handmade appearance.

Butcher block countertops have several hardwood strips bonded together, usually maple. Although cherry, oak, and walnut are also used. They are sealed with specific food-safe oils that protect the surface from water and debris and give the wood an enriching "drink" to keep the wood from drying out and splitting.

Homeowners must be prepared to maintain them with proper cleaning and butcher block oil treatment. The frequency will depend on the oil manufacturer's guidelines and the instructions on the product bottle. These products should be available in any store that sells wood stains.

As with any countertop, a proper cutting board or sheet must be used to protect the surface from knife marks. A butcher block countertop will show dents or cuts from wear and tear more than a more rigid surface. Be prepared for this possibility. It is also fair to consider how young the children are in the house. They may not understand that they should not cut with knives directly on the wooden countertops and cause damage before their parents know what is happening.

Pricing on butcher block countertops will be more expensive than laminate surfaces and less costly than granite, quartz, or hard surfaces. They are also much easier to install. It may be another reason that homeowners find them appealing for their budgets.

Solid Surfaces

What do I mean by a solid-surface countertop? Aren't they all solid?

This category covers concrete, resins, and any number of creative solutions that people have invented. There are many benefits and considerations to consider with all of them. I would highly recommend doing a lot of research on the supplier or company providing them before offering this suggestion to your clients. Some of them are tried-and-true; others could look cool but not be very practical in your client's home. You want to use warrantied products with trusted suppliers and manufacturers rather than the guy who just started into the countertop business a month ago.

I have seen some beautiful concrete countertops with pieces of sea glass embedded in it. It was also sculpted. When the client rested a dish rack on the counter, it automatically drained away water following the swirl pattern. A person can do many exciting things with these types of surfaces, so they are worth considering. Seamless applications are possible, but consider the weight and ease of installation before finalizing the decision. I am sure that your client may not mind any necessary seams once they realize that they would not get the countertops through the front door.

Pricing will range on how customized the solid surface countertop is, the products used in manufacturing, and demand. You can find less expensive options in big box stores, excellent stain resistance, and many design selections. If you consider using their installation services, ensure you know in advance what their policies are regarding repairs or issues, should they come up.

From experience, some of these installation teams come in from out of town. The company cannot service the issue quickly, or worse. They are not inclined to handle customer aftercare at all. Consider the level of customer service as you inform your client where to spend their money.

When it comes to quoting, you can provide a set of drawings and measurements to begin the process. However, to get a firm estimate, the countertop supplier or contractor will need to do their measurements and template for the job. It ensures that they have the right amount of material, knows seam placement and what kind of quirks may need to be worked around.

If you are getting more than one quote, you will have the same people to do their templates. You never want to use someone else's measurements or templates to order a custom product elsewhere. Any errors made could transfer to the other supplier, and they will not be responsible for the error. That could be a costly mistake for you.

We touched on the customer service aspect of the purchase. It makes sense that the real value is not merely in the product itself but the experience of choosing, buying, installing, and service afterward. Many companies are vying for a piece of the pie and will do almost anything to gain a sale. Be wary of this, though. It does not mean your client is getting the best value for the money they spend. They could be paying for a load of problems if they happen to purchase with an unscrupulous business. Sometimes there are hidden costs in the quotes so that they can add unexpected expenses.

In some cases, expenses will happen like extra repairs to the drywall. Cabinet supports that were thought to be sufficient need to be replaced, or cabinetry could need touch-ups after installation. Discuss them as they come up, so the homeowner is informed adequately as the situations come up. Having the right supplier on board will mean that they work with you to keep everyone up to date. Companies who are not on the up and up may not be so quick to inform anyone if issues or charge for items the customer did not get. That is something to look for with all quotes from any trade.

Backsplash

Don't you find the idea of shopping for backsplash tiles exhilarating? There is something about finding the perfect shape, texture, and tile colour to tie the kitchen together. It is the opportunity for more creativity. As designers, we are SO ready to bust loose our pent-up artistic juices.

Like the tile that we discussed with flooring, backsplash tile can be ceramic, porcelain, glass and natural stone. It can have mixed elements that include pieces of mirror or contrasting colors woven into intricate patterns. Some backsplash tile can even mimic fabric patterns. This decorative element truly adds flavor to the kitchen or bathroom.

You can add rustic Italian porcelain with a wide variety of old-world patterns or glass "lanterns" for posh sophistication. Change the contrast a little with some tone in the grout, so the tiles themselves pop out more. Run the pattern opposite to what one would expect. Or mix colors in the same style of tile. It becomes slightly addicting with all the ways that we can play with backsplashes.

We must consider our client's goals and tastes. Before we get too carried away, consider what they are most likely to gravitate towards. Something I have noticed over the years is that people react to the idea of *busy*.

Most of our clients cannot visualize the finished project as we can, so they may have a vague idea of what "busy" will be. Others mean that they do not want it to look busy, and there needs to be real thought into how the project will look to them. The art of being a truly gifted designer is the ability to step into your client's shoes. To see the project from their standpoint, desires and tastes, then step back out and pull it off for them. *This* is what they have hired you to do.

Clients who are particular about perfect or straight lines will less likely appreciate teardrop or lantern-shaped tiles. They will not want tumbled or rough edges to their tile either. Those edges "catch" the grout. They will expect straight grout lines and crisp edges in their tile, so you then know what to steer clear of. Those who like more of a Boho or Farmhouse feel may like a little "rough around the edges" feel or a handmade look. These clients are not likely to want to color inside the lines and find straight or square tiles too stiff and formal.

Tile surfaces can come in sheens from matte to highly polished. Just because it is highly polished does not mean that it is a flat surface. Some subway tiles come with a handmade wavy look to their surface, which will catch the light when installed vertically. Some may like this effect; others may find this busy, yet you would have thought this a simple look.

Rectified tile edges are a crisp and sharp cut to the tile. Tumbled will have a bit of a chunky effect. Bevelled edges mean there is a slight slope at the edge and can create a subtle shadow. Beveled tile can also refer to, for example, a subway tile that has a second rectangle pattern indented or raised to create a three-dimensional aspect.

The thickness and dimension of the tile you select play a massive part if you intend to blend different tiles together. If they do not match in thickness, the installer would have the headache of levelling the tiles on the wall.

Likewise, it can create a nightmare for the installer if the dimensions do not match perfectly. If one tile is slightly larger than the other, there will be inconsistencies in the grout pattern. The installer will pick up on this right away, and you will likely be getting a phone call. The tile store should tell you if there are any issues with this as you make your selections. It is just something to be mindful of.

Smaller tiles are usually mesh mounted for ease of installation. Again, once you add the grout, this means there is a lot more going on visually than with larger tiles. The trick to lessening the busy factor would be to use grout in a non-contrasting color.

Large floor tile is not usually used in backsplashes because the standard height between the lower and upper cabinets is 18". A 12x24 tile, cut lengthwise, would not give you pleasing dimensions to work with. Sometimes, you will find coordinating tiles on the sample board that match the larger tiles but will work better for those applications.

You want to consider how much pattern is in the countertop

while making your selections—the more design on one surface, the less design on the other. Carrara marble looks can be challenging to match up as authentic marble has a different tone than faux surfaces. And you will learn in the fourth chapter; white is never just white. Marrying the two surfaces is the key. The countertop and backsplash are a unit that needs to work together. They can work together in interesting and contrasting ways, but once installed, they need to look like they tie the room together in a pleasing way.

When it comes to the quantity of tile to order, you want to rely on the expertise of the store or supplier that you are using. Tile calculations are never just the square footage of the surface you are covering.

The waste factor is high with tile, at about ten percent, due to cutting. If you have a bevelled edge, you cannot just use that piece's remainder anywhere. You can disguise the top row's cut edge against the upper cabinets, for example. All four sides no longer look the same after cutting the tile.

Tile with patterns, such as mosaics, do not come in exact 12x12 sheets. Calculations are needed to figure out how many sheets of that specific tile you will need to cover the intended surface.

Not all tile is available per piece either. Sometimes you must order by the nearest box quantity, so it is prudent to ask that question when you get your estimates from the store.

Essentially, you should never be embarrassed or too prideful to ask for all the expertise you can. Use the people you have come to trust as much as possible. Double-check that no errors have taken place by carefully reviewing the quotes with them before presenting your numbers to the client. Being patient and thorough ensures that you cover all the bases, giving your client the most accurate numbers and information possible. They will appreciate you for it, even if they are somewhat impatient themselves, and your reputation will grow as well.

Doors, Baseboards And Casings

Your clients usually have a pretty good idea of what they want when it comes to baseboards. Perhaps they are moving away from oak or mahogany to the more modern white or painted options. The doors, too.

To help the clients who intend to keep their existing baseboards and doors, you will need to inform them of the preparation and process to refinish them with stain or paint. They may save money by reusing what they have. They will either be putting in some manpower and elbow grease themselves or paying a contractor to do the work for them. It may not save a lot of money in the end, but it could save some hassle in painting them.

To re-stain baseboards and doors, completely remove all existing clear coats and stains. The baseboards may cause the most headaches while sanding the various bevelled profiles.

If the doors are a veneer, sanding will be almost impossible without going through the fine wood layer into the composite behind. In these cases, it may be easier to use a chemical stripper to remove the coatings. They need to be properly neutralized and dried before applying new stains or clear coats to avoid adhesion or colour variance issues.

I highly recommend doing a stain colour test on the back of the baseboard and an inconspicuous area on a door before applying stain on everything. Having to take it off again would really suck!

Depending on the baseboard's age, they may be very brittle, and they can snap in the removal process. It is a problem because new wood will not stain the same as aged wood. In the case of mahogany, you may not be able to find it at all because it is an endangered wood species.

It is essential to handle the baseboards gently. The existing baseboards and doors are likely to have some damage from years of use. Stains do not disguise that wear and tear. New shiny clear coats may highlight them more than before. The pre-existing clear coat could have been so old that it had become dull and quickly became powder while sanding.

All these considerations may lead the client to either paint the existing woodwork or replace them altogether.

Painting will take some prep. Ideally, you remove the baseboards to coat them; however, they can stay in place a great deal of the time. It does not mean that prep is not essential. The doors and baseboards still need to be cleaned with TSP (trisodium phosphate) to remove dirt, grime and cleaning products. Suppose there are dents, pre-existing nail holes or damage. In that case, they can be filled with paintable wood filler and sanded smooth along with scuff sanding over the entire surface. It means just a slight roughing with 120-grit sandpaper.

It is vital to use an oil-based primer to seal the surface. It prevents stains from leeching through the paint and grabs the wood's surface for a solid bond with topcoats. Sand to smooth any brush or roller marks. Use two coats of top-quality latex paint with sanding between each coat. It gives a beautiful finish.

Do not reinstall the doors until they have adequately cured, as you do not want the tacky paint to stick to the newly painted door jambs. Patience and preparation win every time.

Solid wood doors are an expensive but beautiful upgrade. They allow the homeowner freedom to re-stain the doors rather than paint. However, a stained door does darken areas like hallways when there are several doors to other rooms and closets. It can seem like there is more door than a wall.

Store-bought doors can also come pre-finished or primed, appealing to many when they are renovating. I have seen several homes of a certain age where the baseboards were solid oak, but the doors were white. Builders found a way to offer an upgrade but also cut in other areas. For my taste, I never liked this because the baseboards would then frame the door where the trim stood out more. My eye followed the trim up and down the wall when looking down the hallway. It looked like a bunch of eyebrows!

It is something to keep in mind. When leaving the existing wood trim, I would consider painting the doors a deeper tone, so there was no contrast with the trim.

With painted baseboards, doors, or any other masonry, be cautious if you use a variation of the new wall color. Because they now "match," the homeowner has to repaint them when it comes time to paint again. If they want to do this, then not a problem. However, on average, most folks like the idea of changing the paint up about every five to seven years. Some do not want the extra work of doing the baseboards too.

Once the baseboards are finished, either being re-coated or replaced, a professional installation will see them sealed with a bead of silicone along the top edge. Matching the silicone to the wall paint color is possible, so it is important to finish the painting before installation. Other times it will be clear or white, depending on the material or color of the trim. Ensure that you leave enough time for special orders if you choose a profile that is not in stock at the store.

Sometimes it's fun to be bolder with the baseboard and door colors. I love Iron Mountain by Benjamin Moore. It is a deep but warm grey/black that works beautifully with wood and painted surfaces. I have used this for baseboards, doors and shelving, feature walls, accent furniture and painted floors. It is a statement maker and, in simple designs, can offer an exciting element in the room. In the case of baseboards and doors, it can highlight the fine details. Finding the right balance and statement will be where your creative abilities come in.

The profiles that you choose for the baseboards and doors are a feature in themselves. There are many to choose from too. The wider and more elaborate, the more expensive they are. Homebuilders have been using a trick for years to use the less expensive window trim for baseboards. It is around two inches, but the proper baseboard should be a minimum of two and a half inches up to six.

It is also fun to use a slightly wider header above the door and widen the rectangular door's impact. I love to give doors some architectural interest.

Some homes have wainscoting, or maybe the homeowner is looking to decorate their cottage. Wainscoting is a lovely wood panelling effect that covers roughly half to two-thirds of a wall or room. Staining the wood panelling to match the doors, trim and compliment the flooring is standard in traditional settings. It is often in a simple shaker style or much more elaborate with filigree in a grand home. An additional chair rail or cap will be added to the top to finish the edge.

In the case of a dining room, the finished height for the chair rail coincides with the height of the chair's back so that as guests pull away from the table, it prevents damage to the wall. Hopefully, they do not shove the chair back hard enough to damage the chair rail, but that goes without saying.

In less formal settings, wainscoting has a more vertical striped pattern and often painted. I have a trick up my sleeve. A client had older wood veneer panelling in their basement. We oil-based primed and painted it, which gave it the look of wainscoting. It was a very inexpensive trick to update the room for meager effort or cost. Those vertical stripes also helped add some height to the standard eight-foot ceiling.

I also love to update eighties-style homes with tongue and groove wood panelled walls or ceilings. If the client is up for it, I love oil-based priming and painting these a light color to brighten up the room and give that clean cottage feel. Sometimes the homeowners are so focused on working with what they got. They do not know what they can do with their space.

Masonry

While we are painting existing surfaces, this includes brick. You have likely seen many ways to paint or whitewash brick fireplaces and feature walls in the DIY era. It is very different from wood, even though it is a very porous surface. Whether it is an interior or exterior project, brick is the easiest surface to paint.

All you need to do is wash it, ensure there is no dust, dirt or debris hidden on the surface or in the grout, let it dry, and away you go with latex paint. In the case of exterior brick, you want the surface to be slightly damp and then paint because the last bit of moisture will suck the paint to the surface as it dries completely.

Latex paint only for brick folks. As I said, brick is very porous. Moisture moves through brick a lot, and if you seal the surface off with oil-based paints, the moisture can't move and looks for other places to escape. It builds up and pushes the paint off if it cannot escape, peeling it away in an awful mess. You will see this happen in bathrooms where moisture has gotten behind the drywall. It will push oil or latex paint off the surface in this case something to keep in mind if you are looking at a client's home through the initial consultation.

It is good to take a measured amount of latex paint and play with the proportions of water for whitewash effects. Do not test this out on the brick until you have the consistency you want.

Here is the warning: once you paint brick, there is no going back.

You can power wash the exterior to remove peeling paint and debris. You cannot thoroughly remove paint once you've painted the brick. The choice will be to repaint it or replace it later. When whitewashing, start with an eighty percent water to twenty percent paint ratio and test it on some cardboard or another surface. Add more paint but always add it into a separate cup or pail, and continuously measure what you are doing to repeat the *recipe* when you run out.

With sooty fireplaces, you will need to scrub that darkened area to not mix with the whitewash or paint. Whitewashing will not hide anything but rather lighten or lessen the tones of the brick.

Avoid the pink effect with red brick. It also is essential to play with different brushes and rollers to know what finished effect you want.

A painter will have no issue doing a *trim and door package* for a home but not every painter is willing to do a faux finish on brick. Make sure that you, as a designer, have one or two specialty painters/artists up your sleeve for when this occasion arises. They will need to know in advance, very specifically, what the client is looking for and have them describe their process to them. They will have a very different rate than a typical painter and likely operate on a project cost.

———————

Note: Home renovations can have a bit of a scattered effect for those who are very excited yet have no idea what process to follow. Out come all the latest magazines and clippings of everything the homeowner has been eying up for years. They will show you any number of photos on their Pinterest or Instagram accounts with the hopeful expectation that you can source their every desire. Oh, and within their budget, too! Oh boy.

I have often jokingly said that my clients are like happy little magpies who have picked up bits and bobs of everything that appealed to them and brought it all back to the nest. Then looked at it all and said, "What do I do with all this?"

As I worked through the selection process, I would have rogue thoughts of a fabric or wallpaper. Perhaps it was a piece of furniture that caught everyone's attention.

It does not help to buy that gorgeous lamp with brushed nickel if you have decided to go with a brass look. Once again, the proper order to selections helps save time and money in the long run.

It is quite likely that your clients have helped you out by saying, "I love the new brass fixtures that are out!" It gives you something to think about as you work towards that stage.

———————

Working With Metals

Most of the time, mixing metals does not work very well in the finished design. If the eye has a chance to find the one thing in the room that does not work with the rest, it will. Different metals with the same feel or tone can work on the odd occasion, but it takes some skill and control to pull it off. Knowing when and where to mix things up a bit will keep things looking comfortable.

Chrome- is the brightest and whitest silver metallic look. It is posh, crisp and immaculate in appearance. This metal will not mix well with brushed or rusty tones, so be prepared to use it throughout.

Stainless Steel- a cooler toned brushed silver look. Found in sinks, appliances and taps. This metal is expensive and not often seen in light fixtures. Considered neutral, stainless steel pairs with chrome, brushed nickel and black.

Brushed Nickel/Satin- is a "dirty" or casual silver with a muted warm, luminous finish. This metal is soft on the eye and one of the more popular choices for the look's longevity. It pairs with antique/oil rubbed bronze, black or brushed brass looks in small amounts.

Oil Rubbed Bronze- warmer than black and has a soft brown finish. A moody and atmosphere inspired metal, oil rubbed bronze is in cabins, wine cellars and casual homes with warmer tones. It pairs with black, brushed nickel and antique brasses in small amounts.

Brass- the brightest "gold" metallic look. It is clean and bold but with warmth as opposed to chrome. In the past, brass was used in light switch plates, fireplace accents and doorknobs. It is a trendy metal that could swing in and out of popularity, so it would be wise to use it in areas that are quickly and cost-effectively changed out. This metal pairs with black metals.

Brushed/Antique Brass- a less formal and rustic feeling of "gold" metal with a soft finish. More casual than brass, it lends to an easy-going and warm feel when used in small doses. Trendy, this metal is excellent for feature lighting and blends well with black and sparingly with brushed nickel.

Black- polished or matte, black is always an easy choice for contrast and goes with anything. Creating an anchor in the room, be prepared for your eye to find it quickly because it stands out. So ensure that when you use this metal, you are looking for that effect.

White- polished or matte, white also goes with anything. Less often used in hardware and fixtures, it is still seen from time to time.

There are many variations of the above metals. You will have the job of narrowing them down to work within your design. Make sure you take the time to compare the tones side-by-side to see if they are truly working together. Of course, from one room to the next, a slight change will not be noticeable if one light fixture, let's say, is slightly shinier than another.

Hardware

Select the cabinet hardware at the same time as choosing the taps, sinks and lighting so that you can be consistent with these items throughout the house. The metal selection even comes up in the finishing edges for the tile backsplashes or transitions in flooring. Not only are you working with the tile selection, but also with the overall theme of the home. Doorknobs and hinges are part of this process as well, and like the baseboards, the metal tones will run from one room into the next.

The choice of black, white or stainless-steel appliances also significantly impacts what direction to go with metallics. The challenge comes in getting the metallics to blend without making anything stick out like a sore thumb.

Sinks and taps are often in stainless steel; however, the latest trends are using black or a deep bronze or charcoal tone. Making that decision points you in the right direction for what taps will look the most appropriate and pleasing.

Because the handles, knobs and pulls are all visually in the same area, you want them to look like a complete package. Perhaps the sheen is a little more, or less, in them than in the taps, but if the tone is right, you can get away with it.

Do you want contrast between the hardware and the cabinets? Or would you rather have them blend so that other elements stand out?

From sleek and simple to elaborate and ornate, hardware comes in many styles. As a designer, having an excellent selection to pick from in one or two locations will save a lot of running around. Of course, there are all kinds of websites you can purchase any number of decorative items from. But, unless you are prepared to buy and return, you do need to see things in person to determine tone and quality.

Specialty hardware stores will carry options on doorknobs and hinges that could save you a lot of running around when looking for something above the *standard.*

Lighting

Just like shopping for tile, entering a lighting store is a bit like a kid in a candy store. Everything is lit up like a Christmas tree, glittering and shining and quickly overwhelming the eye. It can be tricky to visually narrow down your selections and adequately see the dimensions or scale of the lighting you need with many samples crammed in above your head.

Once you are used to this experience, it will get a lot easier. For your clients, they will likely be relying on your expertise heavily.

In this case, it may help you shop for your client's ideas online and bring them to your suppliers. Hopefully, they will have the brands and styles you are looking for or have access to them. Once you have narrowed the search down to a few options and stores, you can take your clients with you for their final approval.

How do you know what to look for when it comes to the lighting needs of a home? First, it helps to have the blueprints and see where the electrical is. Is it centered over work areas in the kitchen? Is it located in the spot you want to put the dining room table? How high are the ceilings, and with how much clearance in certain places? (like in the front entry, for example) Do the clients need ceiling fans as well? How much light does each area of the house need?

Remember how I said it was essential to know which way the windows face and whether blinds, trees or overhanging decks block sunlight? It is key to understanding how much light your client is going to need in addition to the natural light in the home. Are pot lights to be installed for the main lighting so you can add decorative focal points in the foyer, over the table and maybe some drop lighting over the island? Will under cabinet lighting help in a kitchen that does not have ample natural light? How many actual light bulbs are in the fixtures you are considering, and how much light will they give off?

You need to know how many lumens you need per room, how much the existing lighting provides or how much to look for, and then keep those questions in mind.

What is a lumen? A lumen is a unit measurement of light coming from a light source. Essentially, it tells you how bright a light bulb is and is stated on the packaging. To determine lumens/sq.ft (or meter depending on where you live), you divide the total lumens by the room's square footage.

How do you know how many lumens there are? Again, you can figure it out by adding up the number of light bulbs in the room, based on their wattage or lumens, then divide by the square footage. If you only have the wattage available, you can use the following chart from www.energystar.gov to help you.

Old Incandescent Bulbs (Watts)	ENERGY STAR Bulb Brightness (Minimum Lumens)
40	450
60	800

75	1,100
100	1,600
150	2,600

Once you know how many lumens the house has been operating with, you can determine whether it needs more or less. Additional task lighting would be used for work areas, as I mentioned before. With this guide, you can see quickly if the home has been within the suggested guidelines or lacking in some areas. You can always get the trusted expertise from the lighting stores you shop with and determine how to improve the fixtures you are hoping to use.

Experts suggest the following for specific rooms based on general lighting:

- Living room: 10–20 lumens per square foot
- Dining room: 30–40 lumens per square foot
- Bedroom: 10–20 lumens per square foot
- Bathroom: 70–80 lumens per square foot
- Hallways: 5–10 lumens per square foot
- Kitchen (general lighting): 30–40 lumens per square foot
- Kitchen (task areas): 70–80 lumens per square foot
- Laundry room: 70–80 lumens per square foot.

One of my pet peeves is the dome lights with frosted glass mounted flush to the ceilings. They serve as a form of soft lighting. I have seen them utilized as an inexpensive option in places like walk-in closets, hallways, and even living rooms when more light is needed. The frosted glass mutes the light, making it difficult to see, but the darn things are painful to change the bulbs. Every time I have ever tried to change a bulb in them, I have had the joke of "how many Jenny's does it take to change a light bulb" going through my head. I always had to ask for help, so I did not drop anything every time!

Consider what you are installing and the ease of replacing light bulbs for your clients. Elderly homeowners, or folks with physical limitations, may not be able to handle ladders. Do the bulbs point upward or downward? Are they easily accessible, or are there multiple elements that need to dismantling to replace a burnt-out bulb?

Installation of fixtures is relatively easy for your electrician. Still, you want to have a conversation about how high to install the light fixtures prior. Task lighting over the island is a good example. Make sure that you consider your clients' height. Tall people will be frustrated looking through or around lighting as they work and are trying to speak with guests on the other side of the island.

Think of lines of sight as well as clearance for people's heads. You cannot think in terms of what looks acceptable to you at your height. You would think that is obvious, but I have had many conversations about how high to place mirrors so that both partners had the ease of use. Lighting is no different.

While you are having the conversation with the electrician, make sure that you relay any extra wishes for your clients in terms of plugin and light switch location. Renovations can include moving walls around, including where the light fixtures will be. It makes sense to consider where and how many electrical outlets and switches are needed. Do any of the fixtures need dimmers? You get the drift.

In addition to knowing how much light a fixture will bring, it is important to plan which direction the light will be traveling.

Light travels away from the light source in a triangular beam. The stronger the light, the farther it will travel unless impeded by an object like frosted glass—these change the distribution of light.

With one new house that I designed, I knew we needed inexpensive light fixtures that did not hang low into the room, but I did not want to lose the light by cupping it close to the ceiling either. The compromise turned out to be domed fixtures that dropped about four inches from the ceiling. It allowed the light to filter down into the room through the frosted glass while also spreading bright light across the ceiling. It means highlighting any imperfections in the ceiling, but it gave me more light to work with and still saved dollars in the lighting budget.

Exploring lighting is quite fascinating, and there are some genuinely artistic pieces to be found. I admittedly am not hugely versed as a lighting expert as this is one of the few areas I have not been a salesperson in. The fundamentals are here for you, and you can continue to research anything I may have potentially missed.

Confidence comes from you knowing enough to guide your client and when also to say, "I am not positive on the answer to that. Let me get a hold of my contractor/supplier/salesperson about that for you."

Accent Lighting

Table lamps, floor lamps, wall lighting and even candlelight all fall under accent lighting classification. Of course, they serve a purpose, but they are for ambient lighting or ambiance. These excellent light sources can provide soft light to give a room mood. For instance, in a theater room or highlighting a beautiful piece of art or a piano. Or provide an added boost while someone is reading.

Some light is directional, like wall sconces or table lamps. These offer light through the center of the room or space, even creating the illusion of more height if directed upwards. Staircases can have mini lights mounted under the nosings or along the stringers to accent the stairs and make it easier to see. Of course, anytime you highlight an area, you want to make sure you do not highlight imperfections as your client will be quick to pick up on them.

A lot of accent lighting has shades made of either fabric, metal or plastic. Each will mute the light cast into the room, but the opacity will determine how much and how far the light can escape. The real issue to watch out for is colored lamp shades. These are not as common anymore, and they certainly put a time stamp on the design in a room. They also cast the lamp shade's hue into the room, which changes the paint tones, flooring and furniture colors. The same thing can happen with unlined colored draperies.

Understanding how to create relaxing and sufficient lighting throughout the home will pay off the better you understand your clients. Do they have a lot of books signifying that they are readers? Do they have an office? A musical instrument? What are their preferences for the theater room? Are the kids going to do homework at the kitchen table or in their rooms?

To figure out how much accent light is needed, the chart highlights the recommendations for each room. Once you know how many lumens the main fixtures give off, you can make up the remainder with the accent or task lighting.

Task Lighting

As a designer, you need to inventory all the potential tasks and hobbies your clients could be doing in their homes. Ensure your lighting selections make this easy for them. Pendant lights over the island, under-mount light "pucks" for the kitchen cabinets, lamps for desks or reading and makeup stations are all considered task lighting.

For one, I am big on as much light as possible in kitchens, closets and laundry rooms. There is nothing worse than going into a poorly lit closet, jam-packed full of clothing and trying to color coordinate an outfit. Every time I found myself in one of these situations, I told the story of one of my most embarrassing and humorous moments.

Keep in mind when a woman finds a pair of shoes or boots that *really* fit well, we are known to buy a pair in multiple colors. When I asked my daughter to organize all the shoes in the front entrance, I did not think too much about it.

I got up early for my first day of work as a color consultant at a large design company as I wanted to make a good impression. I did not want to wake anyone, so I just turned the small light on in the entrance as I got my dress boots on. It was not until about two hours into my workday that I looked down and realized I had on one brown boot and one black.

Yup. It was horrifying. I looked around to see if anyone had noticed and realized that I could not go home to switch my boots. I would have to wear them for the rest of the day. I started to laugh at how ridiculous all this was and decided I would not say anything and just play a game of "who will notice by the end of the day."

They noticed. It wasn't until the afternoon that one of my co-workers was cheeky enough to say anything, but at least I could say, "Oh, I know. I was waiting to see how long it took you guys to notice!"

My clients love this story, but it makes my point. I make sure they consider a better light fixture in the closet areas and the paint to a light shade.

Migraine sufferers and folks with sight issues have a different set of needs altogether. My mother's vision is in such a way that if she gets bright light shining in her eyes, she will get migraines. Headlights at night do this to her. You would think that being visually impaired would mean she would need lots of light to do tasks like cooking or cleaning. She prefers it darker. Knowing what your client may need can help you with task and accent lighting to minimize any difficulties.

Pot Lighting

In the eighties, pot lighting was new to the lighting scene. They were large and slightly bulky but adjusted in direction. My parents installed them at the same time as the new fireplace. They even had a dimmer!

Thankfully, pot lighting has become smaller, more attractive and available in painted or metal tones. I am a huge fan. I love the ability to put light where it is needed most and mix it with beautiful light fixtures for design elements. You can beef up the lighting in task areas like kitchens and dining rooms when you need it, then blend in accent lighting for meals or entertaining.

The pot lights themselves are relatively inexpensive; however, the installation is a lot more. They must go into attic spaces to wire and install them properly. Pot lights are also a little more difficult to change when one burns out.

These twinkling little gems tuck up almost flush in the ceiling. Reducing the need for other light fixtures, and the room becomes visually simplified. When you do spend the big bucks on an attractive feature for the dining room table, then you will notice it that much more as it does not have to compete for your eye.

When you are in the planning stages, it is helpful to consider how many pot lights you genuinely need and what would look the most aesthetically pleasing. Most often, pot lights frame the room. In the case of a kitchen, they follow the footpath through the cabinets. Too many pot lights can look like an alien ship is landing or that there are a lot of "eyes" looking down. Too few, and the pot lights look like lost little distractions without much effect. How many and how far apart they should be will always depend on the dimensions of the room.

There is a simple calculation. Take the ceiling height of each room and divide it in half. Use that number for how far apart to install the pot lights. For example, if you have an eight-foot ceiling, install the pot lights four feet apart. A ten-foot ceiling would be five feet apart. You get the drift.

Having made your cabinet hardware, door and lighting se-lections, you are at the point where all the "bones" of the house are in place. You have got the home to the point where all the main elements are working harmoniously together. Or maybe you've noticed something is sticking out and needs reconsider-ing. That is the beauty of the selection process. Unless ordered or installed, you have the flexibility to refine your choices with the homeowner at no great expense. The lovely thing at this stage is that your client can visually see how the project is coming together where they were lost before. They also understand the *why* behind each item and how it affects the others should they decide to change their minds.

The journey has been a lot of fun so far, but I cannot wait to get going on the next steps of furniture, soft furnishings and, at last, paint!

In The Next Chapter...

We have reviewed all the aspects of fixed furnishings for the new construction or renovation of a house. Or a business, for that matter. These are elements that are not going anywhere if the homeowner decides to sell and move. In the next chapter, we move on to the decorative aspects that are just as essential and often custom. They make the home comfortable while express-ing the homeowner's unique personality and flair for crafting a designed project that promotes your brand.

CHAPTER THREE - SOFT FURNISHINGS

Soft furnishings are the "clothing" of the house and involve fabric items. They give the home layers of color, texture pattern and artistic flair. It can include furniture, blinds, drapery, wallpaper, toss cushions, bedding, area rugs, art, decor and paint. Furnishings can be simplistic, elegant and soft, bold, ornate or eclectic. Soft furnishings are items that are not permanently part of the house and can be changed quickly.

Many items under this category can have a lot to do with the homeowners' culture, preferences or interests in parts of the world, or memories from their childhood. We are in the realm of pure expression. Where you will truly shine as a designer is in your ability to pick up on the subtle, or not so subtle, cues from your discussions with the client. Your ability to see all the ways to make their precious memorabilia stand out while pulling fresh new ideas in is key.

You must keep product selections in the proper order. We have included furniture as a whole entity, even though soft furnishings would traditionally be the fabric covering or slipcovers. This chapter digs into some of the more complicated and expensive choices a homeowner and designer need to make together. It is necessary to plan these elements carefully for the investment, lifespan and shaping the overall creative direction.

Furniture

Up until now, we have been designing the house itself. The bones. The structure that, no matter what we put in the house from now on, we must work with those elements. We are now putting the body of the project into place... the filler, so to speak. The functional style of the homeowner's belongings genuinely makes the client's house their *home.*

There are a lot of styles to pick from and a lot of stores that sell them. Having a good understanding of how your clients live and their tastes, you will likely already have something in mind in terms of furniture. You may surprise them, or they may surprise you. Having some extra cards up your sleeve will keep you prepared for any change of direction. You may think your clients want good quality furniture again after they have had their last piece for thirty years when really, they want to be able to change it up more often.

We can talk about styles and designs all day long. I will be focused more on the functionality of different pieces and understand the differences in quality. Let's face it. You can feed your design addiction in all forms of magazines, websites and retailer's showrooms. I want to help you navigate past just your style or your client's.

Ninety-nine percent of the time, the homeowners are not replacing everything in the entire house. Unless they have lost their whole house to a tragedy or came into a great deal of money, most people will be working with some of their existing furniture. We will likely have heard from our clients very quickly which pieces are staying, which are going and all the creative reasons why.

It could be the husband's favorite chair that has seen better days or great grandma's chaise passed down for generations. Both have sentimental value. Perhaps one can be "saved" with some new fabric and cushioning. Maybe the kitchen table has water stains and a lot of wear from years of raising children. As a designer, your marvellous skills will integrate existing pieces with the new furniture, making it all look perfectly designed that way.

Just like everything else, there is an essential order to selecting furniture. Know what you are working with first so that your shopping trips are more productive. You will know what furniture styles will be better suited, the wood tones you can combine or avoid and the amount of seating you will need to add. You will also know what upholstery fabric will coordinate well with the existing furniture.

Custom furniture is a long-term investment. Custom pieces are usually made by hand with top-quality wood and material. And have warranties on their construction. Their cost is equal to an investment, and so it is more likely that the fabric will wear out before the frame ever will. Custom furniture is more likely to be reupholstered than replaced for this reason. Clients who appreciate their quality will be happier with a custom piece than store-bought and factory-made furniture.

I had the privilege of touring the workroom of a custom furniture business. It was quite impressive to see how the computer created the patterns for each piece, then laser cut into the customer's fabric and carefully stitched them to cover the frame. They showed me how they built the different frames, cut the foam and used the best quality springs to make every component the strongest possible. If the dimensions needed altering in true custom fashion, the manufacturer would adjust the pattern and create it for the client. I was able to confidently tell my clients what they were getting with their hard-earned money.

The wood was from North America using sustainably forested lumber and already acclimated to our climate. (If you are from another country, check where the wood originates from and how it reacts in your environment) It means that imported furniture already manufactured has to acclimate and usually dries out, making it weaker. And in other countries where environmental standards are not a concern, you do not know what types of glues, lacquers or foams have been used.

When you have customers who are more likely to replace the furniture than to refinish or reupholster it, you can still get good quality store-bought furniture. It helps to ask some questions about where it was manufactured, what warranties are available and how much assembly is required. Does the store offer assembly services? If not, who is going to be responsible for that task when the furniture is delivered?

Speaking of delivery...watch this very closely. Ensure that

each piece is completely sealed in plastic and cardboard adequately protects all wood elements. Nothing has been punctured, scratched, torn or dirtied. It is also prudent to ensure that the proper fabric is on the right furniture piece. Custom furniture can take three months from start to finish, and it is not a quick fix if there is damage or an error. Even store-bought furniture can take several weeks to arrive. Clients are usually very disappointed to have issues when they were so excited to have their furniture arrive.

When custom furniture is not an option, that does not mean that you cannot get good quality furniture from the stores. The selection process will be limited to the fabrics, stains and sizes they have available. The good news is they will likely have coordinated looks to help build your design quickly. If your clients like the idea of matching pieces, then it will be a matter of selecting the best look, price and comfort of the furniture on the showroom floor. Unlike custom furniture, you may have the option of returning something if it does not quite work. However, you want to have a clear understanding of the return policy before finalizing the purchase.

Even store-bought furniture can be a final sale when a piece has a customized fabric choice. I once had a client who had just received her leather sofa and, after unpacking it, discovered that the leather she chose went purple/brown in her house. The store lighting had made the leather look more deep burgundy. She had spent all morning on the phone trying to find a way to return the sofa to no avail. She was stuck with it. Be careful to see the fabric swatches at the client's home and in their lighting.

The more eclectic your client, the more original you can be with mixing up furniture pieces. One of my favorite clients was refinishing garage sale or vintage items long before Pinterest or Instagram came along. Her home was a wonderful mix of genres, textures, color and metals. Nothing matched, yet everything went together. She had a real knack for knowing what to keep and what to resell. I still have the painting in my living room that she gave me after she repainted the frame.

The trick with this kind of client is to be just as playful as they are. There is no "right or wrong" to creating an expression of who they are in their home. They need as clean a palette on the walls so that the many shapes and colors of the furniture and other elements can shine. When you hunt for the right pieces, you must keep a couple of things in mind.

Old furniture can have lead-based paints. You cannot sand them without significant risk. If you are unsure, you should get a test kit at your local hardware or paint store. When in doubt, just make sure the surface is as clean as possible, and oil-base prime them. Then paint good quality paint over the top, preferably with a pearl, satin or semi-gloss paint for ease of dusting. Barnboard items or reclaimed wood can add a rustic charm, but the caution I have is an infestation. If the wood is left untreated, you could be introducing bugs into the client's home, which would be catastrophic. It can happen with other items too, so it is always prudent to be cautious and double-check all items to be unpacked on site.

I knew one store owner who had ordered a selection of silk plants for a specific customer. She took them out of the boxes, still wrapped in plastic, and loaded them into her car so she could take them to the customer's house the next morning. The next morning, when she got to her car, she could tell something was not right through the windows. Low and behold, the plants had been infested with spiders. They had gotten to work and created a series of webs all over the interior of her car. When she told me this story, I was horrified and asked how she got all that out. Her car was not her primary concern. She was just relieved she had not gotten the plants into her customer's house and had them go to town there.

One last general note. White or light furniture and shelving will show more dirty fingerprints, where dark furniture shows more dust. Discuss which will be more forgiving for your client's lifestyle as it will be an important discussion to have with them.

Upholstery

There is a difference between what can be refinished or reupholstered and what cannot. The costs involved make it an obvious choice. Unless you have a client who loves to upcycle, refinish woodworking, or sew, you will have to hire out the work. The piece of furniture itself may not have good construction with inferior quality wood. Or possibly the frame has been damaged. If a client is serious about keeping it, the only way to know is to get a quote.

Reupholstering is expensive. It can often cost more than the piece of furniture was originally purchased for. In some cases, such as antiques and heirlooms, the piece's emotional value far outweighs the monetary one. Clients are often shocked at the price tag of refinishing a piece of furniture, so they will either resign themselves to the fact and move forward or dismiss the idea. With the example of the husband's recliner, it would financially make more sense to replace it than refinish it. The upholstery cost would likely be worth two or three new chairs. The price can be the same or more for grandma's chaise. However, faced with the choice of selling the chaise or restoring it, a homeowner is more likely to refinish it if the budget allows.

A quality upholstery shop is not an easy thing to find. In the age of discarding furniture, not that many people have proper training in the trade. Before you recommend someone, ensure that you have seen their work in person and heard from their customers. The cushioning should be the appropriate depth and quality, free of lumps or awkward stretching of the fabric. Piping should be straight and aligned at the seam of the cushion. The business itself should be clean and speak of a high standard. The employees should also be neat in appearance because they can transfer anything from their clothing or hands to the fabrics they are working with.

You know quality when you see that the cushion's fabric pattern lines up with the piping. If the piping is attached and the designs do not line up, then it is not as quality a job as it should be. Make sure you state your expectations when giving the design details to the workroom.

When selecting a fabric, there is a big difference between what you will find at a fabric store and special-order fabrics from design houses. That is not to say that you cannot find upholstery fabric in a store, but the quality will be different along with the price tag. You may not get the same essential information either. Fabric "books" can be borrowed from the design showrooms that offer special-order fabric for custom projects. Please do not assume you can cut samples from them as these books are irreplaceable to the studio. You may not be allowed to borrow samples again. If you need a swatch, they can order one from the supplier for little to no cost.

Upholstery fabric strength is measured in double rubs. Essentially, how many times a person can sit down and stand up before the fabric begins to wear. They have equipment specially designed to recreate this scenario and document the results. The higher the double rubs, the longer the material will last during everyday use. The recommended minimum is 12,000 double rubs for occasional use furniture and can go up to 250,000 or more. Sofas and love seats should have the higher double rub count fabric. A chair that sits in the corner and unused can be less.

Like carpet, the fabric can have directionality to it. It means that when people sit on it or run their hands across the surface, the fibers lay in the direction they were swept. For some homeowners, this would drive them nuts. You want to test the samples that you are considering. Another consideration is how the fabric will "sit." If you grab opposite corners of the sample, pulling them tight, does the material remain taunt, or does it have some give to it? The more a person's butt will bounce off the surface and be less comfortable, the tighter the fabric is. Dining room chairs will use a tighter cloth than a sofa would.

The foam used in upholstery is not your standard stuff. High-density foam is the best for maintaining the shape and durability of the furniture. It bounces back into its original shape without breaking down. The thinner foam is utilized for dining room furniture. Slightly thicker will be used for window seats or occasional living room furniture. The denser foam is for comfy sofas, loveseats and chairs.

Bedroom Furniture

The master bedroom is the sanctuary of the home. It is where a person should feel the most comfortable, relaxed and a true expression of themselves. It is true for every person who is living in the house, even children. When a person loves their bedroom, they can snuggle into bed and sleep better. They wake up and love their surroundings, which starts their day off on the right foot. When they are not feeling well or have a stressful life event occurring, their bedroom's serenity helps soothe the soul.

You and I know this to be true. I cannot get over crisp, freshly laundered sheets. I have my best sleep after I have washed my bedding!

The house's main areas should be designed for everyone who lives there, both in style and functionality. Everything has a flow that works together as a person travels from room to room. The client may prefer to keep that flow in their bedroom or change it up. I have jokingly said that if a person loved hot pink and did not want to use it in the other areas of the house, why not their bedroom? There are ways to keep a look isolated to a room without seeing it from the hallway, but I will cover more in the paint section.

Bedroom furniture starts with the bed. It is the focal point of the room and draws the eye first. The bed's size makes a difference in which wall to place it but so do the electrical outlets. There must be a comfortable amount of space for each person to get out of bed and move about without stubbing their toes or knocking things over. The electrical outlets give you an idea of where the nightstands will go, along with the lamps and chargers for cell phones. Some homes have outlets on two walls, so there are more options. Homeowners love to move their furniture around.

All those questions you asked the client earlier are about to come in handy. Will it make your client nuts to have the window above their head? Are they night owls who are up in the night quite often? Do they want to change to a king-size bed from the queen they currently have? Will it fit the proportions of the room? What style of furniture are they thinking about?

The larger the bed, the more it will visibly fill the room when adding the headboard and other furniture. Solid dark wood stains take up more space than lighter stains, glass or MDF furniture. The floor's depth will determine whether to go lighter or darker with the furniture for contrast. The selection process of bedding and paint color tends to go hand in hand; however, this is another opportunity for layering color and texture.

A fabric headboard has a softer appearance than solid wood. Do your clients like the idea of having something soft to lean up against with their pillows? Will they want a custom piece or store-bought? Construction or ordering timelines may make that choice for you. Still, the selection and options will be greater with custom upholstery. The fabric has the chance of getting soiled, and in the case of velvet, can leave directional rub marks. Are these things that your client can handle, or are they going to want something they can dust quickly? Are they willing to have the headboard steam cleaned when it calls for it, and is the material you selected able to handle that cleaning method?

Solid headboards come in many styles and shapes. Some beds are wide and low to the ground, very sleek and modern in appearance. With clean lines, this Scandinavian or sixties style furniture begs for simple and luxurious comfort. Is this height comfortable to the clients when they get up or down from it? Make sure they try it out. If the frame goes directly to the floor, they have a better chance of stubbing their toes. The client will love this style if they prefer to keep everything organized and straightforward. Still, much like an open concept, it will not take much to create a visual mess with anything that is not immediately put away.

More traditional furniture has detailed woodworking, matching footboards, shaker styles and wainscoting. Antique metal frames are charming and always a showstopper. Antiques can be a challenge in themselves with different leg styles in dressers, tables and chairs. The wood tones are not likely going to match. You also want to be careful about any odors that they give off, especially in items with drawers. Those musty old smells are not always noticeable until you are trying to sleep.

It is fun to be creative with furniture. Reclaiming pieces that blend with store-bought or other antiques is a great way to create a genuine feel in a room, especially a bedroom. Give the homeowners a place to sit and put their socks on but have some fun with it. Give them a mirror to check their appearance in, but why not dress up the frame too? Check your local paint stores for any new and creative project paint they may have. The chalk paint craze is not likely going to be over until there is no single piece of furniture left, not already transformed.

Like other custom furniture, you can also have top quality, handmade wooden furniture made. Amish communities have been perfecting their trade-in woodworking for hundreds of years. It is not just limited to oak. If your clients have something handmade in mind, you can get the ball rolling with true craftsmanship. Again, it does not hurt to know of your closest carpenters and Amish stores. You can get almost anything customized for style and size that will last a lifetime. These pieces are more likely to be passed down to family than discarded later.

I mentioned children's rooms. The little bundles of energy grow into bigger bundles of sass, in my experience. It means that they are going to be needing furniture changes sooner than the adults will. They will outgrow cribs and toddler beds then need something for their almost-adult bodies. They will likely take this furniture with them when they move out too! Keep this transition of furniture in mind when it comes to the expense your client is willing to undertake.

Kids are also notoriously hard on furniture. They color on it, cut it, slam it, jump up and down on it and sometimes fall in it.

The cheaper and lower the quality, the less likely it will last until their next furniture stage. You want to blend the right amount of quality with practicality as you go through the selection process. In some cases, the expense is not a concern, and the client will likely just replace anything that gets damaged. There is no parent out there who does not want the beautiful baby room or sweetest bedroom for their six-year-old. It just does not stay like that, and magazines do not snap photos of the war zone after the kid has been playing in their room.

Children and teenagers need comfort, a place to create, listen to music and do their homework. Their whole lives fit into one room until they get a home of their own, so they require more creative storage space that is multi-functional. And do not forget the friends. Friends will need a place to sleep, and you will look like a rock star if you can fit this need into your designs. Integrating furniture and shelving pieces that can grow with them will help save your clients money in the long run and leave room for changes in other areas. The bed will likely change, but the bookshelf may survive if the quality is there.

You must watch for exposed components that could be sharp, pinch fingers, protrude in awkward ways or be hot to the touch with any children's furniture. Kids do crazy things. I used to jump on my bed high enough to hit my head on the popcorn stippled ceiling. And in those days, it still had sparkles in it. Look at the hardware. Is it manageable for a child? Are there any screws in awkward places that they can wiggle free easily? Is anything going to be a choking hazard, such as cords on drapery, tents, decorations or blinds?

Bedrooms are one of my favorite spaces to decorate, and there is a lot to consider on a personal level. The bedroom is our most intimate of all the rooms.

Dining Room Furniture

A formal dining room will have enough chairs for the entire family to sit easily at the table, as well as a spare chair or two for guests. The table will have leaves that expand the table for entertaining. They are beautifully crafted and usually heavy as heck to move around and ornate in design. Dining room sets will have matching buffets, china cabinets and cabinets for dishes and stemware. China cabinets are often passed down along with the beautiful china dishes within.

Some people have a formal dining room for special occasions and a casual kitchen table or breakfast nook. Others will have only the one and make do with every surface available when their company comes over. Not only will your client's lifestyle come into play, but the amount of space they have as well. Do they like to entertain? How many people do they have in their family that you need to plan your design around? Where do they spend most of their time when there is a meal or party? Do they like to spread out casual style or have everyone sit together at the same table?

I have a relative who renovated a two-hundred-year-old building in Hudson, Quebec. It overlooks the water and has expansive grounds filled with flowers, shrubs and trees. Family and guests can play yard games and sports in the old tennis court flat, lounge on the patio, or walk the path down to the lake. They are a couple who love to entertain, not just their family and casual affairs, but black-tie events or jam sessions in the basement. They are hosts to various people for many reasons, and their home does not have a dining room table. In addition to the fifteen-foot-long island, they have a pool table with custom leaves built to cover the top when they want to sit up to the table. Guests can mingle, sit at the island, eat at the pool table or venture outside to eat on the deck.

As you can see, sometimes it just takes some thinking outside the box and a willingness to let go of a formal idea to get an even better result. But you must know who your client is and what will work for them the most. People who love the big family dinner on Sundays may want the dining room experience. You will have a different approach to designing this room than around a pool table turned eating platform.

You must think in terms of traffic. Serving meals around several people tucked up to eat is tricky. Still, without enough space to travel around the table and from the kitchen, you are asking for some burn victims and swear words. You also need to consider the amount of room between the table and the chair when pushed out. You want to have at least four feet from the table edge to the wall or piece of furniture to fit a chair tucked in with a person in it. A larger person will need more room than someone slender.

Is there enough room for someone to sit up to or get up the table without bumping into walls or other furniture? While you are at the furniture stores, look at the matching chairs to the set and determine how bulky they are. Are they wider than a typical chair? Does the dining room set look like it could disproportionately fill the space?

A large table is a room filler. You cannot see the floor, and if the room is small, it can appear jammed in. For anyone sensitive to feeling claustrophobic, that can be an issue. In the old house I lived in, we had a space for a dining room, but it was not much of one. I had to purchase a new dining room set, and I knew that if I put in a solid piece of furniture, it would look like people would not fit in there. Instead, I bought a glass table to keep the dimensions of the room. My kids were older, so it was not quite the same gong show to keep it clean, but this would be a nightmare for a family with little ones.

You need to know your client, the challenges and positives with the room you are designing, and how to make the best use of space.

Living Room Furniture

Living rooms and family rooms can function the same or

very differently depending on the house. Some homes have a living room upstairs with more formal furniture meant for guests and visiting with the family room downstairs for watching television, gaming or recreation. The furniture for each scenario is very different in style and comfort.

In a home with children, all the furniture will take some hard use. It is not likely going to have any saving grace by being fancier than the other furniture. And knowing that, you will want to steer your clients towards sofas and chairs with stain guards in the material for ease of cleaning. It is not just little kids that are hard on the house. Teenagers and pets are just as capable of creating stains or using the furniture in rather rude ways.

Let's talk about the comfortable furniture first. Families like to read books, hang out with friends, watch the game together and eat rather messy foods on the furniture. They want to be comfortable in this room and not always be worried if the cheesy dust got on the fabric. Polyester materials and leather can be the most user friendly, though leather has specific concerns. Snaps, buttons and nails can all cause scratches on the leather surface, which may be challenging to repair. Some furniture has a slightly worn look to it and can help disguise wear and tear while being easy to clean.

The comfy furniture usually has some puffy cushions, and the "sit" is deeper than that of the formal pieces. Flopping into a chair or on the couch is probably going to happen. As we already discussed, the quality of the furniture makes a huge difference in this case. If the wood frame is weak, one person flopping with any kind of velocity and the wood will snap. Or, if this is a habit, the springs will wear out sooner.

The casual nature of the furniture in these rooms means that you can create a design around it. Sectionals can add extra seating that even has a recliner in them. Reclining chairs and sofas need more space for two reasons. They need room for the feet without hitting coffee tables but still be within reach of them. Two, reclining furniture can also mean there needs to be clearance behind the furniture to recline properly. Some recliners are now designed with the back of the chair or sofa no longer angles back but slides inside the frame. It may mean that the foot comes farther out into the room, so it is prudent to pay attention to this detail when you are at the store.

The more formal furniture should still be comfortable. One is not sacrificing comfort for the sake of fashion or beautiful fabrics. Unless someone is creating a museum-like experience, like the days when covering the furniture with a plastic protective cover was the norm, the homeowners will still want to enjoy their furniture. The living or sitting room will have traditional fabrics coordinated with more intention. Accent chairs are used more than large sectionals or recliners. Settees and chaise lounges were common back in the days of the "parlor" or sitting room, but more modern versions of these still make a stunning statement.

The modern homes with open concepts rather than separate rooms will find a perfect blend of comfort and style where the entire family can still enjoy themselves. Well, perhaps without eating on the furniture. Softer fabrics and cushier sofas pair with more structured accent chairs. Reclaimed wood coffee tables blend with metal and glass side tables. They are mixing up concepts more than sticking to one style, making it easier to make small changes, like throw pillows or area rugs, without replacing everything. These living/family rooms are still more formal than the "guy's den," where they hang out to drink beer and yell at the referees.

Open concept homes mean that you will be coordinating the living room, dining room and kitchen furniture to have a pleasing and cooperative feel. Because all the rooms are visible simultaneously, this is the more challenging design to accomplish. You must maintain the overall vision while still finding individual pieces that stand on their own and avoiding the "matchy-matchy" furniture. Do not get me wrong, they create entire sets of coordinating furniture to make it easy for the homeowner to decide, but it also sells more. Why shop around when you can get the matching love seat, armchair and tables?

There is little forgiveness for having the wrong wood tone in the sofa legs than the side tables. Everything is out in the open and on display. You made the rooms that much brighter for all the fabulous lighting you added so that it will highlight all your furniture and decor selections. Be disciplined in the fine details yet playful in those limits. What I mean is, do not become the magpie who brings everything you love to the design. Know the exact tones of wood, metals and concepts you plan to work with and then allow your creativity to flow in how you put these elements together.

AND... like the pool table turned dining room table, do not forget to look for furniture pieces that can have multiple uses such as: stools that turn into step ladders, coffee tables that expand or lift for games or teenage snack parties, consoles or art that disguise televisions, floor-length mirrors that open to show the jewellery case behind...there are so many ways to add extra function and still have a stunning design. You may even floor your clients with these little surprises.

Shelving & Storage

Every house has some form of shelving, even if it is only inside the closets. One of my favorite ways to upgrade a home is to take existing built-in shelving and give it a facelift. The previous wood-finished boards and veneers are easily sanded, primed and painted into a fresh modern look but oh! When you add moldings and create more space? It is a divine addition that adds width and height to a room.

Most often, we see built-in shelving on the walls around the fireplace. It is easy for homes without fireplaces to recreate this feeling around television and media rather than bulky entertainment units. They are not only suitable for storage but for displaying photographs, books and collectibles. Most magazines will have features showcasing these beautiful walls and their perfectly designed displays.

The trick to this is spacing. If the shelves are too deep, then items get lost in the back and shadows are created. If shelves are too thin, then things will look cramped. The same can happen with the height between each shelf. Too much or too little distance between them will create a busy or empty effect where homeowners are more likely to overdo it trying to fill the space. It helps to know if specific items the client intends to display so you can consider the dimensions. I am not talking about random things but truly cherished mementos that will always hold that space. It also helps because these items can set a tone or theme for the other items that you add.

It comes down to breaking it down into visually pleasing fractions based on the wall's height and width you are working with. Then use practical measurements for the items you plan to use. With an eight-foot ceiling, the more horizontal lines you add, the more you chop up the room. It will leave two feet between each shelf on a floor-to-ceiling shelving unit if you have four shelves. Not including the thickness of the wood and any moldings. Perhaps you would break it into three shelves and a storage unit at the bottom with the room for someone to sit.

Interior Design teaches us that when we work in the ratio of three, it is more aesthetically pleasing to the eye. Keep this in mind as you are working with your general contractor or carpenter. They may have some experience with exciting built-in units they have created for clients. Ensure that you are lining the shelves up to not detract from the fireplace mantle while working with the house's style.

Freestanding shelving is even more functional as it usually holds many more items, many of them books. I am a book lover, always have been. Finding enough space to house all my books became a challenge when I had limited space, especially in a room with many long windows. I had to create my own "built-in" look with freestanding shelving. The trick was to use the same size of a shelf on either side of my entertainment unit. Then I kept all the books and items similar in size neatly on those shelves. As a focal point, these shelves needed to be displayed rather than just used as storage.

Offices, bedrooms, garages, laundry rooms, bathrooms, and closets will have different shelving needs. As you work with your client to determine what those are, consider the shelving and hardware installed in the closets compared to what needs to be added. Adding additional furniture pieces in the room will be expensive. It is essential to see how much storage you can create in inventive ways—the more open the shelving, the more need to disguise or hide clutter. Items with drawers or doors will keep the room visibly tidy.

So much of this seems obvious when you think about it on its own. However, when you are in the planning stages of a large design project, it is easy to miss seemingly simple issues. If you happened to clue-in that your clients are not the neatest people, giving them easy and quick storage options will be necessary. Those who are meticulous about being tidy are going to find it much easier to organize their shelving.

Consider the depth of shelving that you are installing or purchasing. Twelve to fourteen inches is easily workable for books and decorative items. You may need deeper shelving if you are housing electronics with lots of cords. Office equipment can be quite bulky and, therefore, more difficult to store for a clean design. How much work do they typically do from home? Does it involve a lot of printing/scanning/faxing? Are they like us and have many floor plans rolled up and needing a storage space that does not damage them? Does the office also act as a spare room and need to convert easily? Every scenario can call for some creativity.

In any kitchen design, consideration has to be given to a client's ability to reach. Suppose the only storage you have provided in the laundry room is above the side-by-side washer and dryer, and one of your clients is petite. In that case, they will never be able to reach the laundry detergent. There are plenty of quick ways to organize the shelving in a house, but you are there to see the homeowner's needs, plan for them and give them more ease than they have been living with.

It helps to get some inside knowledge with cabinet makers and carpenters regarding custom or built-in shelving. They assist you with designing slider drawers and unique storage space for odd items. Generally, they give you their best advice on pulling off some of your challenges. Use those pro's every chance you get.

Store-bought is easier simply because you can visually see what you are working with and what will work or not. Be careful about mixing pieces with various wood stains, quality and size. Make sure they will hold up to what is stored on or in them. I have an antique typewriter that I inherited from my grandmother. It is heavier than it appears, and on a poor-quality shelf, it would cause it to bow or even break. It would be devastating for any damage to happen to that typewriter.

Garage, Hobby And Theater Rooms

The garage, laundry room and kitchen are all workspaces. We get very busy designing the kitchen because it is indeed the central hub of a house. Still, the other work areas of the house will need attention. Depending on the budget, clients could require help with organizing and designing the garage. Women do not often think about this too much past organizing the storage for the Christmas decorations. On the other hand, men dream of having all their tools perfectly displayed, organized and gleaming for all their dreamy woodworking and mechanical projects. Maybe it is sports equipment and fishing gear, colors that show off their loyalty to their favorite sports teams.

Heck, this can happen inside the house as much as in the garage. As a designer, it helps to have contacts with companies that offer garage packages of shelving specific to these needs. Or closet and shelving companies can help design storage for fabrics, sewing materials, photography equipment, woodworking tools and benches. Your client will likely know more about their hobbies than you will, especially what they will need to make it easier to do them. So, set up meetings with your clients present to discuss cabinet and storage design. Listen to what they have been struggling with in terms of space, finding items and how they work.

You may think it makes perfect sense to hang all the tools on a pegboard on the right side of the garage because there is more wall space there, but they park their vehicle on that side, and they would always have to be walking around the car to get to the tools. The same applies to gardening tools or snow shovels. Is the garage or shed a place to store "stuff," or is it also a workspace to accomplish potting, tinkering or building? How you work is not the same as how others do. Sometimes, the companies specializing in this area will know more trade tricks after hearing how their customers have successfully used their products.

Who knew you would have to design around such things as fishing rods, vacuum cleaners and lawnmowers? Do not get me started on taxidermy.

No matter what your client's passions are, it is not your place to judge. I remind you of this because, well, you must learn how to work with everyone's sense of taste. And their unique personalities. I once walked into a cabin style home with an open two-floor concept and came face to face with an enormous moose head and antlers I have ever seen. There was no doubt that they designed the house to display this giant above the fireplace. I may not be a hunter, well, not since I went hunting with my father as a kid, but it is not your place to pull out the animal activist card when you come across these things.

Less dramatically, maybe you do not cheer for their sports team. Or you hate getting your hands dirty and have not gardened in your life. You must get into the groove with people, and the better you are at it, the more successful you will be as a designer. The more resources you have at your fingertips, the greater your ability to help your clients when you run into situations you know nothing about.

Now theater rooms have become very popular when space allows. Movie watching is one of the top past times for families, and some take it to the next level. Popcorn machines, the sconces on the walls and lighting in stairs, comfy individual reclining stairs and a mini-fridge complete the ultimate theater room. I have had clients who added soundproofing drapes along the walls and went all out on the projector and stereo equipment.

These rooms obviously will have a very different approach when it comes to furniture. Lighting will be low, the sofas or chairs will be about complete relaxation, and the homeowners will need places to place their drinks without spills. How you plan this room will be about pleasure, but also safety. With the room naturally darker, and the desire for minimal accent lighting, you need to design around: tripping hazards, ease of use, and easily clean up snacks or spills. Leather is a good option here. Recliners with cup holders and mini lights help.

Sticking with the proper design, the trick to theatre rooms is planning so everyone can see by staggering the seating platforms' height and the furniture. The top stair or platform should account for the standing headroom of the tallest person in the house. The platforms themselves should be no higher than a standard stair riser, which is no more than 7 3/4", but can be less. The width will depend on the furniture you select, whether it reclines and how many pieces there are. Keep in mind extra seating is needed for any company or friends. Offsetting the seating spacing, rather than one directly in front of each other, is ideal. No one is staring at the back of someone's head, and it gives the feeling of more space for each person.

A fun addition in a theater room is a concession and drink bar. Add shelving on the wall for storing various glasses, liquor and wine bottles. You can design a snack display within the glass doors of a cabinet. It might be prudent to have a lock and key cabinet so the kids do not ransack all the goodies when mom and dad are not looking. A popcorn machine will need supplies to go with, including bags, oil, butter powder, and popcorn. Having a sink will aid in quick clean up so that the homeowners do not have to carry everything up and down the stairs, assuming the theater room is in the basement.

Every room in the house has unique needs and functions differently. Each person in the house likely does too. You can go with furniture selection in many directions, and sometimes, you just need to let your clients narrow it down for you. Getting a client from confused and unsure to feeling confident about their decisions takes some skill. I love to give them little rapid-fire tests, "This one, or that one?" I reassure them that this is just a "love it, don't love it, hesitant whether I love it" reaction I am looking for to sort out their tastes better. It becomes a bit of a game with no winners or losers, which relaxes my clients and lets them have a little fun with the process.

Blinds

Drapery and blinds go hand in hand. Most homes will have blinds, some you may have to work with, and other times, they need replacing. You will need to determine whether the blinds will operate as purely function or design with your clients. For those who do not like drapery, the blinds are not only about controlling light and privacy but adding the only window dressing.

There is a lot to know about blinds. Quality ranges from inadequate and inefficient to warrantied products with top of the art operating systems and beautiful fabrics. Most designers will not waste their time with the first and quite likely prefer which brands they will use for them later. If you do not know what brands you should be hanging your flag with, it is time to research. Decide if you will be selling the blinds yourself, with a significant investment of time and money. Another option is to use a professional studio to handle this service for your clients.

If you recommend a separate company, you should have them do some product knowledge training with you. You essentially want to sell the project, including which style and color of blinds you plan to use with the client, and not rely on the salesperson to do this. Their advice and expertise are invaluable, do not get me wrong. But it can take your design in a completely different direction than you were intending. They may also have a different approach than you would prefer, which can cause some confusion for your clients. It is best to know your way around all the blinds brands you intend to recommend and work with your showroom to help you accomplish this. You will want them to handle the measurements with you on-site to discuss installation, operating system placement and potential issues with every house.

If you are selling blinds yourself, you will be responsible for getting correct measurements and ordering the proper operating system. Plus learning all the ins and outs unique to every product. You will need to invest a decent amount of time in training seminars, which could include travel. Most importantly, you want to have a professional installer who knows their stuff at your disposal. Even better would be to have two in case one is too busy or goes out of business. Whatever you do, do not tick off the installer. Good ones are not easy to come by, and without them, you are out of commission with your blinds business.

Knowing which brands to use will take some research. You want to use products that meet and exceed government regulations on safety and be environmentally friendly. Even custom blinds made with fabric in a workroom must meet these standards. Sadly, too many children and pets choke to death after getting tangled in the operating cords. That is a serious risk that you cannot take. Researching different brands online will give you a good indication of who the award-winning companies are in innovation, safety and design.

I have sold a lot of blinds in my time. I prefer companies that take the deductions themselves rather than rely on my math skills. Deductions are the amount taken off the tight inside measurement so that the blind will fit after manufacturing. Any miscalculation can be a costly error. It is easy enough to make an error in the first place. Having an online ordering system is also more beneficial than a supplier who takes handwritten faxed orders. Again, too much room for error. The online ordering system usually catches issues such as exceeding maximum width or height for a specific blind. It can tell you what control systems are available in the style of blind you are trying to order. It is handier than flipping back and forth in giant product books or relying on your memory—no guessing in custom blinds, folks!

There are two ways to mount blinds. Inside mount, which is inside the window frame, and outside mount, installed outside the window frame and trim.

Inside mount blinds keep the blind inside the window frame and neat and tidy. They leave the window trim exposed and are the preferred placement for installation. Depending on the window's depth or the frame's design, the blind cannot be inside mounted because there isn't the required space for the headrail. Too narrow of space, and the blind will not be adequately supported. In other words, it could potentially fall out of the window. Follow the manufacturer's recommended minimums, which you will find in the product price book and information guide. Suppose the window meets the minimum requirements but is wider than the mounting space (keep the open and closed position in mind for this). In that case, the blind will protrude out into the room to some extent. It could interfere with drapery unless it is accounted for and mounted to avoid it.

Outside mounted blinds will need to clear the window trims or casing and not interfere with the operation of the blind should there be other windows or walls. The blind will also need to have the room to clear the window or partially block the view when it is fully open. They call this "stack." One blind will stack differently from another based on the thickness of the individual vanes or material type. The stack can also refer to the amount of blind sits at the headrail when in the fully open position, as with traditional roman shades. Consider drapery's operation, as the fabric's folds tend to stick out farther than other types of blinds.

New inventions in blinds happen all the time. Headrails now

disguise the roll when a roller shade fully open or pulled up. They are thicker than other headrails and need more mounting space in a window. They can also eliminate more light gaps than other headrails, which means light cannot peek in around the hardware. For migraine sufferers and night shift people, this is a big deal. Outside mount blinds eliminate this issue if the blind is ordered wide enough. It is another benefit of drapery. It takes care of the light gaps at the window's side while eliminating the need to mount the blind in a way that blocks the window casings.

Any blind that has a cassette headrail is considered a form of a roller shade—the blind rolls out of the way. Innovation in blind design has created roller-type shades that operate entirely differently from a standard roller shade. Check out what is available with each brand. One thing to note about these blinds, because the fabric must clear the mechanisms at the top of the shade, there are more light gaps at the side of the window. Most times, there is enough of the actual window vinyl to help lessen the effect. The only other ways to stop the light from coming through is to outside mount them or use drapery to frame the blind.

Windows are the eyes of the home, after all. We want to be able to see out and let light in. However, we do not want the neighbors seeing in or having natural sunlight damage the floors or furnishings. Blinds are designed in such a way to minimize damage with carefully designed polyester blend fabrics and PVC's. Some will let in more light than others, which can also lessen privacy at certain times of the day.

Opacity goes from sheers to fully opaque. Sheers will let in the most light but filter it, so there is not much glare. They do not assist with lessening the heat coming in in the summer and out in the winter. Sheers are lovely for homeowners who love their views and do not want to be closed in. Semi-opaque blinds can range from slight sheer to almost blackout. These are more light filtering, prevent more heat from escaping or entering and typically have the most comprehensive fabric and color selection. Opaque is truly room darkening or blackout. No light gets in through the material, though it can still make it past the head-rail and sides of the blind.

All blinds serve a function, environmental control of light, heat and privacy. Some will be more functional than others, operate completely differently and wear faster too. They can be fabric, plastic (PVC), wood or wood composite. For instance, wood and faux wood blinds are hefty. They wear the strings out far sooner than lighter fabric blinds. It is not recommended that the heavier blinds are fully open except clean the windows, relying more on the tilt mechanism to control light. Certain types of controls are easier to manage than the long cords that contract and retract as the blind is lifted and lowered.

More energy efficient blinds will contribute to the "R" value or insulation levels of the house. They can lessen a heating bill too. These blinds are great for older homes that tend to get overly hot. The same amount of heat the house has coming through the windows in the hotter months will be the same amount the homeowner is losing in colder temperatures. These blinds tend to look like honeycombs from the side. To get a solid idea of how energy efficient one honeycomb-style blind is to another, refer to the brand's information guide. If that information is unavailable, you can call customer service. If you don't receive an answer, you may have a lesser quality brand on your hands.

FYI...homeowners do a lot of research on products themselves. They can become virtual experts themselves and develop some interesting questions about the brands you are selling. Ensure that you do not give any untruthful or made-up answers because they will quickly pick up on this. They may lose their trust in you. It is better to know your stuff or tell them you are unsure but can get that information. Then follow through and provide the answers to their questions.

All blinds will need cleaning, and there are different methods for each blind recommended by the manufacturer. You want to ensure that your clients get a copy of their warranty and clean instructions for their window coverings. Some blinds can be ultrasonically cleaned, which is a particular machine that vibrates the dirt loose. Look into blind cleaning companies in your area so that you can make that referral at the same time as your blind sale. Not all fabrics are covered under warranty if ultrasonically cleaned, so ensure that you inform your client of this when purchasing.

Measuring

How do you measure for blinds? Even if you are using a blinds supplier, you can get a preliminary quote with your measurements and confirm their measure.

Inside Mounted Blinds:

First, measure the mounting space. How deep is the inner frame where the blind will sit? Document this as it determines the kind of blind you can or cannot use. Next, measure and document width first, starting at the top left of the window using the space where the blind will be mounted, moving across to the right. Measure from side to side, exact to the nearest 1/8". If you round up, the blind may not fit, so be careful to use a practical measurement. Then move to the middle of the window and take the same measure. Is it more or less than the previous one? Make a note of it. Move to the bottom of the window and repeat. Is this measurement more or less than the other two?

Windows are rarely perfectly square. The house's movements, how the house was framed, or insulation application all play a part in how square the window is. You want to take the smallest of the three measurements for your blind. HOWEVER, I had a case where the smallest measurement was in the middle of the window, where it usually gets bigger, and the blind was too small at the top and bottom. It is a quick way to point out to a client how out of square their windows are, but when they see a blind fit like that, they always blame you and the measurements of the blind. It is prudent to point out discrepancies of the client's measurements as you measure, so they are prepared for some light gaps or not quite perfect fitting blinds. You cannot mold the blind, after all.

Once you have the three width measurements, take three lengthwise measures from the top of the inner window frame where the blind is mounted to the inner bottom frame. Note all three measurements and take the shortest of the three UNLESS it is significant. You can always stop the blind at the frame, but you cannot stretch it farther if the edges are longer than the middle. Use common sense. You do not want it so long that it sits on the high point at the bottom of the window frame, causing the blind fabric to bunch.

You also want to consider using multiple blinds on more expansive windows, such as picture windows with three individual panes. Usually, one or two panes can open, so having one large blind over this window would mean the entire blind has to lift to get to the controls. Three blinds may work better.

To measure this, you will still need the overall width of the entire window. You then begin at the left of the window; the middle of the inner frame is fine. Measure from the edge to the center of the mullion, the PVC where the two panes meet. There is usually a line separating the two. This measure means that the left blind and the middle blind will meet on this line, minus deductions and the light gaps are less apparent here. Next, you will move to the right side of the window and measure where the right panel meets the middle panel. Then take the middle pane measurement to where you stopped on the left and right sides. In case there is no exact line in the mullion to use as a reference, you can add the two side measurements and subtract them from the overall width measurement. The difference will be the center blind. You can then re-add all the measures to make sure they add up to the overall width.

If it does not add up, it is better to have the two side panels match in width and use the remaining number for the middle blind. For example: Let's say the three-pane window has an overall width of 108," and the side panes each measured 23 1/8" and

23 1/4" respectively, then the middle would be 61 5/8". That makes the sides uneven, though. If we change the side blinds to 23 1/4" each, the center blind would then be 61 1/2".

It is an example only. You must use common sense and use the measurements that make the most sense. Some windows only have one small operable side and one larger pane. You can use the same technique and account for what looks best. It would not make sense to divide a window like this precisely in half where a light gap does not line up with the mullion and allows a stream of light through the middle of the window. Never mind that it would look terrible.

Suppose you discover that the mounting space is too small for the blind you were hoping to use. In that case, there may be supporting mounting brackets available to order. The blind will protrude into the room more, but you are in business if the client is okay with this. Keep in mind that the windows' operating controls may stick out and interfere with the blind sitting flush in the window. If possible, have the client switch them out to ones that will fold out of the way. Otherwise, your measurements will need to include these controls, and the blinds installed closer to the outer edge of the window with the hopes of clearing them with the bottom rail.

Outside Mounted Blinds:

These blinds sit outside the frame and casing of the window. Not only will you need the window measurements, but also the wall around the window. You may need to make a diagram of the entire wall, including any other windows and the spacing between them.

When you measure for these blinds, you need to take the window's measurements, from outside trim edge to outer trim edge, for both width and height. Then you need to measure the distance from the top trim edge to the ceiling. From the left, measure from the corner to the left outer edge of the window trim. From the right, measure from the corner to the outer window trim. At the bottom of the window, measure from the bottom outer trim edge to the floor. Ask your client how high off the floor they would like the blind to sit. If they are unsure and need your opinion, it is standard to be 1/4" off the floor as with drapery.

It is a good idea also to measure the wall's entire width and height. Drapery needs three lengthwise measurements from ceiling to floor to double-check the area is square. If not, the blind could drag on the floor or have awkward gaps. Take 1/4" off the shortest measurement.

Where you mount the blind is then a question of how much room you have for the installation brackets and the type of blind you are using. If you have lots of space between the upper trim and the ceiling, then you can use your best judgment. You can place it halfway between the two or as close to the ceiling as possible. I would caution you from installing too close to the casing, if possible, as it can shorten the room. Keep in mind that the wider and longer the blind, the more money it will cost.

These blinds will also need to clear the window and trim itself in both the open and closed positions. Outside mounting brackets can adjust so that the blind does not get hung up on the trim or any window's operating mechanisms.

Notice if the blind will clear the window from the middle as it is opened, called a center split, to the right or the left, in the case of vertical blinds. Will it lift and clear the window from the top? Or will there be a portion of the blind sitting in the window if drawn completely open or lifted? Where you place the width of the blind can make a difference for this, and additional width or height maybe needs to be added to clear the window. If you are trying to keep close to the window's dimensions, you will still need to allow for some extra width to ensure the blind does not create additional light gaps.

Controls

A blind will always have a control of some sort. The most high-tech blinds will be electronically controlled and can even sync up with a smartphone app. The most straightforward blinds will have a cord of some kind that will hang at either the headrail's left or right side. It is essential to place the control where the client can access it easily and operate it without restrictions. For aesthetic reasons, it is also more pleasing not to have all the controls lump together, in the case of multiple windows or blinds in a single window.

You need to make sure that you specify where you want the control placed, or the manufacturer may default it. Consider whether the client is left or right-handed. Perhaps they have any physical limitations that may prevent them from pulling or lifting a blind, or children will use them.

In one instance, I had a client go to the expense of motorizing (another fancy term for electronically controlling the blind) all the blinds in the house. It seemed extravagant in my mind, considering the space; however, she let me know that she had a condition that would eventually lead to her being in a wheelchair. She was planning ahead.

Thankfully, many blinds can operate as cordless; however, limited to specific widths and heights for weight. I love cordless blinds for how clean they are in a window and easy to use. That is if your client is tall enough to reach the bottom rail when the blind is raised. Usually, they operate by pushing or pulling the bottom rail and leaving the blind in the desired position. If the client is too short, or the blind installed in an awkward place, like a bay window behind a kitchen sink, they will never reach it and get frustrated.

Luckily, the blind manufacturers think of almost everything by creating an extension pole for people to reach the cords. These are great for homes with large high windows where the homeowner does not motorize them but also does not want cords dangling down the wall to reach. I would still recommend motorization whenever I could because it is the most user-friendly and visibly pleasing when it comes to cords.

There are so many types and styles of blinds available these days. I would end up sounding like I was training you in blind sales if I went into all of them in detail. You must decide what avenues you want to pursue as income avenues and want to leave to other professionals. Drapery is another example of custom window covering to consider.

Drapery, Cushions And Bedding

Some folks are against drapery. For others, the room is not properly decorated without it. Just like in clothing design, there are thousands of ways to create window fashion.

Now, there is always the store-bought drapery that you can choose from. Often you will easily find grommet style drapery panels in standard lengths. It can work when you are in a pinch, like needing to sell a home quickly and you do not have much time to get it prepped. It can be somewhat limiting for selection, lengths and operable widths. Using store-bought drapery and hardware will come down to using your design skills to pull the look together in a budget-friendly set of treatments. Apply the information about custom window treatments to store-bought drapery. It applies there too.

When I first started out designing drapery, I knew nothing other than putting fabric on a pole. Yes, I am a self-taught woman. I had a workroom behind me who was willing to answer my questions, do the fabric calculations and point me in the right direction. Every time a fabric rep came into the showroom, I educated myself. I bought myself a drapery book called "The Design Directory of Window Treatments" by Jackie Von Tobel. Another book that I would recommend is "The Encyclopedia of Window & Bed Coverings" by Charles T. Randall.

I did not have the terminology to describe elements of the design for my client. I was able to photocopy images out of the book to create an idea "file." The client could see what I was envisioning for their windows, eliminate what they did not like, and then customize it for them. Trust me, when you say "jabot" to a client, hardly any will know what you are talking about unless they have some experience with drapery. It also allowed me to explain the window treatment design to the workroom with diagrams, measurements, and fabric selections.

The last piece of "equipment" I invested in was Minutes Matter's program by Debbie Green. Not only did it incorporate the exact window covering elements in the program, but it allowed me to create a digital copy of my customer's windows. I could put the drapery design in the virtual window for the customer to see and then sign off before I ordered fabric or work started. The lovely thing about this program is you can create the entire design project digitally. It helps when you have clients who need to struggle to visualize what you are talking about. It takes some practice to get used to the program. I highly recommend taking the tutorials before needing them for a project.

When it comes to designing the drapery itself, it starts with the measurements. Using the same techniques as measuring for blinds, you want to have the inside and outside measurements for all the windows you will be dressing. I highly recommend you draw diagrams of the walls, which do not have to be to scale but with enough room to write your measurements down between elements. You need to know the spacing of windows so that everything is in the proper scale while designing the treatments. It may be prudent to create a measurement template to save time. You want a "fill in the blank" form so that you can catch if you have missed a measurement before leaving the house.

You will need the trim's width around the window, the measurements around the window, and the measurements inside the window, including the mullions' placement. You need to know where electrical plugs and light switches are. You will need to know if there are any wall sconces or artwork to avoid. You will need to measure the distance between each window and where pieces of furniture will be. Knowing how much room you must work with and what dimensions you are limited to will determine where you mount the drapery and how big you are making them.

Make your diagrams as easy to read and follow as possible. Sometimes a client will put a project on hold, and you want to quickly pick right up where you left off, even if it is months later. I recommend having both a laser measuring tool and a tape measure handy for those areas that are difficult to measure with a laser.

You will need to know how much of the window the client is okay with covering, whether they want the drapery to be operable or just for show. In swags, cornices and valances, width and depth play a considerable role in obscuring the window. The width of the valance will have the drapery panels mounted within it. If the width is limited, the panels' width will be too and may not be installed entirely off the window. You want to cover the trim and maybe a few inches in on either side and in the case of operable drapery panels, they can be swept to the side with hardware. The valance's length depends on where it will be mounted and how low into the window it will sit at its longest point.

Drapery panel dimensions depend on whether they are installed on their own or under a top treatment of some sort. For inoperable drapery, I like to work in thirds to determine their width. For example, let's say the window is 36" wide with the trim. We will mount 12" on each side, minus 8" so the panel will sit 4" into the window on each side. We have a total width of 52". If I divide 52" by 3, then each panel is 18"…with a little rounding. If I look at the window, the valance and the wall and decide this is too narrow, I add some inches to each panel.

Suppose the drapery is operable and pulled across the window. In that case, I take the window's overall width and add for the panels' stack when they are open (this will depend on the width of the window and how much fabric there is). Then add 4" for the drapery to overlap each other when they are closed and divide by two.

For example: Using the same 36" window with trim, mounting 12" on either side plus 4" for overlap, gives us 60". Divide this number by two, and we have 30" panels.

To finish off operable or inoperable drapery panels, you want each panel's outside edge to turn towards the wall, called a return or return-to-the-wall. The extra inches added once per panel will be determined by how far out the panel will be from the wall after installation.

You are probably seeing how essential it is to show your clients how the design looks and how it affects their view through the window. With blinds also in place, they could have a lot going on. If they are into simple looks, you will not be giving them a five-layer look between blinds, drapery panels and layered swags. The more traditionalists may be looking for that.

One of the most challenging drapery designs I ever did was a seven-panel bowed bay window. The client wanted sheer drapery as well as layered swags along the top. Sounds simple enough, right? Well, it was the angles and the lack of space between each window that was stumping me. I did not have a lot of mounting space either. We had to get everything just right because this was a rather expensive job outside my typical trading area. Any errors were going to mean costly trips back and forth, reordering fabric, waiting on the workroom again and ticking off the client to boot.

Thankfully, my client was patient enough to allow my workroom and me to work through the design and special order a pattern for them to work with. Installation day almost had me the color of an eggplant; I was holding my breath so much. It went off perfectly and my client was ecstatic! It pays to take your time and stay organized.

Drapery design comes down to fabric selection. You can have the most beautiful swag in mind but if you have chosen a fabric that will not hold the pattern, frankly it will look like hell. That is where I loved having my workroom on standby if I had any concerns. Some sheer fabrics need a training thread to control the shape of the folds in extended designs. When you do not have your workroom available, a phone call to the fabric rep or your fabric retailer should get you some more information. It is their job to assist you in any way they can. It is to their benefit to sell the fabric.

The fabric's width is also a crucial element. It tells you how many seams you may end up with. When designing drapery panels, cornices, swags, and any design with some width involved, it is essential to know. Like in operable drapery, panels that will close over the window, those seams can be less appealing. There are 118" wide fabrics available, mostly in sheers, for this reason. All the information is on the back of the fabric sample or the book's back when all the fabrics are the same width.

Fabric is listed as upholstery, drapery or multipurpose. These are vital designations to know whether the material you are considering is suitable for your project. An upholstery fabric may be the perfect shade and pattern but horrible for the way it would hang. In the same breath, a multipurpose material may be suitable for upholstery. Still, because the double rub count is lower, it is better off in a toss cushion than in seating.

The back of the fabric will also list the pattern repeat dimensions. It is the width and length of the pattern before it repeats itself. Why is this important? The material will need to line up, so the patterns match perfectly, creating the need for more fabric. Larger pattern repeats mean you will need more fabric than smaller ones. When designing the smaller window coverings and soft furnishings like cornices, swags, toss cushions or chairs, it is essential to have this information. The pattern may be too large or small for the scale of the project.

Just to keep us on our toes, the fabric can also be railroaded. Another term to look for on the back of the fabric sample. It means that the design of the material runs width-wise on the roll rather than lengthwise. It can result in more seams, confusion on how much fabric you will need and costly errors if you miss this detail. The fabric book may show the material in how it is supposed to look rather than the direction it comes off the roll. That is where I got into the habit of looking at the back of every sample a client was considering before I sold them on it. It saves a lot of time in reselecting later.

Fabric selection is so much fun. Like shopping for tile, there are so many colors, patterns, sheens and combinations to pick from. Some fabric books arranged with pattern combinations are already displayed stylishly for you, making it easier to co-ordinate multiple soft furnishings. It can be overwhelming and time-consuming in the early planning stages. In some cases, it may be better time spent scouting the fabrics you would like to use before bringing your client along.

Showrooms may only be open to the design community and require appointments to attend. Fabric manufacturer show-rooms are even better because they usually have a yard of every fabric, so you can play with how it hangs and holds in folds. You can discuss your designs and the overall vision for color and pat-tern with the staff and get their recommendations. They know their way around a lot better than you do and can show you fab-rics that you may not have considered otherwise. When you are ready for a second appointment with your client, try to arrange for the same staff member to help you, so they are already up to speed. Then the both of you can work with any changes the client wishes to make. Two heads are better than one. In some cases, you will be able to borrow the fabric books for a short amount of time so that you can see the fabrics in the client's house.

Ensure that you or your client do not cut samples from these books as they are irreplaceable for the supplier. Manufacturers only produce so many, and sales reps only hand them out to spe-cific clients. When they are all gone, no one can get more. Being respectful of your supplier's sample books will keep you in their good graces as a designer. It can even earn you recommenda-tions if they have business opportunities in your trading area.

Once you make your selections, make sure to document all the details about them, including: brand, supplier (in case sev-eral stores offer them), price, color, SKU and stock availability. If you cannot get the fabric for three months, it delays the drapery job for five to six months. Your client may not be willing to wait. You must continue to check stock and availability on the fabric if you are not ready to purchase it or place it on hold. Any product holds will only keep the material for a short amount of time. If you suspect that you will be short or stuck, it may be wise to place a hold until your workroom gets you the quote and your client pays their deposit.

Embroidered trim can add detail to the inner edge of drapery panels, the hem or finish the seam where there are two fabrics sewn together. Some trim is simple, while others have designs sewn into them or even thread tassels, beads and crystals hanging from them. You can be as elaborate with them or simple with them as you like. Traditional draperies from Europe are a good example. Tie back draperies with an elaborate silk rope and finish with a large tassel. Typically, trim is sold in yards or meters. It will come down to your client's taste and style and their home... and your interpretive skills as a designer to know how much or how little to use.

Pleat styles vary. Pinch pleats are typical with sheer draperies but modernized with stitch placement and the number of pleats. There are many designs found in Jackie von Tobel's books. If you have an idea of a design, it may be worth discussing it with your workroom to create it. Either way, the drapery panel's pleat style, or header, is the primary design element for drapery panels. It determines how the fabric will fold, how rigid or fluid it appears and how intricate it is. The more elaborate the stitching is for the workroom, the more it will cost.

When you give the design elements to your workroom and ask for a quote, you must include how full you want the drapery. It means how deep and how many pleats or folds there will be in the fabric. For example, if you were to order no fullness, the material would only be lying flat. However, two times fullness means the fabric doubles upon itself for the same width. Two and a half times fullness is preferred and can go up from there but could get deep and heavy. I stuck with two and half times thickness as it was luxurious but less expensive for my clients. It also determines the number of folds the panel will have and how deep the return-to-the-wall will be.

Drapery Hardware

Drapery hardware is the mechanism used to hold the window fashions in place. They can be as simple as the pole and brackets, the finials to dress up the exposed ends of the rod, and they are used to hold back the drapery panels. Hardware also ties into the other metal or wood elements in the home. It's like a lovely hair clip or set of earrings to complete the outfit. Without them, even the most beautiful look is not quite complete. The hardware serves a purpose, of course. It includes grommets and rings, pullbacks, rods, brackets and finials. These selections tie the drapery design together and give the more functional aspects of the drapery some pizazz.

It starts with the pole and brackets for drapery. In the case of a set of sheers with an additional set of panels, you will need double rods and brackets designed to hold them both. But let's not get ahead of ourselves. When calculating the pole's width, we must look at how far past the window the drapery itself will be sitting on either side, plus the window's width. We need to add at least four inches, two for each end, for the pole to rest in the bracket. The finials or caps will need space for installation. That will depend on the finial for how much you will need to order on each side.

Drapery poles come in standard lengths and then cut to the appropriate size. So, once you have added up the overall width you require, you must select the next pole size up from that width. In some cases, two pole pieces are spliced together on the same treatment with a splice's help. The splice is open on both ends and allows each part of the pole to slide in either end. Angled splices and various hardware pieces are available to help connect poles in the case of bay windows. It is good to see all the parts available in a hardware line to see if you can utilize them from the same manufacturer within the selected finish.

Drapery poles also come in different thicknesses. It is essential to make sure that you are lining up the same dimensions in drapery grommets, rings and passing rings. Passing rings are designed to continue along the rod without getting hung up on the brackets. Yes, you would need to order the passing brackets as well. Of course, there are different rod systems for sheer draperies installed with gliders and hooks. These systems have an operating loop cord, much like a blind. They are hidden by the drapery header and do not have finials. Your supplier or showroom will have a catalog of what is available for these relatively inexpensive operating systems.

Drapery rings and grommets are the pieces that connect the fabric to the pole. Calculating how many you need comes down to the number of times the cloth folds in the design. You will need a ring for every time the fabric ripples and comes back to the rod. It may be challenging to know the exact number until the drapery comes back from the workroom. I was ordering my hardware in advance. When the drapery arrived, we were ready to install it as quickly as possible. That meant I was estimating the number of rings in advance. (Grommets are punched into the fabric at the workroom, and they included in their quote)

Knowing the fullness of the drapery, I knew there would be pleats every two, two and a half or three inches. I would then take the flat width of the panel and divide it by the thickness. I then would add a few more per panel for the ends. It was always better to have a few more rings than less, so I erred on the side of caution and ordered spare.

Finials are the dressing for the drapery pole. Some finials are little caps to finish off the exposed end of the rod. Others can be very ornate with carved wood to look like pineapples, branches, fleur-de-lis or acorns. These shapes are not limited to wood either. You will often find them in many metal finishes and sheens as well. Some of my favorite finials include glass and crystal, but the price tag comes with the glitz. The style of the drapery treatment and the fabric will help determine which direction to go. If

LAUNCH INTO INTERIOR DESIGN

the homeowners like simple drapery panels, fabulous finials are a great way to add some flair without being overly flashy.

When it comes to finials, you must look at the dimensions regarding whether it will fit if the window is butting up to a wall or another window. It only makes sense to have one set of finials when there are multiple windows, like bay windows. In some cases, windows butt up to a wall on one side, and you can only use one finial, and likely a tie back as well. Keep in mind that tie backs and finials are sold in pairs and charged for both in most cases. Ensure that you are also charging your client for two. You can leave them with the extra pieces or save them for on-hand stock on other projects. How you handle spare products in your business is up to you.

Valances, Cornices And Swags

What is the difference between a valance, a cornice and a swag? A cornice is a hard surface box with fabric and padding mounted to it or a finished decorative wood box that caps the top of a window. These can have other fabric elements like a swag or brad nails added to them. The edges are cut into any shapes or designs to add a different visual line in the window. Cornices can be relatively simple or ornate. Some mimic or match the crown molding, and others can have metal scrollwork installed to have an old-world effect. If you have the products available or know artisans who can make a custom piece for you, you can create a truly one-of-a-kind cornice.

Valances are softer than cornices. They, too, cap the top of the window treatment; however, valances tend to have fabric and padding wrapped and attached to a board. Valances can have layered features with a tight padded fabric on the main body, with a sweep of material added for a little flare. Valances tend to be more popular than cornices for their versatility but also the expense. Because the framework is not part of the design, they are much more affordable to build. Valances are also easier and lighter to install. I have put quite a few valances in my clients' homes over the years, and you can install the fabric wrapped board with "L" brackets and then Velcro the decorative fabric piece in place. It is so easy. After installation, you use a fabric steamer as you should with all custom drapery to remove any small wrinkles or creases developed in shipping and handling.

Swags are constructed much like a valance with a fabric wrapped board for a header installed on "L" brackets; however, swags refer to the swooped fabric design. We often see them in sheers and can look a bit like campaign banners. You can use the main drapery panel fabric for a soft look or a contrasting fabric for more visual impact. Swags can be layered so that multiple swags are on one treatment, with each slightly overlapping the previous one or staggered. There are many ways to design swags, depending on the fabric selected. They can create a very formal look, rich and moody or casual country.

Calculating the width and height of these window coverings is easy. Just fit it over the drapery panels, and done. No... it is not quite that simple. You do need to know where you are placing the drapery panels. But while you were calculating the panels' dimensions, you were also keeping the valance in mind. It is trickier when you do not have much space to work with outside of the window. Once installed, the window's view is obstructed, something a homeowner can be sensitive about. Again, I liked to work in thirds.

Let's cover a 36" wide by 60" high window with 2 1/2" trim, with 18" of mounting space above and lots of room on the sides. My inoperable drapery panels will be 19" finished width with 2.5 times fullness and mounted 8" past the trim with a tieback. To determine the dimensions for the valance, I know I need to clear the installed panels underneath. For width, I add the 36" of the window, 5" for trim (two sides) and 16" for the extra width of where the panels will sit. This is 57". I would then round this to 60" so there is 1 1/2" clearance on each side.

Now this means that the valance is the same width as the length of the window. It may seem a lot but let 's continue with the height of the valance.

Adding the window height of 60" plus 5" for trim (top and bottom) plus 6" above for where we are mounting gives us 71". Divide this by three, which is more visually appealing to the eye. You get 24" when you round it out for the height of the valance. Which means the valance will hang about 15" down into the window.

I would now get out my graph paper and do a to-scale drawing of the window design the treatment. If my goal is to make the window appear larger, this would surely do it. Visually, you would not know where the trim of the window is because the valance and the drapery panels are disguising the sides and top. If the valance looks too low, we have mounting space to move it up higher. However, watch that you do not need longer panels now also. It seems like a larger window with a beautiful window treatment. However, if my goal is to keep the window a little more accurate to its dimensions, I would lessen the panels' width, both in the fabric and mounting space. Then adjust my valance width. Then I would redraw the window treatments to scale and see how it looks. Once you get the hang of it, you will automatically know which will be more appealing.

It took me a lot of practice, patience and erasers to figure out window covering designs. I did not have a guide on what would look better or how to calculate the measurements. I taught myself. If you have mentors who have given you precise formulas to use, tricks up their sleeves to assist you or just some great advice, take it. Soak up as much information as you can. It is only the method I used with great success because I was not breaking any rules. My customers were repeatedly happy. I had a great workroom who assisted me with the fabric calculations, and away I went. My confidence and willingness to try saw me through a successful career in drapery design.

There are so many elements that you can add to the window treatment. I investigated every example of drapery design I could get my hands on and put the plans into a practical understanding as I worked with my designs. Your client's home may allow for the more elaborate creations you develop, including the fabulous fabrics that go with them. Other clients will call for a set of simple drapery panels. Yet, the material can make them gorgeous in their simplicity. And when you finally get to use those designs you have been dying to try, or fabrics in the colors that most are too nervous to have on their windows? *Oh boy, look out!*

Drapery design is one of the real expressions a designer has in creativity. It is true fashion. A place where you can be as original and unique as your clients trust you to be. There is a lot to consider between the measurements, fabric selection, design, creation and installation of drapery, but the result can be stunning. Window treatments of all kinds are an investment for the home to save the furniture, flooring, and energy. But they sure are an attractive way to do it!

Toss Cushions & Bedding

While I was ordering my drapery book, I realized a second book by Jackie Von Tobel, "The Design Directory of Bedding," was available. I thought, well, why not? I was going to educate myself in drapery, so it only made sense to learn about custom bedding. Once I received my books and started flipping through, I was pleasantly surprised to find many custom cushion designs.

Toss cushions are not just for the living room sofa. They can be accents to bedding, including neck rolls, which can be quite handy! Pillows are in window seats, extra cushions for occasional chairs and even floor cushions for kids to lounge on. Heck, meditation cushions are trendy too!

It is great fun to visit your favorite home furnishing stores and find all kinds of treasures in the pillow aisle. Pillows come in every size with sequence, tassels, silk, faux fur, intricate patterns, weaves, and stitched scenes. These pillows offer up untold dreamy room schemes just waiting for you to discover them. They are relatively inexpensive for the labor that goes into them because you are buying products already finished, likely in mass production. To get store-bought pillows to match perfectly to other fabrics you are using can be tricky, and you may spend some time touring different stores looking for the right fit.

Cushion and bedding shopping with your client can be an excellent way to get them involved in designing their home. Most have been itching to dig into this process from the beginning of their renovation or redesign plans. It is a good idea to discuss what you are both looking for before diving into the sea of choices. It will lessen the "magpie effect" from liking everything and selecting nothing. It is not just the color or fabric that you have to consider. Are the pillows just for show, casual and meant to be put aside, or are they going to be used for back support, head support or any functions like meditation?

The firmness of the pillow, whether store-bought or custom, is vital information to have. Polyester blend and down pillows will come with different densities or firmness. The softer the firmness, the less support there will be for backs or necks. Test this while you are shopping with your client and discuss as you are deciding on placement.

It is standard to layer pillows rather than having the same size for everything. Again, the more formal or traditional the client's home, the more layers you will have and the more elaborate the pillows will be. A casual home may have fewer pillows and keep things simple in terms of comfort and style. I say this a lot, but it emphasizes the need to work within your client's tastes and how they function in their home. Always moving cushions out of the way so they can sit down or get into bed may turn into more of a pillow fight than a luxurious, perfectly designed room.

Again, the rule of three keeps a pleasant balance. Let's face it, sofas and beds are boxy looking items. By adding cushions, we soften those lines with cushions that mold to all the lovely curves of our bodies. It says, "Hey! That looks like a wonderful place to get into!"

Let's say that we want two larger 24"x24" pillows for the sofa and two 18"x18" complimentary pillows for the love seat. We are already aware that the larger pillows will not look as good on the smaller furniture as it would on the sofa. Yet, we still want to add another layer to the cushions with a second set. What is a better dimension to use?

Well, if we take the 24" cushion and divide it by three, we get 8". If we take the 18" pillow and divide it by three, we get 6". We are not trying to have a large difference in size between the larger cushions and the smaller cushion. We want to have a casual layer. So, we then take our 8" and multiply it by two. 16" is then two-thirds of the size of the 24"x 24" cushion and the same with 12" being two-thirds of the 18"x18". If adding a third pillow, you can look at the dimensions again and decide what works best. Usually, the first two pillows are for comfort, while any additional pillows would be decorative.

Layering pillows on a bed is similar in how you stagger the sizes but different. You are working with the actual bed pillows' dimensions. Standard, queen and king size pillows will all have different dimensions to work with. Still, you can use the same calculations to figure out the accent pillows.

Finding the perfect cushion according to size, color, fabric, and shape can be done, but it is more challenging in a store. However, if you cannot find what you are looking for, you have entered the custom world again. Not every client will have you designing custom items like bedding or pillows. Be prepared to be asked for this service.

One of the first questions you need to ask when designing custom cushions is whether they understand the cost. Custom pillows will be significantly more expensive than factory-made store-bought pillows. They can be anywhere from four to six times more expensive depending on the fabric, detail and type of filler used. The second question will be which pillows are for practical use and what is decorative only. It will tell you what insert you will be using.

I had a client that insisted that we made every pillow with a down insert. Down pillows conform to the body without lumps and bumps and can easily be fluffed back into shape. Feather inserts are less expensive but can have pokey feathers sticking out of them from time to time. Down pillows cost more but are less likely to have that problem. Watch it, though. Clients may be sensitive to smell or even have allergies to them.

In custom pillows, you still have to work with the sizing of the inserts available. Your workroom, or whoever is supplying the inserts, will have a catalog for you to choose from. Once you know that, you can determine what size is most appropriate for the area. You can visually expand on the pillow's dimensions depending on how the sewing of the slipcover. Essentially you are designing slipcovers. Some will fit together like an envelope, close with buttons, where others have zippers.

Hidden zippers are disguised within the seam and give a beautiful, finished look. From then on, you are only limited by what you can come up with in your imagination. The more custom work you can introduce into a project, the more creative and unique it will be. It is not for the faint of heart because there is more room for error with expensive furnishings, but when you get it right, oh my, is it beautifully worth it.

In The Next Chapter...

Do you feel your creative juices tingling yet? You have gotten a definite taste of what some of the exciting, and sometimes more complicated, aspects of interior design are all about. You know how to select custom or store-bought furniture, along with some cautionary knowledge to save you some trouble. You know more about custom blinds, drapery and cushions, along with how to measure for them. And, even more importantly, you know how to find the resources to further your training in each of them.

In the next chapter, we delve into more decorative treasures that we will use to finish off the entire design. It includes area rugs, wallpaper, art, décor and *finally* paint!

CHAPTER FOUR - THE DRESSINGS

Here we are! The last chapter focused on beautifying the client's home. I hope you are excited to round out the remaining decorative elements with useful information and tips to make you a successful and sought-after designer. These items are the juicy goods that decorators and homeowners crave and drool over and have the most fun shopping. As expected by now, I have some advice based on experience with area rugs, wallpaper, art, décor and mostly paint.

Time to dig in!

Area Rugs

Area rugs can be as luxurious or as practical as you want. It can be an afterthought for some people on where to put a carpet. In some cases, to hide the scratches on the living room floor. Or maybe they find their voices echo and need to buffer the noise with an area rug. For others, an area rug is a beautiful piece of art and is something to be cherished for the investment they made.

Visually, an area rug helps frame a seating area into a more cohesive space, but the rug's size will depend on the room's size. It is ideal for containing the sitting space within the area rug dimensions with at least twelve inches to spare on the outer edge. This will include the sofa, loveseat and accent chairs, as well as all the tables. It only works in large open spaces, however. You can use the same effect in medium rooms by using a rug large enough to tuck six to eight inches under the furniture's front legs. It may not contain all the tables, but it still defines the sitting area. In small spaces, a small area rug works under the central coffee table. I would caution you, this creates a tripping hazard and can make the room appear smaller.

Apply the same rule to dining room settings. Again, watch for how traffic moves around the room or table area and select a rug that allows for ease without tripping.

You will have to be inventive to work with oddly shaped rooms or different furniture layouts in some living room layouts. If you have a long narrow room, try to give more visual width with the area rug and furniture placement. You may have to have the rug tucked under the main piece of furniture and not under the rest. No matter what improvising you must do, you want the finished result to look neat, polished and without awkward features sticking out.

Area rugs are also used in bedrooms to showcase the bed. When working in thirds, if you use two-thirds of the space, the headboard and side tables are left without carpet. But more of the rug is exposed at the foot of the bed. If the rug sits so that one-third of the bed is on the rug, then more of the rug is revealed at the sides. The size of the rug will depend on the size of the bed. I recommend leaving enough area rug exposed for the client to step out of bed without tripping.

Hard surface flooring is hard on the feet, beautiful, but cold and hard, especially in a bedroom. Getting out of a warm bed and stepping onto a cold surface does not appeal to most people, and this is where area rugs come in very handy. Simple and plush area rugs are about comfort and adding a soft layer to the bedding and draperies' design. Or in reverse, if the bedding is simple, the area rug can tie into the draperies in the subtle tones of the color palette you are working with.

It is another chance to get our hands on craftily designed color and pattern and bring a room to life as designers. Of course, there are the functional benefits of having an area rug. Still, no matter what, they add another decorative layer. Selecting an area rug for a room is like picking a single piece of art. It is one area that I found homeowners get overwhelmed in the most. The rug design truly sets a theme and can rule out other fabrics in pillows and drapery. Unless a client has already selected an area rug, it is better to have the custom pieces designed before the area rug. If you are using store-bought cushions and curtains, then you can select the area rug first.

Keep in mind, there is no hard-fast rule about anything, as I have said before. If your clients have difficulty making decisions with soft furnishings, try switching the order of your selections. Once you have the ball rolling on one major item, it will be easier for the others to fall into place.

Area rugs can make a striking statement or add a soft touch. They can be a casual shag rug, textured woven wool or a traditional hand-woven silk rug with tapestry patterns. They can be used as an accent piece like in bedrooms or be the main attraction in living rooms. Runners can be used in kitchens, entrances, and staircases to help warm the feet and prevent slips.

Function can always have design, but not all design can have a function.

Knowing what kind of rug will be most suitable will come down to how the clients live in their homes. If they have young kids, then you want rugs that are stain-resistant and easily cleaned. Perhaps allergies are a consideration. You will need to pay attention to the fibers and the construction of the rug. Like wool, natural fibres have specific smells, and it may take some time for new rugs to lose that odor.

Proper care is just as crucial for area rugs as it is for installed carpeting. Knowing what you can and cannot do in terms of cleaning will have to be strictly followed to maintain the manufacturer's warranties. If your client is not likely to maintain the upkeep, they may want to select a rug that works with their cleaning style.

As a designer, you will need to have several stores and suppliers for area rugs in your pocket. Some stores will have a selection on hand, either hung in racks or stacked on the floor. More will be available in catalogs or online, but not getting your hands on them for accurate color depiction and feel is not ideal. It is important to be on the same page with your client about what they like and do not like when it comes to color, pattern and feel. If your client is into abstract art, you will not likely select a traditional oriental rug. Knowing that your client loves teal, the rug allows you to bring in pops of her favorite color without overdoing it throughout the design. Organizing your thoughts will help keep area rug overload to a minimum.

In some cases, stores will allow you to take the area rugs home for a trial run as long as it is promptly returned and not soiled. I highly recommend this if possible. Seeing the colors in the home, even without other key elements installed, can show how much color or how bold the pattern comes out. Often, I can tell when a client loves or dislikes something by the expression on their face. They do not even have to say anything. I ask them their opinion, letting them tell me what they see. If they do not like the rug, I reassure them that my feelings will not get hurt but ask them to elaborate on what they do not like. With their responses, I can then reconfigure my game plan when I start looking again.

Of course, you will have brought several to try and perhaps minimized the search. Keep the process light and fun, and avoid getting too caught up in any indecision your client is having. You may be used to this process, but for others, making all these selections is mind-boggling and stressful. Especially when there is budget pressure (there is always a budget) and one partner is stricter. You can even be the instigator if you take sides. Ensure that you are empathetic to both your clients' needs and concerns. Confirm your understanding of where you are at in the budget and reassure them that you can work within style and cost to achieve a beautiful home.

The same stores offering in-stock area rugs are also likely capable of ordering custom area rugs. In some cases, the pattern is available in several sizes to work with your area.

Tip: Always be open to being pleasantly surprised. You never know when you will find something out of this world, crazy, never have you seen it before in the world of décor. Keep your eyes and mind open to possibilities and your eyes peeled as you browse the shops. It is the unexpected where things can get interesting. Just when you did not think a color scheme would ever look good together, someone has pulled out all the stops and found a way to turn it into a trend. Suppose you are fortunate enough to have a client who loves to mix it up. In that case, you can crack your knuckles and dive into the unpredictable and exhilarating scavenger hunt that is interior design.

Wallpaper

One of the most drool-worthy elements in design has got to be wallpaper. It can revert even the most seasoned interior designer into a three-year-old at Christmas when the sample books come out.

Wallpaper has evolved WAY past the silk vinyl with shimmery florals termed "blue hair lady" paper. Textures range from matte, embossed and various sheens to full glitz with crystals embedded in them. You'll find them in woven grass, paper blends and even vinyl.

Like fabric selection, patterns move a room into a specific color palette and theme and make no mistake; wallpaper has an endless selection. The difference is that the design is now spread upright along an entire wall where the pattern's effect is on full display.

One of my clients' biggest concerns has been whether the pattern would be too much once it was installed. Honestly, that is a valid question. I found I was describing the effects of a large or small scale pattern on the room and the eye for less visual people.

A large-scale damask wallpaper can help fill a large room, even if used only on one wall. Yet, it can still be busy with the pattern having more contrast than the client would like. A small-scale floral can look quite busy on the same wall because the number of elements in the design has just increased.

You need to consider the scale of the room and the scale of the wallpaper. Think of the overall effect you are aiming for — or, in some cases, trying to avoid! There is a photo of the installed paper in the sample books and the range of colors available in any given pattern. Grouping complementary accent papers within the same color scheme are common, so you can mix and match without the fear of getting the tones wrong.

How a paper looks on the wall is very different from how it looks laying flat in a book on the table. Sheen will influence the color as well as the intensity of the pattern.

> *Tip: Stand the sample book upright so you can see*
> *how the light plays down and across the paper. It is*
> *crucial to see it in the home's lighting as well. Go the*
> *extra step of ordering a sample roll so you can see*
> *the pattern in a larger format before making a final*
> *decision.*

The repeat of the pattern, large or small, can make an enormous difference in the quantity that you need to purchase for the job. The designs may match, need to drop or not matter at all. It is called *pattern repeat.*

Straight Match means that when the strips of the paper are hung on the wall, the patterns directly line up with one another. There is less wastage when this paper is installed than if the design does not line up.

Drop Match means that the next strip of paper will need to be adjusted or 'dropped' for the patterns to line up. It can mean more paper is required to cover the entire wall and needs to be accounted for in calculations.

Random Match means that the patterns will line up regardless of how the next strip is applied to the wall. Wastage is minimal.

Where do you find the details about each paper? As you flip through the sample books, you will notice information on the back of each sample page. You will find the information on how the paper is 'matched,' the roll's width (which affects your quantity calculations) and installation instructions. If the information is not on the back of the paper sample, it may be on the back of the sample book itself. It would likely mean that the entire collection of wallpaper has the same measurements and installation instructions.

Some papers come pre-pasted, which involves wetting the paper in a tray, 'booking' the paper's sticky parts together to activate the glue and applying it to the wall. Others require pasting the wall with a clear wallpaper adhesive or clay in specialized cases. Follow these instructions precisely, or it could result in a costly replacement of the paper.

Installation of wallpaper can be done by homeowners themselves, with some patience and the proper instruction. Unless you have a lot of experience hanging wallpaper yourself, I would not recommend offering to hang it for your client.

Tip: You must find a professional wallpaper service that you can trust and who has specific training in hanging wallpaper.

Walls are never straight or flush. Angles can be tricky, and whole bathrooms can be the toughest to paper due to the multiple fixtures and plumbing. The pro will know how to manipulate the patterns to work around obstacles and challenging walls to get the perfect result to base your career on. Guaranteed, should there be a bobble, or a misaligned strip of wallpaper, it will be a glaring issue for your client to stare at every day. A professional is your best bet to a beautiful outcome.

Calculating how much paper you need is a tricky business. The length of the roll and the width are often, but not always, a standard 21" wide x 16.5 ft long (approximately 28 sq. ft.) per double roll. Get into the habit of ALWAYS verifying the paper's dimensions as you can have expensive miscalculations leaving you with way too much paper, or worse — not enough!

NOTE! Wallpaper is priced per single roll in the sample book but ONLY comes as a double roll bolt. Industry standards changed, but the books, for whatever reason, did not. Don't get confused. When you see the price per roll, double it. That is your cost per double roll. If you are unsure, double-check with a salesperson to verify the paper's information before you quote your customer. No, you cannot just order a single roll if you are short. Your calculations must be as accurate as possible.

The steps for calculating the quantity of wallpaper you need is:

1. Multiply the width and height of each wall you cover (add wall totals together if papering more than one) to determine the square footage. Subtract the square footage of any doors and windows, but not for small outlets or plumbing fixtures.
2. Find the pattern repeat of the paper. Determine if the repeat is small (12" or less), then divide the square footage by 25 or if the repeat is large (13" or more), then divide by 21.
3. The total will give you the number of SINGLE rolls you need. Round up fractions to the nearest even* number... but never round down unless you are confident you don't need that much. Take your new total and divide by two to get the number of double rolls you require.

For example: 8x12' wall = 96 sq. ft divided by 21 for pattern repeat = 4.57
4.57 single rolls become 6 single rolls divided by 2 = 3 double rolls
* even numbers calculate into complete double rolls as you cannot order single rolls.
**Calculations based on York Wallcoverings website: https://www.yorkwallcoverings.com/wallpaper-calculator

The texture, weight, and type of paper can make a difference in the ease of hanging the paper. Some are more difficult to cut.

Others are difficult to hang. *Always account for the chance of error and order at least one extra double roll of wallpaper.* It is better to have too much than too little.

Dye lots are never going to match perfectly from one manufacturer's batch to the next. It means that if you order paper and run out, and the supplier is now out of stock on that batch number, you can have a color variation on the wall. You MUST verify that all paper is of the same batch number BEFORE installation begins. If you do need more paper, specify the batch number when ordering and its availability. Also, make sure that your installer knows not to start the project until you have confirmed.

As you can see, not having enough paper can pose expensive problems and delays. Double-check your calculations with the wallpaper salesperson and your installer before ordering. Make it a practice to order an extra double roll whenever possible and leave it with the customer if they need a repair.

Not all papers are meant for every space. Commercial wallpaper is required in commercial areas for fire rating codes and heavy-duty wear and tear. If you are working on a commercial project, ensure that you are using commercial wallpaper sample books when making your selections. Or inquire about the commercial use of the paper you are considering before specifying it on your project.

Even residential wallpaper must have practicality when considering its placement. Grasscloth, for instance, is costly but gorgeous. You would be better installing it in places where there is little wear and tear as the surface is exposed. Rubbing of laundry baskets in a stairway will leave a noticeable wear mark over time. You will also need to consider grasscloth can pose a problem for allergy sufferers.

Papers with anything you can pick off, such as crystals or fibers, should not be hung in children's rooms. You just know the little tykes will have a hay day with that, and heaven help anyone should they decide to start eating them too!

Wallpaper adds a beautiful textural element in comparison to paint. With so many patterns and colors to choose from, you can bring life and depth to an otherwise ordinary room. Knowing your stuff when it comes to installation, pattern use, and client reservations will make you an expert when it comes to wallpaper. Sometimes you will need to be more conservative, and others — we can be as lavish or wild as our clients will allow!

Art

The number one most personal thing that a client will select for their home is art. It is not likely that they have hired a designer or decorator every time they hang something on their wall. Many people do not feel good at decorating because they just buy it without rhyme or reason when they see something they like.

There is nothing wrong with that. I have often said that art picks us. Avid art lovers will appreciate many modalities and artists, showcasing them proudly in their homes and offices. Someone who is following their instincts while they are selecting art will quite often naturally choose pieces that work wonderfully together. Perhaps even accidentally. The marvelous diversity of art means that it is a true expression of the people who live or work in a space. It is as personal as the clothing that we choose every day. We look at these pieces to appreciate their details, stirring up emotions and, sometimes, memories.

The people who have trouble selecting art for themselves have truly lost touch with their taste. They have no idea what they like anymore, and you will know when you have this person in front of you because they are always looking for you to choose everything for them. Perhaps that is what you were hired to do. They may still want to be a part of the process and are relying on you to guide them truly. To bring out the expression of who they are with your excellent design and interpretation skills.

So how do you develop a skill in selecting art when it is so personal for every client?

You must know who your local artists are, who the more well

known and less known maybe. How much fun is it to have a working relationship with a group of artists in different crafts! To bring your clients to their talent and then celebrate when they purchase from them? I find this thrilling. To support local talent or self-made artists from all walks of life and celebrate their art in my client's home is very satisfying. It is helping two people instead of just one.

Suppose you sell a lot of artwork. In that case, the artist may give you a finder fee or a percentage; however, this would be a special arrangement.

In some cases, you can find artists on Instagram or other social media apps. You want to make sure that you are purchasing from the original artist or a properly licensed business. Many companies are selling knock-offs that don't benefit the artist who created the piece. Ethically I find it sad and would not support a company like that. When you do have a reputable artist or company in your contacts, you can purchase from the selection they have available or possibly commission a piece. That way, if you are looking for a specific size, you can have an original created for your client and their home.

Store-bought art is also valid. Many companies recreate multiple prints from artists' originals that they obtain licensing for. The sizing will be limited, and you will not get an original piece. Still, these days' manufacturing techniques apply all sorts of texture to imitate the original as closely as possible. It even supports the artist and gets you a less expensive option.

Framing is an expensive element of art or photography. More expensive pieces will have a framed canvas, where less expensive will show the canvas's edges. But not all frames are apples to apples. Shoddy workmanship or material can mean it isn't well made and damages easily in shipping. Whenever you purchase artwork or photography, you want to inspect the frame on all sides, including the back. Are there spaces where they should butt together tightly? Are staples sticking out of the back? Are there scratches, imperfections in the finish or dents? Is the artwork installed correctly?

Even open-sided canvas prints can have quality construction, and you can tell when you flip the piece over. The canvas is stapled and folded to fit tightly to the frame. The print itself is straight, not off-kilter or unbalanced. A proper canvas will be stretched over a frame after the artwork is complete. You will see the outside edge of the painting on the wrapped edges. Less expensive versions will have painted edges of a canvas after it is wrapped on the frame. Cheap art will have blobs in the same colors to mimic the artwork, but this is a sloppy technique that I would watch out for.

Art in any form is about evoking emotion through expression. It can be an investment for more well-known artists, especially those featured in galleries. It is a wise move to be familiar with the galleries in your trading area, or even in other cities close by. Not only is this a culturally enriching experience for you, but it keeps you in touch with the community.

I was visiting my aunt in Hudson one year, and they took us on a sightseeing trip to Montreal. I loved it. The atmosphere, the cobblestone roads, the street vendors with their jewelry, photography, souvenirs and trinkets all enchanted me to snoop at everything. We made a point of visiting the less well-known shops and art galleries, strolling at a relaxed pace. We walked into one art gallery as they were just setting up an artist's show for the coming weekend. I happily started making my way through the nooks and crannies with accent lighting directed all the beautiful paintings, mouth-blown glass sculpture and photography. It took a little while for me to realize I was alone, so I went in search of my family.

I discovered my aunt and uncle in negotiations for a painting at the very front of the gallery. Freshly hung, it was the first thing they saw. The artist was the same as the art show and happened to be the artist they followed for several years. Every time they came across one of her shows, it was sold out. Not this time; our timing had been perfect. The owner did not know what to do as the show had not started yet. She was on the phone with the artist when I approached. I got the full story as we waited to see if the artist would sell it to them that fast.

Luckily, they could buy the painting and leave it on display for the show's duration. Long story short, not only was there a story to how my aunt and uncle knew of the artist but now how they came upon the painting with us was too. It is displayed above my aunt's piano in their living room to this day.

When I travel, I tend to buy art or jewelry. Or both. It can be a favorite past time for art hounds, and you may have quite a collection to work with. Piecing it together can take some sifting. Looking for color and themes that work within your design is obvious. All the pieces are likely going to be loved treasures with stories, and it takes some careful steps to weed out the ones that will not work. If some pieces are truly special, then you will need to incorporate them, whether it is in the same room or a different one. Stay open-minded and be creative. Perhaps you can change the frame and matting to be more up to date. Maybe you can create a collage on a staircase that will be more interesting and eclectic without other furniture or soft furnishings to coordinate around.

Group family photos in this way. These are tricky to work with because they tend to be very posed and formal. I am a fan of finding more creative photographers who use more relaxed and unique ways to bring out moments within a family than traditional portraits. I especially love using a favorite family spot, maybe a lakeshore or mountain range from a family photo and having an artist create a one-of-a-kind painting. There is more heart in these personal touches that genuinely add to the story of the home. These pieces are the unspoken memories shared between family members and appreciated by the homeowner and guests alike.

Décor

I have a confession to make. I adore decor. That sounds vague...let's try that again. I love home decor shopping. I just can't get over the satisfying feeling of treasure hunting for the perfect throw, set of decorative vases or unique wall hanging that brings life into a room. The more unique and less "known" an item or theme, the more thrilled I was to discover it. I was responsible for decor purchasing for the design business I managed. I found specific furniture or art items for clients and created showroom displays full of prizes for our retail customers.

It made little difference whether I was making personal selections for a house or shopping for extensive décor selections for the business. I was using the same skills to coordinate my projects.

Home decor is classified as: vases, statues, trays, wall hangings, candles, candleholders, lamps, art, accent furniture, throw blankets, pillows, poufs, signs, mats, bathroom accessories, knick-knacks, picture frames, hooks, faux plants and flowers and anything else that you can think of. These items can be inexpensive grabs from the dollar store for a patio table or collectible heirloom pieces found at an auction. Home decor is accumulated over a lifetime, rather than in one fell swoop, so the challenge is to shop the client's belongings for what will work in the design and what will not. Then you are off to find additional home decor pieces from your favorite stores.

You are on a scouting mission. If you are looking for one or two items, then your shopping trip may be quick. However, suppose you are looking for several things and are trying to piece together a theme. In that case, you could be in for a more extended challenge. The fun is in the discovery. Suppose you are more open-minded about what you are looking for and use metal, color and size to guide you. In that case, you can be pleasantly surprised when the perfect item shows up unexpectedly. Be especially careful of this if you are shopping online. Tones and colors are usually quite different in digital images than they are in real life.

It helps to have a good visual memory of what you have seen and where you saw it. Your mental catalog will come in handy when you are shopping for several clients. It will save you a lot of time, making you look like a decorating wizard for pulling the perfect find out of your hat!

A lot of times, a client wants the fun of going with you on these shopping trips. If you shop your selections before getting together, you can put the items on hold and set your date with your client before the hold expires. It ensures the things you are interested in will be there when you show up together. It also gives you a starting point of why a client may like or dislike the selections, where you can then regroup with a better idea of what to look for together. By purchasing your final pieces, you can still review them in the home with other decorative elements and furniture and then make a return if necessary.

Keep in mind stores are happy to take returns on items that are not damaged or past the return deadline. Be careful not to dent or scratch any of the items. Keep all packing material until you are sure you will not need it for a return. While you may have a good relationship with the store staff, make sure that you do not abuse it by excessively returning or abusing their return policies. I know of designers who purchased items to return everything after a photoshoot was over. That is not ethical and does not help keep your favorite stores in business.

Be a good back scratcher because I guarantee you that the staff will help you more when doing profitable business. When you have a situation where you must ask for an exception or return more than you planned, take some cupcakes with you. Better yet, surprise them when you are not asking for any favors. Do not be the designer who always borrows their samples but never purchases anything with them. Do business with the companies who support your business.

There are going to be clients out there who just cannot be pleased. They pull apart every angle to find a fault in the size, shape, color, finish or price. Then look to you to find the magical item precisely opposite to the perfect one you just offered them. Worse is when they have done that with every item brought to them, and you must return everything. It is frustrating for you and for the stores you bought them from. It happens from time to time, but it is not the right time to start bad-mouthing about your client to store staff. Trust me, that will get back to people, and you want to keep your reputation respectful and reliable. Understanding relationships with your retailers will help ease everyone's consternation and quickly find solutions to please the client's tastes.

When working with decor items, you must consider how much room they will take up. Consider, too, coordination with other things and how much "stuff" you are planning to display within a room. A large room with very few small items will look bare and out of proportion. A small room with too many items will look stuffy and heavy. You can also create some very awkward vignettes (another fancy word for displays) by paring too large an object with too small of one. Your aim is to create visual appeal with balance, interest and pops of texture and color.

Tip: Stagger pieces in thirds and threes to maintain balance within the display. The smallest item is one third smaller than the medium one, and about two thirds smaller than the largest.

Staggering your decor pieces does not mean that everything must match perfectly in shape and size. Displaying a bit of pink quartz on top of three coffee table books does not mean you need three pink quartz pieces. It may mean that you have a soft pink frame around a favorite photo of the client's grandchildren on the shelf with some smaller books. Staggering is about creating balance without overdoing it in pieces or awkward sizes. Sometimes the only way to know is to get in the room and play with everything. Some pieces will work better than others, and what is fun is when something you thought was going to be too outrageous turns out to be the perfect element to kick off the theme of the room.

Cultural and historical items do not always marry well together in one room. A broad sword collection does not blend well with tie-dyed pillows and peace sign artwork from the sixties.

Your client may have a rich family history or culture that they want to ensure is incorporated in their home. You must find unique ways to display treasured items. The challenge is to give these items the space to tell their story without taking over the whole room. I have found several interesting artifacts in people's homes, and sometimes you can only work with them.

I once did a paint color consultation for a police officer who had worked in the Arctic and was given a narwhal tusk by the community he served. There were lots of indigenous sculptures, photos and pieces of art throughout the house. It obviously all worked well together as a theme. I would not start putting Buddha statues or Navajo throws in their home. That is an extreme example, but you get my drift.

Every item in the house does not have to be of that one style or theme. Suppose I were decorating around this couple's collection. In that case, I could weave in neutral artwork with an interesting approach to tree paintings. I could use natural fiber area rugs for texture. I could add pops of nature-loving colors like green, yellow, orange or red. I could add a coffee table with reclaimed wood. A coffee table book with the photographic history of the area he served would be perfect. I would avoid adding extra artwork or decor items of animals. Floral patterns, pastel colors and a lot of traditional furniture would also fight their style.

Decor pieces are easily changed out when a homeowner decides it is time to change things up. Determine what they have already been living with, so you know what direction to go and what to avoid. While it is so much fun finding all these fantastic little prizes to decorate with, it is essential to follow the proper selection steps first. The very last thing to choose is paint color.

Painting And Color Selection

Painting is one of the quickest changes that anyone can make to a room without redecorating it completely. It is not a quick and painless task. Still, homeowners and professionals are painting to make a cosmetic change in a home about every five to seven years. They may do one or two rooms at a time or the whole house, but a fresh paint job is a thing of beauty to walls that have seen better days.

There is a lot more to consider than just picking out a paint color that you like. If it were so simple, more people would be doing it successfully on their own. Not to say that people cannot choose their paint color on their own; instead, it is the more visual homeowners who are more successful at getting it right the first time.

The process I used while doing color consultations was like how I approached most decorating consultations. I had the client give me a tour of the house, viewing what elements they wished to work with and how much light they had in each room. It included what window treatments they had and how many trees were blocking the sunlight and the windows' direction. I was looking for any underlying issues that were going to take more repair or prep for their paint job. I asked questions about any other changes that the homeowners were planning to make to flooring, tile, countertops and cabinets.

The answers I got gave me direction on what colors may work best, how deep I could go and whether the client would be daring enough to try something drastic. It is incredible how much you can pick up from a client by watching their expressions and reactions as you discuss their home. You can tell when something has been aggravating them, exciting them or making them nervous. I got good at reading their faces and adjusting my ideas to suit them better. There have been plenty of times that I have had clients jumping up and down and hugging me in relief once we had finished our scheme.

Developing your confidence will take some time if you are new to the game. By being open-minded and friendly, you are approachable when the client has ideas of their own. They are unsure what they are doing and trust you to hear them out without shooting them down. Having a designer in your home is the equivalent of having a magnifying glass to their lifestyle. Some homeowners will care more than others.

Sometimes the client had a solid idea of what they wanted, but it was outside of their comfort zone to pull it off without becoming garish. Most of the time, a client is playing it too safe because they do not know what else could work in their home. I quickly realized that lighting is the first thing to figure out with color consultations. The homeowner's personality is the second. That includes the significant other. Usually, after you have those two things figured out, the color will fall into place.

I have thousands of consultations under my belt from the last fifteen years, but there are a couple that stands out.

One of my favorite bedroom consultations was for a couple in their late twenties, early thirties. They were painting their master bedroom and attached ensuite bathroom. I immediately fell in love with the headboard, matching side tables and tallboy dresser for their bamboo frames and rattan accents. The existing paint color was a very safe builder beige, and they were ready for something new. Thankfully, the tile in the ensuite was relatively neutral in warm colors, so I knew I had a decent selection of colors to work with. Their bedding was cream without much pattern. Everything complimented each other very well and did not have anything standing out to give the room some pizazz.

As I started pulling paint swatches that could work for them out of the fan deck, I watched to see what looked too bright or loud, too dark or too close to what they already had on the walls. I held them up at the angle they would be painted on the wall rather than flat in the light. The paint looks completely different based on the light's angle, so it is essential to view it as if it were painted on the wall...or at whatever angle, a surface may be. I also test the colors against the bedding, flooring, bathroom countertops and tile. As I found colors that had potential, I would ask the clients their thoughts and carefully watched their expressions as they looked at the swatches.

I like to offer several tones or depths of the same color range, complementary colors if there will be more than one paint color used and my wild card. I almost wink to myself as I pull out a color that a person would not usually consider but that I know would look fabulous in the room. It is what I did that day.

My clients were trying to find something to warm up their bedroom and keep it cozy. I pulled out a color called Pilgrimage Foliage by Benjamin Moore. It is a rich red-orange but in the "burnt" range of color rather than the bold primaries. I knew that the tropical bamboo style bedroom furniture would stand out against the color but without too much contrast. The bedding could stay or, if they wished, along with any bathroom towels and accessories.

When they saw the paint chip, their mouths dropped open as they looked at each other and then me. I could tell that they loved it! We decided to find a lighter complimentary tan for the bathroom, so there was a "breather" from the bedroom. I suggested getting some tropical plants to add pops of green in the room. The color gave the room a rich, spicy effect without being too devoid of color, too flashy and or entirely obscure for their space. It was not a cookie-cutter effect and did not take any more time to discover than deciding between beiges.

The last thing I do is pull out the larger individual paint swatch from my designer kit. We could see all their colors together without the other colours' visual complication on the fan deck this way. Suppose they are truly satisfied as I move these around the room against their furniture, draperies and fabrics. In that case, I will cut a swatch and create a consultation sheet with their colors attached and include where each color is going and where to stop. I also like to recommend the paint brand, sheen and professional painter if needed.

I reiterate to my clients the quality of the paint, tools and the painter. Suppose they are painting themselves but using good quality paint and sundries. In that case, they will be relatively successful with some instruction. If they are using low-quality paint matched to another brand's color, you cannot guarantee that the tones will come out the way you intended. The painters you recommend should be using the brand and sheen you have specified if you recommend quality paint. Ensure that you know what they will use, what they will not and whether they will change things when you are not looking. There are many tricks in the painting trade, but we will go over those later in this chapter.

Sometimes you will be picking colors with a client, and what you feel will be too much is exactly the look they are after. You need to keep in mind that there is a color for every personality out there, ones that you would never imagine using in your own home. It is not your position to tell a homeowner how wrong they are. It is your job to work with what they love, tweak it to work with their space and show them options that they could consider. In some cases, the only way to get the color they love into the room is through accessories. You can run up against an off-color in the cabinets or baseboards or simply have a spouse that refuses to agree to the color. I have a story for both scenarios.

I learned my lesson about trying to steer my clients when it came to their taste in color. I drove to a home on an acreage in the countryside to help my client select paint for her entire house. She was a dentist, single and loved to entertain her friends with their children at her home. She went so far as to have a playhouse with a climbing wall and was known to spend the night in the playhouse with her friends' children while they drank wine in the house. I knew that she was a special breed, to begin with. As we walked through her home, she kept asking for more color as everything I showed her, although quite colorful by most standards, was more muted and softer.

What I quickly realized was that she was a dedicated color person. Nothing less than the brightest colors would do. Not only was she an outgoing, playful and adventurous kind of woman, but she had a very stressful job, and her home was her happy place. She had beautiful maple plank hardwood floors, five-inch baseboards and newly installed concrete countertops with pieces of blue sea glass embedded in them. I realized that she had all the right bones to pull off the intense colors she was craving, and I decided to let go and go for it!

The primary color throughout the house was a rich and magnetic teal blue, one you would find in Caribbean waters. She chose a different color: purple, yellow and a lighter blue for each bedroom upstairs, each loaded with character from the dormer windows and sloped ceilings. I knew her painters would think this was nuts, but they got to work when we gave them the paint selections.

I will often have clients send me photos of their finished projects, thanking me for helping them. I did not think much about not hearing from this client, but I was hoping that we had made the right decisions. Within six months or so, I got a request to come out to the same area for a color consultation and discovered that it was my dentist client's parents. She had referred me to them after they saw what we did in her house. I mentioned that I was curious to know how that job had gone, and they offered to sneak me into their daughter's house while she was at work. I assumed they told her on our drive over and was relieved that they had the security combination.

When I walked in, it was my turn for my mouth to drop. The paint color was stunning. It perfectly highlighted the Cape Cod-style feel of the house, the wood floors, the art collection she gathered from her travels around the world and just glowed in the light. I knew after that that there was a way to pull these intense clean colors off in homes and would jump at the chance to work with them again. The trick is not to mix them with muted tones that have been "dirtied" with black or gray tints.

Not every consult goes so smoothly. As I mentioned, sometimes a husband and wife do not agree on what they like or tolerate in their house. It can be difficult finding common ground, and without choosing sides, you can become a little bit more of a mediator than you want to be. Make a point of hearing what each has to say. Ask why they don't like something the other suggests. If one is cutting the other off before they can finish, ask them to humor you to understand better. In a way, it is like giving two separate color consultations at once, and you have the spectacular job of marrying the two once everyone has shared their two cents.

Again, that will take some practice to be confident in these situations. If you do happen to agree more with one spouse, then be as diplomatic as possible. Give the reasons why you are going in a particular direction over another. Then find creative ways to incorporate some of what each is wanting.

Sometimes, there is no helping the situation. Sometimes you must treat the person who scheduled the appointment as your client when their spouse is not happy about your presence.

I went to a client's home who was having difficulty selecting a paint color for their home. When I arrived, I could see why they were having trouble. Everything had been painted white for quite some time. The walls were not the only thing. The carpet was white, the tile around the fireplace and the backsplash was white, the linoleum was white. The only color they had in the house was the deep red cherry cabinets, baseboards, window trim and fireplace mantel. I immediately knew that we needed to soften the contrast between the wood and all the white. I could not do anything about the carpet or tile as that was staying, but I could find a balance between the two with the paint.

That was not the challenge. The challenge was that the wife was sick of it and ready to paint with color, and the husband insisted that everything stay the way it was. And when I mean insisting, I mean sitting in the corner of the room, scowling at me with his arms crossed over his chest and muttering as his wife and I moved around the house. I had to whisper because every time he heard me mention a color we could paint, he "put his foot down" very vocally. It was uncomfortable, even now trying to write about it. The best I could do was work with the wife and let her hash the results out with her husband after leaving.

Under these circumstances, as a designer, you need to work with the house itself, do your best to work with your client's taste, and find ways to compromise for them. Sometimes, one partner decorates one room or part of the house and the other partner decorates a different section. I never knew how that consultation worked out, but I know that it was uncomfortable for everyone. You also must respect the fact that you may have clients who are in abusive relationships. Respect your client for having you in their home, do your best to offer your services and realize that you can't decorate some situations away. Still, you can make a person feel better in their home.

Personalities And Color

I have discovered that when it comes to color, there are four types of personalities. As I said, after you figure out how much light you are working with and how much light your clients prefer as they function in their house, you need to work out their personalities. There are the types of people who will paint color on their walls and have neutral furniture. Some people will have colorful furniture or accessories and neutral colors on the walls. Other people prefer not to use a lot of color and stick to a mono-chromatic color scheme. And then…. there are people who love to have color on every surface they can see!

I will offer more insights into each personality. One is not better than another, and people change over the years. Marriages, deaths, new children or a renovation can quickly open possibilities to people where they thought they were stuck within a specific range of color. I will go over the color personalities in the same order as I mentioned above.

Personality One:

For practical people, they know that furniture is a long-time investment and that their tastes in color may change over the furniture's lifespan. They keep to neutral tones of beige, brown, cream and grays to make it easy to decorate around. It does not mean they are boring. It gives them plenty of options for both color and more neutral shades on their walls. The furniture can also be in any range of these colors to add more contrast or inter-est, usually against the flooring and cabinetry. Style or theme is not limited by these selections either. Any number of decorating ideas will work as the furniture sets the stage for pattern and color as loud or subtle as they please.

Most clients are afraid to use color in my experience. They think it will take over the room and make it too dark, too loud or too flashy. Some are willing to give it a try with your guidance, and you will know it by an eager expression on their face. Others will consider your ideas but back away. Sometimes it takes a moderate change this time before they are ready for something bolder the next time they paint. The conservative clients are more likely to keep their walls painted within a comfort zone. But, with a little push, they will go deeper, or in a slightly different color family, they had not thought of before. The more playful clients will try out new color palettes they have seen in magazines or show homes to determine if they will work in their home.

They are not likely to start any trends amongst their friends; instead, they are typically people who have seen something they like and want the same feeling in their own home. You will likely hear, "My best friend Molly just painted her house. You helped her pick her colors, and I was hoping to do the same in my house!" There is nothing quite like the grapevine to help your business when you have successfully helped clients with their decorating and design needs. They will talk you up to everyone!

These types of clients are ones who truly need to see the results before they feel confident in trying it for themselves.

For these people, the paint color and some soft furnishings are more decorative than the furniture itself. They like to change up the pillows or the area rug more often. They are also more likely to change their paint around the five to seven-year mark.

Your job is to help these clients use color in playful, comforting, charming and stylish ways that they could not see for themselves. Especially with the neutral palette they have been working with. It may mean you are coordinating paint, soft furnishings, artwork and even new furniture, but these clients will be relieved to find a style of their own with your help.

Personality Two:

Not that different from Personality One, these people like to have a comfortable and practical approach to their furniture. Still, they are bored with the same old neutral tones everyone else has. They want to make more of a statement and enjoy rich tones like burgundy, sage green, navy blue, burnt oranges and yellows. They enjoy making their rooms cozy. Depending on the style of furniture they have purchased, their homes can be traditional, formal, or casual.

Still being practical, these clients tend to love color a little more, though in subtle shades rather than bright ones. They know that they will love colorful furniture for years to come, planning to decorate around it and freshen up the paint from time to time rather than get creative on the walls.

It does not mean they are boring either. You may see more patterns and color in the window treatments, area rugs, cushions and artwork. They appreciate balance without overdoing it. You will likely hear comments like, "I don't mind a bit of color." or "I don't want to feel like I'm in an asylum." While they may want neutral colors on their walls, they will use various shades and are not afraid to go a little deeper. The beiges get a little richer with warm tints; the grays have more undertones to complement the furniture's color. "Snug as a bug in a rug" is the saying that comes to mind for these folks.

For these people, the furnishings are more important than the paint color. They are more likely to keep the paint color and apply a touch-up coat of paint than select an entirely different color. Their furnishings are likely to stay for several years, opting to create a new look when replacing the furniture. If they change paint colors, they will likely remain close to their color but lighten or darken it.

As their designer, they will ask you to work within the feel they have already created for themselves in their home. However, push the color and tone boundaries a little to freshen up their look. The real test of your skills will come if they have brought you on board to help them create an entirely new look. It will be a challenge because they will have no idea where to start as it will feel "from scratch." Knowing what their new "look" should be could involve deciding on neutral furniture. However, it could also mean that you are still using colorful furniture but with more modern styles. It would stay comfortable, but the remainder of the furnishings are more up to date.

Personality Three:

The people in Personality One and Two are likely to use various ranges in their paint color. Personality Three is all about keeping things light, open, and airy. They prefer to have as much light in their house as possible, which means their furniture, soft furnishings, and window treatments will be on the lighter side as well. They will prefer to keep color to a minimum; however, when used, the color pops, creating a focal point in the room.

They are minimalist in nature, enjoying plants, natural wood grains, and simplistic patterns in their homes. The furniture may have comfortable and functional fabrics, exotic woods and simple lines. However, they can still be modern, traditional or comfy. These types enjoy texture in their area rugs over loud designs and often like photography or art that reflects nature. While they keep their furnishings to a minimum when they use something in the room or on the wall, it makes a statement, so they are not afraid to use abstract art for the "wow factor."

In paint colors, people in Personality Three will be the clients looking for white-on-white color schemes, off whites, creams and warm grays. There will be very little contrast between the walls and the baseboards, and sometimes it is the same color but in a different sheen. Live plants with lots of greenery bring fresh air, and contrast brings the outdoors in, and yet the view outside is part of the "artwork" in the room.

In truth, we all go through phases of these personality types at different stages of our lives. Spouses can have other traits that somehow have to come together cohesively in their home. As their designer, you will exercise your restraint skill, knowing the perfect items to add and what to leave as a blank canvas. Adding black or the rare pop of color or contrast will help anchor the room, which can appear like nothing is grounding it when everything is the same tone.

I have found that a person's profession often dictates what they find comforting in their home. People with hectic, stressful and overwhelming jobs and who deal with many people or think quickly on their feet tend to come home to a serene and visually quiet space. They want peace, to unwind and let their minds and bodies rest in their home. People who work in cubicles, do a lot of repetitive work or do not love their jobs as much tend to have more going on at home. It gives them more excitement and the chance to feel playful.

Personality Four:

You guessed it. These are the wild child people to thrive in anything and everything fun, creative and colorful. They are the rare breed, the inner kid who refuses to let life stamp them out. They are adventurous and will be the people who pull you out of all your safety nets to join them in their shenanigans. For a lot of us, we would walk into their home and think, "Wow! I love this, but I could never do it in my house."

These people buy colorful furniture, whether it is for comfort, modern style or a statement piece. They will refinish reclaimed wooden furniture and use bright, dynamic patterns for contrast. It does not stop there. Their paint colors are brighter, bolder and used on more walls. The art, drapery and area rugs are no different. There is simply something going on everywhere you look in these clients' homes.

As I said, the other three personality types would be going nuts in a home with all this going on. Most likely, these people have found the same type in their spouse or partner or have found one who does not care and lets them do what they want. For the people who have no idea how to pull it all together, they are the true but lovable magpies of us all. They see something they like and bring it home, not knowing what they will do with it or where it will go. Those with more constraint and skill can siphon through the visual barrage and create an eclectic and original personal expression in every inch of every room.

It would almost seem envious for those of us who crave being free of the box, wanting to be carefree like a kid again. Or in some cases, the client's culture is rich in color, and they bring in fabulous colors shimmering in silks, velvets and metallics. There is no hard-fast rule with these folks because somehow, they have managed to pull it all off without a care in the world.

Your skill as a designer will be in controlling the clutter. The magpies will need help sorting through what works and what to eliminate to create a more purposeful overall design. They may be relatively attached to all their baubles and trinkets as they have likely been collecting them for quite some time. I confess, even I have been an avid rock, crystal and seashell collector. I have them in displays or vignettes all over my house. They are not exactly a part of my "design," but they are part of me. You will need to find creative ways to use items that look less about clutter and more about deliberate creations. Pinterest can help you out there if you get stuck.

To help the clients who seemed to pull it all off, they likely are looking for a fresh set of eyes to help pull off a change. These folks have used so much color in so many ways that they may not know what other options they have but sticking with their preferred form of expression. You will need to be thinking outside the box with these folks. They have brought you in to add your creativity to theirs and change things up a bit.

I know of a woman who frequently changes out her art prints and stores the spares underneath the house's beds. She loves playing around and is always finding something new that she loves.

These personality types are more likely to be the one in hundred, "I would never have thought of that" kind of people. They aren't likely to set trends because most are not brave enough to jump fully into the deep end with them. They will be ahead of the game in design innovation and inspire others with their unique ideas. They may be artists, inventors, sculptures, carpenters or designers themselves. Other people will look to their style and take bits and pieces to incorporate into their own homes.

Working with the four personality types will keep you on your toes. Just when you think you have gotten the hang of how to work with each, something will pop out of nowhere, and you need to be innovative enough to keep up with your client. Of course, no one fits each personality perfectly. Sometimes a client will want all the bells and whistles in one home, and the next, they want it to be simple and serene. Or a spouse will allocate the basement to their wife's wild and woolly ideas if he gets the room above the garage. Maybe you will have a too conservative client in their style one day and a bohemian nature lover the next.

That is the delicious aspect of interior design. Each person is unique, and their home along with them.

Trends

You will see fashion trends in everything from clothing, houses, hairstyles to cars, boats and dog beds. The retail industry thrives on our thirst for creative expression, comfort, luxury and color. Some people enjoy flipping through a magazine and seeing what is new and exciting, casually taking note but not investing their energy in it one way or another. Others are avid about it. They need to be on top of the latest trends, and if they have a project in the works, they want to be the first to have the hottest items.

Not everyone can afford to cycle through the season's latest designs and models. Some can. The talented interior designer that you will know how to incorporate the fashionably new with the timeless classics. Clients will give you a clear idea of how important the latest trends are and whether you will be working with them. Rest assured, you had better be on top of the trends within all the design fields you participate in.

In some cases, when a person is finally ready to purchase the item they have been coveting, it has already gone out of style. It can happen in lighting, metal finishes, wood tones, fabric patterns and paint colors. Every year paint companies put out their projected color trends based on many consumer and business trends research. Sometimes, in my opinion, they hit it right on the head. Other times, I shake my head.

Color is a very personal selection for the interior and exterior of a home. It is impossible to nail the "Color of the Year" for every person out there. The goal is to get enough interest in the coming year's color palette, so the homeowners come into the stores for paint chips. Which, in turn, turns into paint sales. It's brilliant marketing, marketing that you can tie into your business acumen as well. For one, you should know what the new color selections are for each paint company that you recommend. Expect to be asked what the latest trends are. Some clients are mildly curious; others are passionate about it. You can easily access brochures at your favorite paint stores, but sometimes they host color reveal events that could be a fun outing for you too.

The thing about trends is that they are only relevant if they work in the house you are painting. Lighting plays a vital role in what a color will look like in the home. And personality determines whether the client will like it. Most times, there will be a way for you to use the idea of the color trend rather than the exact color the paint companies are suggesting. By changing the color to be more subdued, lighter or darker, you may incorporate the "idea" of the color trend but stick with what the house can handle. Other times, there is no way to manage this new trend without completely replacing all the furnishings and repainting cabinets, baseboards and doors.

Often, the discussion of color trends comes up around the sale of your client's home. "Are you decorating/renovating/painting for yourselves? Or is your intention to sell?" are the first questions I ask. Homeowners are always concerned about the value of their property. When they paint, the clients want to make sure they are not automatically outdated, which is more of a concern if they intend to put their house up for sale. They want to appeal to as many potential buyers as possible who are likely viewing show homes while seeing other homes on the market. An older home will look that much older with a color scheme from ten years ago, which immediately brings down the asking price. An older home with a fresh and current color scheme will show well and appeal to the buyers who are up to speed on current trends.

If the client is painting for themselves, they work within their tastes without appealing to other people's opinions. When you are selling, the opposite is true. The homeowner needs to think about a marketing plan and less about how much they love their lime green walls in the kitchen. Color trends can pull potential buyers in without much expense. The challenge is not to end up looking the same as all the other houses on the market. Be appealing but be unique. If everything is beige and smells like cookies, later after a buyer has viewed five homes, the details blur together.

Keep color trends realistic. Use them when the house allows, and the client is willing but be careful not to paint them into a corner where they must repaint their home every year.

Trends also color placement. There was a time when feature walls were all the rage. Then came the time when people wanted their homes to feel more straightforward and unified. I found that if a client lived with one color in their house for twenty years, they were often ready for color and feature walls. The clients living with feature walls were moving back to one or two colors in their house. Going through open houses and show homes or visiting home builders and design studios helps get a feel for new trends.

Tip: Be careful what walls you use for feature colors.

Feature colors tend to be darker, brighter, more colorful, and more interesting than the house's main color. Walls that have more interest to them are tempting to use as feature walls, but you need to look at how practical it is. Very high walls will mean a scaffold or large ladders are required to reach the top. With feature colors changing more frequently than the main color, this would not be a tempting repaint. It is more inconvenient for clients who aren't able to manage this easily on their own. Some homes have rounded corners. It is not as appealing to have a cut line with the two colors on these, especially if they are on an outside corner where people can sit and see them straight on.

Color trends can be fun and give you quick references for color ideas with your clients. Understanding how color works, especially when piecing a home design together, is crucial to a successful outcome.

Color Theory

It is not difficult to go online and get information about color theory. Color theory is the science of primary, secondary, tertiary and complementary colors working together. It is used in everyday life more than you think!

To bring you quickly up to speed, I will explain the definitions of each and tint, shade and tone. Most of the color theory you will have learned has been in elementary school art class when you learned how to mix colors. Artists continue to study and perfect their mixing technique but also use it when mixing paint. Those who are exceptionally skilled can custom match by eye using careful measurements of just the right combination of pigments.

The primary colors are red, yellow and blue. You can not create these colors by combining any other, which is why they are called primary. Secondary colors are purple, orange and green because you can make them by combining two of the three primary colors. Tertiary colors are blue-green, yellow-green, yellow-orange, orange-red, red-purple, blue-purple. They are created by mixing one part of a single primary color with half a second.

A tint of a color is created when white is added, which lightens and adds a milky effect. Add black to create a shade of a color. It will darken the color but still leave some of the intensity. A tone is made by adding gray (or black and white combined) to the color to deepen and create a softer effect. With a tone, the ratio of black and white (also gray) will determine how drastic the color will pull towards a tint or a shade.

For the most part, you will not be aware of the amount of pigments going into a can of paint. I had the added benefit of knowing how the pigments, or tints, worked and saw how the colors I was suggesting were mixed. Do not be one of those designers who shows up to a paint store with their color theory knowledge and dictates how the paint is tinted. It is not the same thing. Unless you will compensate them hourly for your "custom" ideas, it is better to leave them with a sample of the color you are hoping for and allow them to match it for you.

It is almost impossible to match fabric due to the nature of the weave, texture, sheen and folds. A fabric has multifaceted elements because it moves into folds, ripples or shapes where the paint surface is generally flat.

Color theory is essential for you to know to understand why color appears the way it does and what you are looking for to adjust it in the right direction. The most crucial part about color theory that you will be using is how the colors complement, coordinate, add contrast and fight with each other.

Complimentary colors are opposite to each other on the color wheel. Red and green, purple and yellow, orange and blue are all complementary to each other. It means that when mixed in the paint world, they create gray. (a good tip if you are tinting or using pigments- use a complementary color in small amounts to make a tone without adding black or white) But, when these complementary colors are side by side, they make each other oh so happy that they burst. That may be a little dramatic, but it gets the point across. Complimentary colors look their best when their mate is close by.

It means that when you are thinking of using a beige neutral for the walls when the client has seafoam green carpet, you bet your bottom that it will go pink if there is a red pigment in the formula. There is a way to know whether a color will pull pink, blue, orange, yellow, green or any undertone you are trying to avoid. Hold the paint chip up to the complementary color that would bring it out. If the paint chip now heads in the unwanted direction, you know you need to select one with different undertones. If the paint chip "behaves itself" and stays neutral, then you know you are safe.

Suppose a client calls you up after a paint job and says, "Oh Sally! I could have sworn that my paint chip wasn't pink, but now that I've painted it on my walls, it is pink everywhere!". In that case, you know that it could be a combination of the light bulbs, flooring or furnishings that are bringing out those tones. That is why it is always crucial to finalize a paint color in the home in multiple rooms at all times of the day. It is also vital to hold the paint chip upright, as if it were already on the wall, rather than flat in hand.

Colors play with each other, and we know that if we stick a paint swatch on the existing paint color, there is a pretty good chance that their interaction will skew how the new paint color looks. Once the old paint color is gone, suddenly, we see the new color in a different light, without the effect of whatever was there before. In some cases, all is well, and everyone can carry on. But in others, the client now sees undertones they are not so fond of. I recommend painting a swatch on a tester board, adequately labelled on the back with the paint color name and number, so you don't mix them up with other samples. Once dry, move this independent board around the room. Rest in on doors (if left unpainted) against furniture, cabinets, flooring, window treatments and tile. Look at it in the light of day, see how bright it goes in full sun and how dark it looks at night without much lighting.

Colors will also change from one wall to the next simply from the angle of the light. It helps to move the sample board around the room and decide whether it is friendly in all situations.

If your client is not in love with the paint after the job has started, it is important to remember a few things. The paint color will not be its accurate representation until two full coats are on the wall. Panicking the moment it gets rolled on the wall is normal but not helpful. A very light color will look white when it begins covering a dark one, the subtle nuances of the new color losing the fight against the old's intensity.

For example, let's say you were thinking of pairing a light gray-green neutral for the main color and a deeper and more vibrant green feature wall. Your eye would see the color in the vibrant color. The other would just look like an off white. That is until seen away from the feature wall. The subtle colors cannot compete, but it still works because they are in the same family.

A monochromatic color scheme is using various shades, tones or tints of the same color. These schemes are very soothing, creating opportunities for soft contrast between the furniture and wall colors. It does not mean they are boring; playing with contrast within the same color palette makes interest and focal points. Clients who have busy and stressful work lives appreciate these spaces.

A triadic color scheme is any combination of colors of the equilateral triangular points on the color wheel. These color schemes are less common unless you are working with Personality Four, who needs color everywhere. Purple, orange and green are at the three equal and opposite points on the color wheel. It may sound loud and a little wild, but using more soft-spoken hues could be an excellent combination between furniture, window coverings, and wall color.

Analogous colors are happy neighbors on the color wheel. Yellow and green or red and orange are good examples. Again, these could be a wild ride of color when used in the right shades and appropriately coordinated; the analogous scheme can be charming and playful.

What I found is that homeowners want to use color but get a little nervous. Most of my color consultations ended up using a lighter and darker version of the main color, with a third color for interest or feature walls. I had a lighter and darker version of the main color to control how dark the color got in poorly lit areas and how bright it was when there was lots of light. For instance, hallways and staircases have less light than, say, a kitchen facing midday sunshine. The kitchen can afford to have a darker color where it would become overly dark in other areas of the house.

You never know when this information may come in handy. The knowledge helps prevent you from making some boo-boos or how to fix them. Color wheels are convenient to have and can be purchased at most paint and arts and crafts stores. You may not be using them when you are in consultation with your client. You may still turn to your color wheel from time to time when stumped for ideas selecting coordinating colors for your design board.

Psychology Of Color

Understanding how colors work or do not work together gives you the fundamentals as a designer, so you have the confidence to work around many scenarios in your client's home. But there is a lot more than just the science to consider when selecting colors with people. They have a personality of their own, tastes that have developed all their lives. Some folks are even known to have a change of heart about a color palette after they have seen it in someone else's house.

Psychology of color is about how a person typically reacts to specific colors. They may associate a color with a situation as well. It is essential to know how a person may feel when they experience the colors you are suggesting.

I had a local veterinarian call to schedule a color consultation with me for her business. She instructed me to work with her staff as she would be too busy, and they were eager to repaint. In situations like these, I knew that I would be getting various opinions and ideas about what would look good in their clinic. I was not expecting magazine clippings, but I got them as we discussed options around the staff room table. I was quite surprised to see that all the staff agreed that they loved the idea of a red feature wall behind the front reception area.

"Have you considered what your customer's reaction to that might be?" I asked. In my mind, I knew that in this setting, people would associate the color with blood, and that is not a comforting thought while you are dropping off your beloved pet. They all looked at me with a curious look in their eye.

"What do you mean?" One asked me.

"Well, this is a business, and you have to consider the overall image of the brand for one thing. That wall is the first thing that you will see when you enter the clinic, and people may react poorly to red." I was trying to be as diplomatic as possible without rudely shooting their idea down. They all just shook their heads, not understanding what I was referring to, and I decided to carry on with more ideas. I knew that in the end, it would be the veterinarian who made the final decision, and I could make more recommendations after my tour.

The staff took me around to each consultation room while I noted the baseboard, flooring and cabinetry colors. I had a reasonably good idea of what direction I would point them for the doors, door trim and walls, but it came down to the feature wall behind the main desk. While I was standing in the entrance discussing the options, I noticed a customer coming out of one of the exam rooms. I asked if it was okay if I got her opinion on a color we were considering, and I showed her the red paint swatch in my hand. I will admit that the young lady was a little emotional from having her pet vaccinated, but I needed to make a point.

Her hands flew up, and she rather unhappily and loudly said, "BLOOD!" I thanked the poor girl and, with a secret inner smile about how well my point had been made, turned to the staff members who were still standing with me.

Before I could say anything, the staff said, "NOT RED!"

I put together a lovely selection of calm and earthy colors that not only did not remind anyone of the more grotesque aspects of a veterinary clinic but was functional and modern as well. Everyone was happy, and no one had to call me with an emergency color fix after completing their paint job.

Psychology and color association is one reason I find out what the clients do for a living. Doctors, nurses and most veterinarian staff are not likely to come home to red walls. Or choose scrub green either. It isn't likely you will resort to drama to get your point across like I did. You will know better and offer other color ideas that work with their furnishings. It goes further than knowing what color will remind your client of, for good or bad. You need to know the physical reactions that go along with color as well.

Vibrant colors that will stimulate the brain and increase heart rate are reds, oranges and yellows. These hues are stimulating, exciting and upbeat, making them excellent choices for spaces that need high energy. Like gyms, restaurants that serve breakfast and lunch and in children's play areas. Bright variations of these colors will have the same reaction. They can stimulate appetite, amorous feelings and uplift a person who struggles with depression. On the flip side of that, they can overwork the brain of a person exposed to them over extended periods. Someone who works from home may have difficulty staying in their office to get their work done. Children will not sleep well if they are in their bedrooms. People who suffer from anxiety or high blood pressure may find these colors overwhelming in spaces where they must spend more time. These colors are not used in prisons or psychiatric wards because they can bring out aggression in people.

These colors help businesses give their customers the impression that they are exciting, eager, and energetic about what they do. They help grab the customer's eye, and we all know that we associate red with the idea of a sale! It is important to keep branding in mind when selecting colors for a business. It ties into their business cards, apparel and marketing. The color consultation is part of a marketing strategy, not just a decorating opportunity.

Soothing and calm colors that lower heart rate, relax the mind and slow breathing is blues, greens and purples. These hues are gentle, relaxing and remind us to slow down. They remind us of the ocean, the blue sky, green grass, trees, flowers and fresh air and are gentle on the eyes. They remind us to stay grounded, peaceful and soothe anxiety. These colors are lovely in bedrooms, especially if someone works night shifts and sleeps during the day. They are also used in offices, hospitals and nursing homes as calm neutrals but still adding some color. On a morbid note, green shades are used in hospitals because you can see blood better to clean surfaces properly. They are not suitable for people suffering from depression as it adds to their "blue mood." These tones can seem cool or chilly in certain lights, which is excellent for a room that gets a lot of sun or too hot in the summer but adds a chill to a cold room.

For businesses, these colors imbue trust, loyalty, profit, and honor to their customers. Using them in their marketing strategy gives the idea of class, sophistication, intelligence and trust.

You can never tell why a customer likes one group of colors more than another. They may even surprise themselves when you offer a color idea that they had not considered but love. Maybe they fell off a yellow bike when they were kids, and they associate yellow with pain. Maybe their grandmother drove an orange sports car, as mine did, and they have loved orange ever since. Perhaps the feelings of anxiety around red and orange make them uncomfortable, but yellow is happy and pleasing. It is a wonderful challenge to find unique ways to help clients select a color for their home.

Tip: Be careful in how you describe colors to your clients.

Just because you find blues, greens and purples to be cool colors do not mean that they make your client feel that way. Maybe they make them feel snug and comforted. The moment you add comments like "pink undertones," "cool," "hot," or any other version of YOUR interpretation of color, the client will react. They could steer clear of a color that would genuinely work for them.

If done well, your job is to coax the nuances of your clients' tastes out of them and bring it to life in their home. It is NOT to tell them how "this or that" their color is before selecting it. Keep your personal preferences out of it until you truly know that a color will clash with their furnishings. In that case, you will show them why it is not working and how to move them into what it does while keeping their preferences in mind.

Be considerate, creative and unique ideas that include your client in the process. They hired you for your talent in how well you put together color schemes and furnishings. In most cases, they just want your guidance so they can keep their focus in the right direction. In some cases, they will want you to go in with your concepts so they can pick one and run with it.

How To Choose The Right Shade, Tone Or Tint And Where To Put It

You know what colors your client likes and what turns them off. You know all the elements of the design you have created this far, and it has come down to the final selection of paint colors. You know how much light the house gets and from what angle, you know your client's preference for dark or light colors and where the client hopes to add some interest. You are now at the point where you have an idea of the color range and scheme you will use.

There are many ways to skin the cat, as they say. It comes down to how much contrast you intend for the space. Unless you are using a monochromatic color scheme, you want contrast between the furniture and the wall color. A comfortable room will have a blend of light, mid and dark between the furnishings and the wall colors. It can include metals in lamps, wood tones in tables and flooring, and color in furniture, carpet and paint. Unless you design something striking like a black and white color scheme with pops of color, you will be blending contrast between all the items.

As before, it starts with the flooring and any built-in cabinetry that is in the room. How light or dark are these elements? Are they wood-toned or painted? How light or dark is the furniture? What is the space used for?

Let's use an example to illustrate better what I mean.

The flooring in the client's home is a medium toned oak hardwood that runs throughout the main level but changes to a travertine tile floor in the kitchen and bathrooms. The painted cabinets and baseboards are in a medium creamy/beige color with deep brown quartz countertops and travertine backsplash. The client has oil rubbed bronze light fixtures, lamps and a glass coffee table with metal legs. Their furniture is medium sage green with deep copper accent pillows. They have had a deeper beige than the cabinets but are wanting to change things up a bit. Using the balance between light mid-dark theory, the client has many medium tones, with metal elements and countertops being the only dark pieces. The paint has been relatively light. With the amount of natural and artificial light they have in the house, they can afford to go darker in the living room and kitchen. Not only will the cabinets pop more in the kitchen, but the living room furniture will look less like islands and more like a cohesive room.

For dramatic effect, I would suggest a deeper copper tone in the living room to bring in more of the scheme's cushion color. It enriches the green in the sofa and creates a cozy space to relax together as a family. By carrying the same color into the kitchen,

I would wrap the color behind all the cabinets, which happen to be in an "L" shape and back onto the living room half wall. With the baseboards and cabinets being the same color, and because the baseboards travel throughout the house, I would either use a lighter shade for the remainder of the walls and hallways.

This color can go in several directions. I do not necessarily want to repeat the same color they have already been using. I could use a shade up from the furniture color and use a sage that keeps the house from being too dark. I could use a warm browned out gray like Benjamin Moore's Weimaraner or Pashmina to bring out the warm tones in the new paint color but compliment the remainder of the furnishings. I would not go too light because the wall color would start competing with the baseboards and doors, which could even bring out unpleasant tones and make them look dirty.

Light furniture and dark flooring mean you can use medium paint colors. Light-toned flooring and furniture give you lots of room for light, medium or dark colors if you have enough light to pull it off. Dark furniture and flooring can mean you need to lighten things up, but you may not want to do that in a theater room. As a designer, you will be playing the room's function off of the depth of color that will be appropriate but interesting.

With colorful furniture comes the challenge of keeping the room married together with the paint color selection. Just because the furniture is pastel blue does not mean that the walls should be another blue shade. It does not mean that you automatically get out your color wheel to see what complimentary colors work with blue. You must work with the lighting very carefully and consider how it reflects the paint color into the room.

I once got a call from a ticked off father-in-law. His son and daughter-in-law had decorated the house they were renting from him, and he had not seen it until they moved out. I could see the reason for his consternation when I arrived. The rose-colored carpet was going to be a challenge for anyone, granted, but she had painted all the walls rose pink and then installed rose-pink curtains too. The room *breathed* pink, and it was suffocating. I could only imagine what the furniture was like in there. The light coming through the pink curtains added to the effect, bouncing and reflecting even more pink through the room until I felt like I was choking on it.

I have seen plenty of homes with traditional pastel furniture, plush carpeting and the slightest mint green or pink toned paint on the walls. They have a very formal effect. When you try to modernize the room without forcing the clients to purchase new flooring and furniture, you will neutralize the pastel tones out of the paint and maybe give it a little more depth.

The paint reacts to light and does it differently depending on the light's angle and the surface it is hitting. For instance, if you are painting color on a ceiling, it will be darker overhead than on the wall. It is better to use a lighter tone than the wall color to keep the room's height open. Often ceiling paint is flat, so it does not highlight imperfections in the drywall or the paint application. There is just more forgiveness with flat or eggshell paints than there is with the shinier ones.

It helps to think of the windows as flashlights where the light's angle comes in and hits the sidewalls the most and diffuses the farther away from the window it gets. It will highlight imperfections and give those walls the illusion that the paint is lighter and diffuses, darker. That is unless there is another window. How the light plays out in the room will determine how light or dark you go on specific walls. The window wall, again unless there is another window, will be the darkest. If you go too dark with the paint color on this wall, the light will keep your eye from discerning the color there. Think of going to the eye doctor with their light tool shining in your eye. You can tell there is color there, but not really what it is.

I like to place the darkest colors where they get the most light, showing them off in all their splendor. It does not always make sense because I do not want to highlight a wall when it is not truly the room's feature wall. In those cases, I will use the darker color on the fireplace wall, for example, and maybe wrap it around to a feature wall to group the room. Other times, I keep it to the fireplace wall only.

When a room is long and narrow, I have a trick to bring the short walls in closer and widen the space at the same time. Yes, it is only with paint. By painting one end wall and one long wall in a deeper color and the other two in a lighter paint color, I create the look of width. The darker walls visually run together. I've used this handy tidbit in more than one basement of my clients' older homes.

It helps to be visual as a designer. You can picture the effect of the paint on the walls before it is applied, and you can adjust it to make the most out of the space, light, and balance needed. Painting can solve many problems when appropriately planned, but even more importantly, when applied correctly.

Paint, Sheen And Basic Application

Baseboards, doors, window trim and cabinetry are usually painted with a soft sheen like a pearl or satin. Still, in some cases, they are in semi-gloss or a gloss. It makes them easier to wipe down dust, grime and fingerprints. It is essential to use good quality paint no matter what the surface is, but you do not want to scrimp on this paint. It takes the most wear and tear and is usually the least favorite thing to clean.

Often the walls will be painted one sheen down from the baseboards. For example, if the baseboards are a pearl/satin finish, the walls will likely be eggshell. In most cases, the walls are eggshell. It is the perfect amount of sheen for easy cleaning; if the paint is quality, it still hides most of the wall's imperfections. In some cases, the baseboards and millwork are painted in the same color. The difference in sheen helps differentiate between them. If you decide to use the same sheen on the walls and trim, please consider sticking to a pearl or higher in sheen as eggshell or flat paint on baseboards is genuinely awful to clean.

Wall sheen can be anywhere from flat, eggshell, pearl/satin to semi-gloss. Often, gloss is reserved for millwork and cabinets, and even semi-gloss is rare these days. Walls are not easy to wash either, but the quality of paint makes all the difference. Budget restrictions often make people choose lower quality cheap paint brands because they think, "paint is just paint." It could not be farther from the truth. You can have a low-quality eggshell or pearl that shows every wipe mark or burnish (where the paint has become polished from wiping hard). You can have a high-quality flat paint that washes like a dream.

The difference is in a fancy ingredient called titanium dioxide. This chemical element is responsible for the color retention, strength in pigment, and paint's overall washability. It is not cheap stuff. The more titanium dioxide in it, the more the paint will cost and the better the paint will perform. The paint companies who charge less, sometimes significantly less, do not have as much of this chemical in their paint and use fillers instead. The filler is called sodium carbonate, which is essentially like baking soda. It is cheap but also gives the paint a rougher finish. So those unfriendly chalky marks you get on the wall after washing are the filler showing its unpleasant side. You cannot remove them without repainting either. I speak from experience.

It is vital information as you are recommending paint colors and the actual paint to your clients. Trust me, it is the first thing that will wear in the house and the most frustration your client will have if they have used low-quality paint.

When it comes to washing the walls, a clean cloth with some warm water and the tiniest bit of dish soap is all that is needed. Using any other chemical cleaners can affect the paint's chemical makeup and start breaking it down on microscopic levels. These chemicals can also build up over time and create adhesion issues when it does come time to repaint. The new paint can blister or bubble on the walls. That is why it is a good idea to first was the walls with TSP, or trisodium phosphate, and then rinse well to prep before painting.

Deeper and vibrant colors could need a deep-based primer to accomplish the proper color on the wall. A deep-based primer is tinted explicitly to the color you are using and applied before the paint. It also helps keep the number of coats to a minimum. Again, cheaper paint will mean more coats and, in the end, more money spent. These are things to keep in mind when you recommend multiple intense tones for children's rooms or businesses, as each color will need its own primer, and costs can add up for your client.

Bare drywall must be primed before being painted. Self-priming paints are not designed to seal surfaces, and yet so many will try to cut corners and expense by trying it. From a liability standpoint, be very careful what you say a client can and cannot do when discussing paint applications. When they cannot get their paint to shop showing lap marks or roller marks for those not in the trade, they may turn to you for paint advice. Ensure you are only speaking from proper knowledge and refer them to your preferred paint specialist before you get yourself in hot water.

I once had a client call me up after he started painting to tell me that the paint was running down the wall as he was trying to roll it and that it was not consistent. I could not solve the situation over the phone and went back to his house to look at his walls. It was a hell of a mess, to be frank. He had been dipping his roller first in the paint and then in water before rolling it on the wall. To top that shock off, he was adamant that I instructed him to do it. He misheard something that I said, but I knew, without a doubt, that I had not instructed him to paint like that.

Painting walls takes proper cleaning, prep and patience. Baseboards should be removed or at least taped off to protect them from overzealous brushes and rollers. Paint should be applied in small sections at a time. Start at the left or right corner of the wall and move in three-foot-wide sections by painting first a floor to ceiling "W" and then filling in that area. Some paints will allow you to cut the entire room in (meaning you paint the edges of the wall at the ceiling and floor) and around electrical outlets before painting the central part of the wall. Others require you to paint into a wet edge, which means you must cut in the floor and ceiling within the three-foot section you are working in. As you work across the wall, you are blending the areas so that there are no "stops and starts" apparent on the wall.

It is better to load the roller with paint then roll it off in the pan once or twice. It is so the paint isn't oozing or dripping from the roller. Start mid-wall with the roller, rolling up to the cut-in, down through where you started. Continue towards the floor cut-in, then angle back up to the ceiling. It moves the paint from the middle of the wall and spreads it evenly on the wall. It is better than working a blob of color at the top of the wall to the floor. It keeps a person from over-rolling the paint and creating lap or roller marks.

You also do not want to press too hard on the roller head as it moves across the wall. Think ballet, not rock and roll. If you happen to need more paint to fill in the three-foot section, load the roller with a little less paint than the first time and use the same method. When you are ready to move into the next three feet, make sure to blend the last stroke out into the new section and then start there with fresh paint. Do not roll paint randomly in the middle of the wall or roll the paint too far. It will dry too quickly to blend out properly. You also do not want to leave drip marks or have so much paint in an area that it begins to sag. "Sagging" is kind of like a ripple of paint moving with gravity. It means you left too much paint on the wall.

After finishing the first coat, you should wait two to four hours between the first and second coat. Yes, *you always need* a second coat. Paint is not washable or sturdy without the second coat, and the color will not be as intense. Anyone claiming you need just one coat is cutting corners and trying to save time and a buck. As a designer, make sure that you are watching your painters closely for this trick. I never recommended a painter to a client who pulled that stunt, and if I caught wind of it, I never used them again.

Most of this is information that most designers will not use personally, but it is good to have in your back pocket should you need it. Remember, do not offer advice on the application, installation or maintenance of a product unless you are a hundred percent sure of your suggestions. It could land you in some expensive legal issues and the proverbial hot water.

In The Next Chapter...

You have made it a long way! By now, you can tell there is a lot more to interior design than just picking pretty things and putting them in a house. You've got the golden nuggets of where things can go very wrong or wrong depending on the information you receive from others. You have walked the proper steps from selecting cabinetry and flooring, countertops and tile, baseboards, doors, furniture, custom blinds and drapery, cushions, bedding to area rugs, and wallpaper art, décor and paint. It was no small feat to make it through all that information.

As you put all of it into practice, you will be able to refer to any section in this book and refresh your memory on the guidance you have received. You also know a lot more about yourself as a designer, your prospective clients' personality, and who you will include on your team of contractors and suppliers. I hope you feel like you are well underway.

The next chapter covers the process of putting all these elements into place. As I mentioned before, the order of selection is not necessarily the order of installation. You will find details about the importance of becoming a trusted advisor, how to build a timeline and communicate with your contractors, suppliers and tradespeople, and finally, how to wrap up the project with a neat little bow.

CHAPTER FIVE - THE PROCESS

Have you heard the expression of getting the cart before the horse? You have seen it. Knowing what you now know, you recognize it when clients choose paint colors before they have their flooring selected. You know when you have your flooring installation booked before you have the flooring delivered and you run into an availability issue.

Not only is this about keeping yourself organized, but it is also about knowing the timelines involved for various aspects of shipping, manufacturing and delivery, as well as installation. It is about having solid communication skills with all your suppliers and trades and keeping your client in the loop on how the project is progressing. It is rare to have a project go off without a hitch, and it is more common to have a hiccup or two. You get to manage the whole show... the good, the bad and the gorgeous.

Trusted Advisors

Becoming an interior designer takes a lot of dedication and patience. There are many elements to learn and learn well. Not all of them learned in a classroom. The industry changes with every change to environmental regulations and standards, changes that you must continuously educate yourself on. If it interests your client, you can bet they have been researching information online before asking you about it.

Acting professionally and being considered a professional in your field are two different things. Of course, you must work professionally to be respected and believe me, and it carries you a long way. The solid advice and creative ideas you can provide your clients will build your reputation and your business towards being highly respected and sought after as a designer. You can wear all the latest fashions, have fabulous shoes and dress the part. But honey, if you don't know what you're talking about, the "fake it until you make it" could lead to some costly and unfortunate mistakes.

Every designer has a unique road to gaining the experience they need to develop their business with a solid reputation. I freely admit to being an expert in some areas and having only a basic understanding of others. I did not sit back and let all my contacts do all the work with my clients; I educated myself along the way. I made sure that I was soaking in as much information as possible that I would easily pass on to my next client when needed.

There is a big difference between being known as a designer, which may gain you some very hard-won clients, and known as a trusted advisr. A trusted advisor is a professional who has earned the trust and admiration of their peers and clients. They know their "stuff," sharing this valuable advice with their clients and often having successful outcomes. A trusted advisor is the person that people turn to for advice when others' advice has gone astray. They are not afraid to tackle a conundrum and problem solve it until there is a better solution. And trust me, that better solution can take some honest advice that can cost the client more money for fixing the issue than if they had come to the trusted advisor first.

How do you become a trusted advisor? Why is this what you want to be known as?

Becoming a trusted advisor takes time because it will be through word of mouth that generates this status. First, a designer needs to be professional, friendly and honest from day one. Not just with one client, but all of them. Start in your business with standards of: transparency, trust, honesty, integrity, fairness, a sense of humor and appreciation for your client's money, time, and wellbeing that sets you apart from the other designers—especially ones who are hell-bent on making money or advancing an ego-based image of themselves. You know when you run into a salesperson who is genuinely interested in helping you and one who is looking at you like a process for financial gain or a burden. Operate your business and uphold your standards. Your clients will recognize the quality is not just your decorating skills but the value in the service you provide along with it.

Being a trusted advisor is not about ego but rather a mutual and successful fulfillment of need and supply to build a relationship with your client. In the end, if it turns into a simple transaction, the relationship ends there. Those who have developed a rapport with those clients will not hesitate to recommend you to their friends, family and colleagues when they ask about their project. If you have done your job right, they cannot stop talking about you and how much they love their house. Even if there was a problem or two, they are more likely to overlook them because they trusted you to handle the situation, and you followed through.

There are two reasons why it is beneficial to you to become a trusted advisor to your clients. If you have not figured it out already, one is for the repeat business. As word-of-mouth travels, you will either get more business or see your business trickle down until you work much harder than you should be to gain potential clients. Referrals and repeat customers are your least expensive form of advertisement and the very best kind. These people are priceless to you because your efforts generate interest in the form of unsolicited clientele and new projects to keep the momentum going in your business. It means that your calendar and your bank account are full.

The second reason it is essential to be the trusted advisor is... competition. You are not the only designer out there. In fact, for new people in the field, this is an intimidating fact. There are more experienced, busier and more well-known designers out there, for sure. But they are not you. Each of us has a unique flavor to bring to the table when it comes to design, and some clients will fit better with some more than others. There is enough pie for all of us. Yet, it is a competitive world we live in, and we need to find as many ways as possible to stand out in the crowd for the least amount of money spent on marketing.

While you may see flashy magazine ads, radio advertisements or bus signs of your competition, know that these marketing tools cost a lot of money. They can blow a marketing budget for a whole year or two on just these items alone. Being a trusted advisor means that while your potential clients see and hear all these advertisements, they listen to Aunt Jean. Why? Because she is busy recommending you, and she just loves how her renovation turned out and could not have done it without you. Your reputation is better built from the mouths of happy clients than it is with a dazzling picture of yourself on a billboard. Your competition will have no way to compete with you, and you will not be bothered with them. They can do their design business their way, and you yours, but loyal, happy clients will generate yours for more profit.

Trusted advisors are the go-to people not only when a new project comes up but when a client has a simple question or wants some guidance. It may take up a bit of time to maintain service with your clients as time goes on and you are more sought after. I can assure you; these small conversations are worth your time and energy. Even if they are just stopping in to say hello or offer to have coffee with you, it is worth fitting it into your busy schedule. These people are now professional friends of yours, affiliates in their rights, ready to sing your praises to anyone who mentions interior design or decorating around them. You intend to maintain those initial standards and provide the best genuine service on an ongoing basis that will set you apart from others.

The highest praise you can get, the real sign of success, is being recognized by other designers, suppliers, salespeople and artisans. Those who hold themselves to the same standards as you do and create a network amongst yourselves. As trusted advisors, you then have a community of people to give advice, get feedback and bounce ideas off of. These people are your kin, not your competition. They can help generate leads between your businesses when you are more suited to a project or need to source a product. Two heads are better than one. The people and companies in these networks are your support groups who genuinely want to see you succeed just as much as you support them. Call it mutual back-scratching in the places you cannot reach by yourself.

Prospecting For Clients

Marketing yourself in today's day and age is vastly different from placing newspaper advertisements or mail out fliers in the mail. Do not get me wrong. Some design firms with the budget to do high-quality mail-outs, radio ads, and bus bench signs can generate stunning marketing campaigns. With the budget to go with it! Most of us just starting need more budget-friendly options that will grab the attention of potential clients.

It has become a digital society of social media with people having a short attention span for advertisements. My writing career and my design company started at the same time when I decided to try submitting an article idea to my local newspaper. Blogging was not the social norm back then, but that's what it was in print form. I gave them three article samples, and voila! They paid me for a weekly article. I began putting all my creative juices into potential design projects and useful tips for readers to use when selling their home. It was the best, and cheekiest, form of advertising I did. I gained a following that I did not even realize, and it put me in the spotlight for potential employers as well.

I allocated some funds towards an advertisement in the telephone. When my ad expired, and the telephone book company called to renew, I asked them, "How much are you willing to pay me to have my business listed?" The salesperson did not quite know how to take that. You see, my newspaper article was paying me to advertise my business. I admit I am proud of how clever I was for thinking of it.

In today's marketplace, everyone is advertising themselves through social media. Whether through a blog, sharing and selling home decor products or direct advertisements. It is relatively affordable if you know what you are doing. The key to becoming recognized is through regular and familiar targeted advertisements. It means you need a consistent logo and "look" to your ads, as well as quality photography of your projects. If you have not completed any projects yet, rearrange and design rooms in your home and get good quality photos taken. It is better to use your photography if possible, but make sure to give any photographers credit for their pictures if you use them. You do not want to get into hot water there.

You also do not want to mislead your clients on what your skills are. Your photos should represent you and your business, your abilities and your standards. Once you put that image out there, that is what people will be expecting from you. Make sure that what you advertise is what you can deliver. Canva is a great app that is useful for creating posts and advertisements on your social media accounts. You can purchase the ability to use different photos, or upload your own, and place various templates over the top with creative fonts and symbols. It creates interest, gives you a professional advertisement and saves you time and money.

Facebook and Instagram ads are linked if you select them when setting up your ad, but you will pay double for it. Be careful to deselect the "post to Instagram" if you only intend to advertise on Facebook. Your post will automatically go on both platforms if you leave it selected, but the cost doubles along with your potential reach. You also get to choose your target market. It will determine how much money the ad will cost you. You can select a specific geographical range within your trading areas like a neighborhood, city, state, or province. You can also choose particular categories like home improvement, decorating, renovation etc., to narrow down the types of potential customers you are trying to reach. Last is setting a timeline for how long you want the ad to run. Once you state how long you want the ad to run for, you will receive a total cost of the advertisement and an approximate "reach" of customers. If you do not want to spend that much, you can lessen the trading area or the length of time the ad runs. Or both.

I learned a trick that can help get you maximum reach but not spend the ad's total amount without lessening your reach. When I finished creating my ad, I would let the ad run for a day or two, carefully monitoring how much it cost me daily, and then I would cancel the ad. No, it was not running for as long as I intended it to be. Still, it reached out to the maximum number of people in the target area without being too repetitive. You want your business to be viewed regularly, but you will get the highest turnaround from customers in this time frame. You can then opt to start the ad again in a few days. Keep in mind that the total at the bottom of the ad will double if you are using Facebook and Instagram. Do not let this be an unfortunate surprise.

The idea is to generate business with real leads and gain followers to your Facebook, Instagram, and other social media accounts. You can regularly engage with your clients on these sites by sharing related products, information, industry changes, and favorite trends. The more you can engage them in a fun and relatable way, the more they will share your posts and spread the word about you. The more followers you can gain without spending money, the better. Do not get me wrong, you will need to spend money on marketing, but the trick is to do it smartly.

Aside from social media, people need to see you in person. It is essential to see the latest show homes, keep up to date on new flooring, tile, carpet, fabrics, and paint colors by visiting the related businesses and their salespeople. Attend their design and product events when they send you invitations and make sure you are on their mailing list. Fundraisers are always going on. If you can support one or two by providing your time or at least a donation by attending a dinner, do it. But when you go, make sure to mingle and ask people about their interests. The better you get at striking up a conversation, the more people will open to you and offer information about potential projects they have going on. Sometimes, you cannot help them personally. Still, you can provide a referral for one of your other trusted advisor friends.

Always keep your business cards on you as you will be surprised how many times you are at the grocery store or getting gasoline and bump into someone you want to give one to. With that in mind, make sure you are always presenting yourself in the best possible light. Do not travel around town in your PJ's and messy bun, thinking no one will judge you. If you run into the client you are trying to woo at the mall, you want that opportunity to put your best foot forward. It doesn't always mean you are dressed in your work clothes, but it does mean you should take pride in your appearance. In some cases, like at the gym or doing yard work, you just cannot help your appearance, but it is something to keep in mind.

The more creative you are with getting yourself seen in relevant circles, the more people will recognize you for your profession. Chances are, someone will be willing to give you a chance with small projects. If you are savvy enough, you can turn the small project into bigger ones by upselling other services you offer, if not now, later down the road. Color consultations are great for this. It is a relatively inexpensive service you can offer that gets you in the client's home. Then you can see any other glaring needs they may have. Using your trusted advisor skills, you can ask the right questions that lead to understanding how motivated the client is for any further changes in their house. Worst case scenario, the paint job goes perfectly, and you get more consultation work. In the best-case scenario, you get to replace the window coverings, called back for a future project, and the client has referred you to three of her friends.

How Do You Find People To Add To Your Network?

Your network is a special place reserved for special people. Not everyone belongs there, but when you find someone genuinely interested in sharing business opportunities, or source products, they are worth keeping close. You will know them by their ongoing success, work ethic, honesty and understanding of the importance of being a trusted advisor themselves. They may not use those words, but you will catch on to how they operate by speaking about their business, clients and love of what they do. They, of course, want to make money and be profitable. Still, they are doing something they are passionate about and will not risk their business's reputation on anything less.

You will learn that some people operate with an "everyone is out for themselves" mentality in some cases. Those folks will likely have a different sort of network, one based on undercutting the competition, stealing projects at any cost, and attempting to sour others' reputations. These are not the kind of people you want to waste your time or energy on, never mind associated with.

Again, finding qualified, eager, and helpful staff in your trusted stores is a good step. These people are passionate about service, understand their role in giving you the best product and price possible and are happy to see you come through the door. Developing this relationship can lead to referral business between the two of you when you each have customers or clients who need services. You may be the first person they call when new stock or samples arrive from their suppliers, which gives you an edge with your clients who are keen on having the latest trends. They will also go out of their way to assist you with any issues that you are having. Do not be afraid to drop by with a coffee or snack once in a while. Offer them spare tickets to fundraising events so they can network as well.

Fundraisers are an exciting experience when it comes to networking. A great many business people attend these events to mingle with fellow compatriots and competitors alike. Some will be quite passionate about the causes they are supporting and be involved on committees and donating large sums of money. You may contribute your time and some funds to causes close to your heart. You may find that having this in common opens the door to creating professional relationships with others. Even attending dinners mixed with silent and live auctions can be rewarding if you can break the ice with strangers at your table. Therefore, it helps to bring along someone you know but is also good at starting a conversation. These are not the places to overindulge in alcohol, though, not for you or your guest. It is about presenting yourself and your company to the masses. You must make the right impression.

There are other networking groups that you can join or attend. Find them by asking questions at your Chamber of Commerce, who will likely have a monthly networking event themselves. Other groups have a membership fee, but the goal is to provide leads and educational conversations within the networking group before giving them elsewhere. It can be very beneficial if you are part of the right group. The price tag is an annual fee and a substantiated business that has been operating for some time. Usually, you will attend a few of these different chapters as a guest to see if the group fits you. Frankly, to see if this form of networking is a good fit for you. You will then go through an interview process, but remember you are interviewing them as much as you are. Do not be discouraged by this, though, as it does not hurt to apply. Once accepted, your company will be the only interior design/decorating business allowed to join to avoid competition within the networking group.

Do not think inside the box when it comes to finding your people. Supporting youth sports by attending matches, events, fundraisers or just donating time or money can get you in touch with other businesses and clients alike. Look for new stores that are opening. Try doing business with some of the companies you see advertising on social media. They may tell you if the advertising is working. Heck, try out a social media firm specializing in advertising for you if it fits your budget. Attend their "how-to" classes yourself. You may meet other business people there that work nicely into your network.

Whatever method you use to market your business, make sure that you have a quick pitch that gives just the right amount of confidence and interest. You want the person to ask you more questions, not run away with an awkward glance over their shoulder to make sure you do not follow them. You are not trying to bombard anyone with too much information upfront, but rather, a friendly and casual information drop that includes why you love what you do. And then, you make a point of allowing the other person to do the same. Ask open-ended questions that offer more information in the answers besides a yes or no response.

Introductions are hard when you are self-conscious and just starting. I get it. I was there once. But most people are not looking to bite your head off and do not mind holding a conversation with you. Starting a conversation with a customer or client who has just walked through your door is slightly different. There are different types of shoppers out there, and the only way to know who you have come through the door is to say hello and ask them what brought them in that day. Some will just nod, say hello and carry on, clearly not needing your help unless they ask for it. Others will come straight to you and inquire about your products or services. And some are a combination of both, depending on their mood that day. If you have said hello within the first ten seconds of them coming through the door, you have started on the right foot. Once you have offered your help, you will know whether to give them some space first or come to their aid right away.

A trusted advisr can "sell" themselves without being pushy or instant. They manage to share what they do, why they are passionate about it. They show how they can help while showing genuine interest in the person they are talking to. After a quick introduction, an exchange of names and a handshake, a trusted advisor asks what brought that person into their business and how they can help. They pay attention and remember small details from the conversation. They pick up on nuances that give away what a customer likes or does not and then act upon them. They use statements like:

"I recall that you said…"
"I remember you saying…"
"If I remember correctly…"

Then they repeat back affirming statements that they understood the clients' needs correctly.

This approach can be applied whether the client is in your establishment, on the phone. Or you have bumped into a prospect on the street. It helps to make notes as soon as the meeting is over so you can keep track of these small details. Whatever happens, you want to get the person's name and contact information so that you can follow up with them in a day or two. Some will not want to share this information because they are worried; they get bombarded with unsolicited emails or telephone marketing campaigns. It is better to say what you intend to do. A follow-up to see how their project is going is expected in a couple of days. Reiterate that their information in their database is protected. Be sure to make good on your promise. Only add customer or client emails or contact information to subscriptions if they have agreed to do so.

As you gain more clients, word of mouth and a full schedule, your confidence will grow. It is crucial to keep yourself organized and prioritize your time to manage tasks efficiently, both for your client's project and for your business. Suppose you know that you are more creatively sharp in the morning to do marketing or writing projects for your social media accounts. In that case, you know not to schedule other tasks during this time. You also need to schedule a time for networking, product sourcing, banking and paperwork, and self-care. You can delicately say that you are not available on specific dates or times to your clients. Asking for them to respect your time means that you will mutually respect theirs as well.

One more noteworthy thought as a trusted advisor is how you charge for your services. In the beginning, it is hard to ask for adequate compensation for your services. In truth, it is intimidating to think that you are relying on your clients for income. When you are gaining experience, it is tempting to undercharge for the sake of being in the starting phases of your business. It is a mistake. One, because your clients will also tell their friends and family what you charge. Know what the going rate is for your type of services, and do not get too carried away being lower or higher than the average. Know your value so that your clients see it also, and you will be more successful in getting your asking price. Be reasonable with how you bill out for your time as well. It takes gasoline to drive to your client's home or to the stores that you are shopping at for them. Minimum charges for the first hour are reasonable for both of you. Then incremental charges are based on the time that you are spending on their project. It is merely a suggestion. You can determine what works best for you. I am saying that your services are worth being paid for. Just be clear about your fees upfront, so you and the client are not surprised with a disagreement in the end.

Communication

There are just as many fingers in the pie as there are elements to your design project. More actually. There are salespeople, suppliers, and installers all playing a part in how the timeline has affected the project. The only way to stay on top of all the moving parts is to make sure you are up to speed on: ordering times, installation dates, length of time the install will need. Including how everything may potentially overlap. It means that you had better brush up on your communication skills to fully understand where everybody is at without misunderstandings, which leads to delays.

They say that to be a good communicator, one must first be a good listener. I wholeheartedly agree. When we slow down and make a point of listening to how our client discusses their home, their desires and what they need you for, you not only get information about your role and their house. You get to understand them better too. Make sure to follow what they are saying, ask questions, and add your input when giving you a chance to speak. Do not interrupt people if you can help it. I have had more than one excited client get rambling about their lives, their house, their spouse and kids, and eventually, I get them back on track. It takes a little suave maneuvering of the conversation without being rude or impatient.

Sometimes, it's you that must do the talking. Clients want to hear about your experience, what projects had remarkable outcomes and how you came to be doing what you do for a living. They want to know who they are welcoming into their little corner of the world and whether they can trust you inside of it. It is not the time to get boastful or overshare in your personal life. Be open, honest and genuine while trying to keep the conversation on track with the project. If you are charging by the hour, the more you talk, the less likely you will feel like it is fair to charge for the quantity of time you are in the client's house.

Communicating With Suppliers, Stores And Contractors

In the initial stages, you will be shopping for anything from flooring to paint colors. Whether this involves the client or not, you know where you prefer to deal and who you prefer to deal with once you are there. We have gone over the type of relationships that you are trying to develop. Still, it is essential to know how to keep communication lines open with these people as well.

Before going into a store or supplier, you need to understand what the project timeline is and it's needs. Do you need installation, or is the client completing the project themselves? Do you have someone in mind already, or will you need a referral? Do you have a clear idea of when you will need the product you are shopping for delivered?

The salespeople are going to ask you these questions when you arrive. It helps them give you a better idea of what items are on special-order and require longer ship times or coming from out of the country and getting hung up in Customs. It is a good idea to have the salesperson check on the product's availability before borrowing samples. If you have a rough idea of how many of the measurements you will need, they can use this to tell you whether there will be enough supply to meet your demand. Ensure that if you place a product on hold, you know when this hold expires and make a note of it in your client file.

If possible, get information, quotes and ETA's on the product in writing so that you can refer to it when your memory is playing tricks on you. Emails work just if you keep them organized in client files, so they are easy to access later. Once you make an order, clarify the shipping dates with the installer and the contractor to coordinate this between them. Your planning for the flooring to be installed with the installer does not help if the framing and drywall are not complete, now does it? Again, try to clarify the details in writing with the installer, supplier and contractor so that everyone is on the same page. Be careful that the contractor keeps you in the loop on direct conversations with tradespeople. It helps you know when there is a change of plan and why to keep your client informed.

You may run into a hiccup of a discontinued item, the stock is not enough to fulfill your order, or the shipment will not arrive in time for installation. It is either your chance to shine or become overly stressed. Be prepared for these types of occurrences by staying in touch with your suppliers. Follow up with them on a scheduled date that gives you room to make a contingency plan, should you need to. If there are any changes, be sure to calmly notify the client and any relevant tradespeople who may be affected.

While you are problem-solving, it is essential that you keep a level head and your demeanor pleasant. Your image as a businessperson should be one of professionalism, courtesy, understanding, intelligence, composure and organization. How you speak to people will either get you closer to what you need or farther away. You may get what you want, but you will have to spend more energy driving a hard bargain or being overly insistent. Know when to put your foot down and maintain the standards you have set for yourself in your business. I would instead give the salesperson or supplier the benefit of the doubt than always second-guessing them.

Tip: There is always a solution if you stay calm enough to find it. Sometimes, it works out even better than the original plan!

I have personally found that the calmer you remain, the calmer your supplier, salesperson, tradespeople and client will be. And when they are not staying level-headed, show them your smile and tell them that you trust in finding a solution. Bring them back to calm rather than join them. Sometimes, it is better to get as much information about the issue as possible and then take some time to calm down about it. Venting should not happen to anyone inside of your professional circle. It is not a great idea to vent anyhow, but sometimes talking through the problem will bring you to a solution you did not see before. Make sure to be in the right frame of mind when you call or visit your suppliers, installers, contractors and clients and only when you are back to a regular heart rate.

The more you trust the people in your business circle, and they trust you, the easier it will be for everybody to achieve your goal. They want to be your top pick when it comes to goods and labor, and you want to be their top pick for referrals. These relationships are just as meaningful as the relationship you develop with your clients. Without them, you cannot do an outstanding job yourself. These people will help share the burden of the work that needs to occur, saving you a great deal of effort and sleep.

Communicating With The Client

Once you have secured the project with the client, your involvement becomes about communication between you. Having a clear understanding of the client's goals will boil down to how well you both communicate.

You must have a contract that plainly states how you will be charging for your time and services. You need to explain in simple terms your hourly rate, flat service charge and any discounts you will be passing along both verbally and in the contract. Do not leave room for interpretation. Be transparent about the frequency they will receive a bill from you and how the charges will incur. If you happen to get into a situation where they dispute the invoice, you want to have more than a verbal conversation to go back to. You also want the client to sign both of your copies of the agreement, signalling they understand everything you have discussed, as outlined in the document. If there is an amendment to the agreement, make the changes on both copies and have the client initial. In the end, you get a copy for your file, as do they.

My tendency to be anxious often had me nervous whenever my client was nervous. I learned that it got worse if I did not ground myself before my meetings by spending a moment to collect my thoughts, slow my breathing and have a little personal pep talk. I also made sure that I had eaten well so that my blood sugar levels were not dipping and causing me extra impatience. How we handle stress or absorb others' energy significantly impacts how we communicate with the people in our day. It is best to know ourselves before interactions with others, especially in a professional capacity.

It feels a little like being a counselor of sorts. Still, your job is also to provide reassurance about the project as it is progressing. The client may be just as involved as you are, which means that those extra set of hands may be helpful, or slightly in the way. Homeowners get excited about the process and can venture out independently without you knowing what they are up to. It means random samples are appearing, and new opinions from friends come out of the woodwork. Suddenly, the neighbor has become an interior design expert and has camped out in one of your meetings. It also means that they have many questions based on anxiety over the project's outcome. Not only do you get to handle the bundle of energy that is your client, but you also get to manage the people tagging along.

In the initial meetings, it is a good idea to set a parameter for how you work. I always made it clear that I catered to my client based on knowing what they like, disliked and how they live in their house. I informed them it was my experience that, while their friends and family mean well, the client has hired me to assist them. They trusted my ability to visualize the project and skills to bring it together based on their home's personality and people. It is a fine line where a designer can quickly insult the wingman/woman the client has invited, thereby insulting or embarrassing the client. If you are good at communicating your ideas and why they work, you can bring the friend or relative on board by asking them to visualize the design. The quicker you can get them on board instead of being the watchdog, the better. Your client will feel more at ease without a push-pull of vying opinions at the table.

As the project progresses, depending on the job's scope, make sure to have an agreed-upon number of updates through each week and month. By showing the client that you have been following up with suppliers and keeping track of trades, they will feel less concerned and that you have everything under control. Of course, they are curious little cats and love to show up on-site to inspect the progress. One cannot blame them for wanting to see with their own eyes that they are well looked after and see what you have been visualizing all along.

Seeing a dream realized bit by bit could make a person impatient for the finish line. I see people start to go nuts when they live in the mess of construction and installation but are finally seeing some of the more beautiful elements in place. Often, there are many steps left to go before everything is clean and polished. It is when the clients start pushing to make everyone hurry it up, especially if there have been delays with trades or installation.

Your skills at refocusing the client's attention to positive aspects of the job will help take the pressure off everyone. Reassuring the client that everyone is working on getting the project wrapped up as quickly as possible will calm them down. How you manage this will come down to your tone, the words you use, and the conversation's timing. You will need to assess how anxious or upset the client is before knowing how to approach a resolution for them. You may not have a solution yet, but you still need to get them to a point where they tell you what the trouble is so you can begin to solve it.

If your client is in the middle of a panic attack angry, now is not the time to point fingers and assign blame. If you have discovered an issue, it is best to get as much information as possible and see if you can find an alternative solution before contacting the client. When you do, apologize if you have made an error and admit it. Your role is to inform them of the issue, provide a possible solution and allow them to make some conclusions for themselves. Even if it was not your error, but someone on your team, apologize for the inconvenience the issue is causing them. The more you show the client that they can still rely on you to solve, the more your trust will remain in place. Please don't make the mistake of plopping the issue in their lap or placing the responsibility on someone else. You will lose their trust, and your credibility will diminish.

Sometimes the reaction is blown way out of proportion, and you are taken aback by your client's behavior. It helps to take a step back and look at it from their perspective if you can.

You may have just informed them that the light fixture they wanted for the front entrance came in in the wrong finish, and you are getting a stronger reaction than you expected. I have often found that there is something more going on in the client's life that just reached the tipping point by adding one more problem. Perhaps a death in the family, an unexpected financial hurdle or a car accident has blown up their ability to handle any further stress. The project's issue may be truly crucial or a minor setback. Take a moment to consider other circumstances.

Allow them to blow off a little steam, without tolerating any abuse, obviously, and instead of reacting to the emotion behind their reaction, listen to the words they are using. Are they hinting that they have a lot of stress in their life? Are they sharing personal information that could explain their anger or anxiety? Are they blaming you for things that you are not responsible for?

My recommendation? Empathize with the client. Say to them, "I understand. I am listening to what you have to say." Wait for the client to give you a chance to talk and keep the subject to the project unless they offer more information. Sometimes clients will share more about their personal lives than you would expect, but this shows you that you have gained their trust.

If they continue to be upset in one form or another, ask them if they can give you some time to find some solutions or get more information for them and call them back. Suppose this is happening during a meeting or consultation, attempt to step away to make necessary phone calls and give them a moment to collect themselves. Sometimes, people just need the chance to get over the shock of an issue.

I have had a client about to have her drapery installed the same day her sister passed away. She went ahead with the installation anyhow. Sure enough, there was a snag in the fabric, and when she called to tell me about the problem, her attitude was rather sharp. Instead of reacting to the client's emotion, I focused on the issue at hand, started making phone calls to the installer and workroom, then decided to remake the panel for her but leave the current one in place for her privacy. When I called the client back to let her know how I handled the situation, she apologized and told me about her sister. She was grateful I was willing to fix the issue so quickly for her.

If you intend to provide top-level customer service, then you should not be intimidated by problem-solving any issues that come up. Letting your client know how you handle problems in advance gives them an expectation that may keep them a little calmer in the event of a problem.

Why is it important to value your client's feelings or reactions? Your attitude speaks volumes about how trustworthy you are in your business and how important your clients are. If you come off cold or unconcerned, the client can take offence on top of being upset and then the emotional state elevates instead of dissipating. Your goal is to bring them back down from their excitement and get back on track with the project's vision. Allow them some time to adjust to any changes that need to be made and make a point of moving on yourself.

Not everything is bad news. I was once on a consultation with a client when the phone call came his grandson was born. It just so happened to be his birthday too. I did not have his full attention, and I made a point of finishing what we were discussing and leaving so he could get to his family. Not only did I get to enjoy his happy moment, but I had personal information to have meaningful conversations about in the future.

There are situations where the client needs to cancel the work or decides on a different direction than initially discussed. Heaven forbid, but they may need to release you from work as well. It may be upsetting for you. Depending on the relationship you developed with the client, they are more than uncomfortable needing to inform you of their decision. On goes the professional cap again, and you get to be gracious and understanding. Allow them to tell you what has changed and ask them if there is anything that you need to do differently. Welcome the opportunity to do business with you in the future and keep all bridges intact. You can be upset or even mad in the privacy of your own home, but never more than polite disappointment with the client. Trust me, how you handle it will be the source of more than one conversation they have with people in their lives.

Communication In The Digital Age

The last area that needs discussion is appropriate forms of communication with your client. In the age of digital devices and smartphones, we have become accustomed to shooting off an email or text about anything and everything that comes to mind. Clients themselves will likely communicate with you in the same way. You must decide upfront what you are comfortable with and set that expectation with the client for you both.

Do you intend to allow them to text you on your personal or business cell phone? Are you going to be available twenty-four hours a day, seven days a week? Will you be more likely to send emails and texts or make phone calls? Do you prefer to send written messages to keep the client informed or meet in person? What preference does your client have around these issues? If they are a couple, who should you be communicating with, if not them both?

Let's face it. It is incredibly convenient to text people in your personal and business life because you assume that you will get a quick response. That does not mean that it is appropriate for either your client or yourself. If you get the clients' cell phone numbers, it is best to ask permission to text them if you intend to communicate that way. On the flip side, be prepared to get a text on a whim whenever your client has a question or an idea. And if you are a busy designer, that can mean several clients are texting you throughout the day. And that is if they are polite. I have had a client text me after business hours where I had to make a point of not responding until the next day.

If you intend to be available by text, set a polite boundary about your business hours and that you only respond during that time. Then make a point of turning your phone off for text alerts. I must caution you that when you decide to make an exception about this, you open the door to texts outside of regular business hours.

Emails are not only an acceptable form of communication

between yourself and your clients or business-related colleagues, but it is necessary. Email helps provide detailed information vital to your project. Save it under the client files you create in your email account. The better you are at communicating through email, the more informed everyone is and the fewer surprises everyone has as the project progresses. Suppose you are not very good at composing letters. In that case, it is better to have personal conversations and keep notes about your discussion. I recommend that you go online and search for business letters to use as a template.

When it comes to emails, it is acceptable to inform your client of problems that have come up, but it is better to make a phone call or tell them in person. It leaves little room for misunderstanding the tone or context of the email or text. In some cases, people's reading comprehension is a bit dicey. They tend to misinterpret the message you are trying to convey. If a client is having trouble following your emails or does not seem to be answering the questions you have, it may time for in-person conversations.

Keep all written communication that you have with your clients and business circle. It is a reference to fall back on when you cannot remember specific details. Keep in mind, your client and compatriots can keep everything themselves. You want to make sure that everything you write is professional, straightforward and easy to read. Do not leave any guesswork to what you are trying to say and keep the language you use easy to understand. You may have a vocabulary that could impress a university professor. Still, you do not want to make the recipient pull out a dictionary every time you send a message. Also, keep in mind that your client may not know the terminology commonly used in the industry. Break it down for them in layman's terms.

Response time can be a bone of contention when you are busy. It pays to highlight the expected response time to phone calls in your voicemail message. Leave an automated response for any absences or holidays. Include contact information in the case of an emergency. Providing alternative phone numbers or emails is a good idea if you have staff that can assist while you are away. If you are running your business solo, it is wise to check your messages once a day and include this practice in your automated response. It will help set expectations and boundaries and keep you from getting an overwhelming backlog of emails and messages when you return.

Communication is vital to running a business and developing relationships. Still, good communication skills are what keep them alive and well. When one method does not work, changing your approach may be the ticket. The more relaxed and confident you are in dealing with conflict or problems, the quicker the resolution. It does take a bit of experience to get the hang of all the personalities you will run into. Still, I can assure you; you will learn to navigate most of them if you stay true to the standards and intentions you have set for your business.

Creating A Timeline

Interior design would seem like it was all about selecting the perfect furniture, area rug and paint color, wouldn't it? We dream of getting to put all the fabulous fabrics together to pull off an exquisite window treatment or designing a kitchen worthy of drooling over. We likely didn't expect the timeline to be as much work as the design itself. I doubt anyone thought they would show up with a magic wand, and *poof*, everything is perfectly in its place with a little pat on our back for a job well done.

So, what is a timeline in the interior design business?

The timeline is tracking the construction, selection, shipping, and installation of a project's renovation or design. You bet you had better include some check-in points with your client to review and report the progress made and leave plenty of room for any changes. Having a clear understanding of when to place orders, shipping times, and installation means you know what is affected by any adjustments. Trust me, and they will come up.

Having a good idea of how long the overall project will take also means checking in with hired contractors.

Every project is different in scale and complexity. The more complex the project, the more involved and detailed the timeline will be. Suppose it is a simple color consult with a professional painter you have recommended. In that case, you will likely only be setting up reminders in your calendar for meeting the client and contacting the painter with the referral. Next, a follow-up with the client and painter when the job date is approaching, then once more after completing the job. Ask to take marketing photos of your work!

Suppose the job entails a full-blown renovation. You are hired on the job from the initial design through demolition to completion. In that case, you know you will need serious organization skills and a timeline that keeps everyone on track. At the very least, it will keep you coordinated and on task, especially if you have several people involved.

I am a fan of Microsoft 365. When I created my website, I could add a blog and subscribe to Microsoft 365 for a small monthly upgrade fee. Microsoft 365 has tools like: Microsoft Word for word processing, Microsoft Excel for creating spreadsheets, Planner for task scheduling, and you can sync your calendar too! While it may take a bit of time to set up, I find it saved me a lot of time in the long run. Follow the tutorials when you are first starting, so you are not immediately frustrated.

I personally love Planner because you can create a board for each design project, a "bucket" for each subject like flooring or drapery. Tasks move quickly by dragging them into other buckets. As you fill in tasks, it tracks automatically in the program's charts and calendar area, so you do not have to transfer information. Under the "charts" tab at the top of the screen, you can see each task's progress and whether it is behind or late. The "schedule" tab shows you all your tasks on a calendar to track the dates concerning the tasks.

I run my business solo and do not have employees or assistants at this point. Once a business is successful enough to have staff, I would recommend giving them access to the Microsoft 365 programs. You have interaction within each "app," including your employees, making it easier to maintain your company's tasks and appointments.

Now that you have some tools to help you document your tasks in your timeline, you will need to know when to schedule what. You will need to know how long custom items typically take to manufacture and how long it takes to install them. You need to know your contractor's availability and how full their schedule is. If they are behind in their schedule, you can bet on a delay with your project. They can rarely stop one job to complete another. The following is a set of projection examples to give you an idea of what you may have to schedule around.

Ordering Timeline

- Custom cabinetry- two-three months for MDF, four to six months for solid wood.
- Quartz/Granite countertops: One to three months depending on slab availability.
- Laminate countertops- two-four weeks once all templating is complete.
- Custom Drapery- two-three months depending on how busy the workroom is.
- Custom Furniture- two-three months for true custom some special-order furniture may be
- Custom Blinds- two-three weeks, depending on stock levels of fabrics with the manufacturer.
- Flooring- two-three weeks, depending on stock levels and delivery location (local suppliers can possibly ship within three-four business days)
- Lighting- one-two weeks unless custom.
- Tile—one week to three months depending on availability, shipping and manufacturing, as

they are often shipped overseas if the supplier is out of stock.

- Baseboards/Trim— immediately if a basic profile is selected, two weeks-two months for specialty profiles.
- Custom Pillows—one-two months, depending on fabric availability and workroom schedule.
- Area Rugs—one-two weeks for previously made special orders, three-six months for hand made.
- Commissioned Art—two-three months unless the artist is in high demand, it could take much longer.
- Special Order Prints—two to four weeks unless they are out of stock and waiting on manufacturing new prints.
- Custom Ironwork (railings, features, etc.)— two-four months depending on the project's scope.
- Custom Woodwork (shelves, barn doors, etc.) — one-three months.

It is crucial to add the dates to your calendar or timeline when you get a supplier's delivery date. Also, set a reminder to follow up with them no later than at the halfway mark so you won't be surprised by delays. Perhaps you have developed a solid relationship with your supplier. In that case, they may be ahead of the game and update you without your prompting. The ordering timeline I have provided is a very general idea of what you may expect. Installation timelines will vary from contractor to contractor and the type of product they are using. Still, the following information should give you an idea of what to expect.

Installation Timeline:

- Cabinetry installation: two-seven days depending on the number of pieces
- Countertop installation: one-two days
- Custom Drapery installation: one-two days
- Custom Blind installation: two hours to a day depending on the number of pieces and style of blind
- Custom Furniture Delivery: one-two hours
- Flooring installation: One day to two weeks (One room of carpet may take one to two days, where hardwood flooring could take two weeks with nail and glue installation)
- Lighting installation: two-three days, depending on the number of pieces and complexity of wiring required
- Tile installation: Two to three day for small jobs (A whole house could take from one to four weeks depending on the complexity of the tile pattern)
- Baseboards/Trim installation: two-seven days depending on the size of the job.
- Custom Woodwork installation: one week to one month, or longer for complex installa tions like spiral staircases
- Custom Ironwork installation: two days to two weeks
- Paint job: two days to two weeks, depending on the paint job's size and the weather if they are painting outside

It seems simple enough, right? Ensure you get the horse before the cart. Otherwise, you could have thirty-thousand dollars worth of custom furniture arrive before the flooring installation. You risk having it get damaged by the installers moving it from one room to the next. Installing the blinds before you paint the trim and baseboards means they will need to be removed again and re-installed at an extra cost. Documenting each element's progress helps avoid costly errors that come out of your pocket, not the client's. You need to monitor the contractor's progress if you intend to use them on more than one of your jobs.

Your timeline and schedule will help you understand how much room you have before accepting any further design projects and where to schedule them once you do. Clients will appreciate your services as a professional designer the more organized and prepared you are. By avoiding headaches for yourself, you are doing the same for everyone involved. It also means that you have your timeline to fall back on when something unexpected occurs and create quick solutions. Much quicker than if you were winging it by the seat of your pants!

It would be best if you made notes about the information you receive from suppliers and contractors verbally. You can easily track down written information such as emails, invoices, statements and messages. Still, when a verbal conversation has taken place, I highly recommend that you immediately take notes about the discussion, either on your smartphone or in an agenda. It is easy to think you will remember all the details of what was said. Still, I can assure you that when there is a misunderstanding, two people will not remember the same conversation the same way. It is better to have notes to review to catch errors on either of your parts. It also holds the people you are working with accountable for what they promised with less conflict.

The Wrap Up

A day will come when all the meticulous work you have done to coordinate every detail of the project comes to fruition. The crew has completed the final cleaning. The furnishings and decorative items are perfectly in place in precisely the spot you planned them for. The design is complete. Your baby is ready to be turned over to the homeowner for good. You are about to get paid!

It would seem like there would be little left for you to do, and perhaps it is accurate as far asyour interior design skills go. But in terms of your business, you want to take the opportunity to get some fantastic photos of the house before the homeowners have the chance to mess it up. I say that lovingly, but I know that the perfectly staged home you have put together is about to be lived in.

Break out that wide-angle lens. If you are not comfortable taking photos yourself, hire a local photographer. They will come to the house with all the proper lighting equipment to make your work shines. You will need the homeowner's permission, of course. Still, these photos' intention is for marketing material on your social media accounts, portfolio for future clients and printed promotional material. You may get the permission out of the way in the initial contract agreement between you and the client. It may save you some money to arrange a trade of services with the photographer. The more you promote their photos through your marketing avenues, the more exposure they get, and they may see the value in that.

When looking for a photographer, look at their own Instagram and Facebook accounts and their website. You want someone who has an eye for artistic shots that promote items, which you may want to highlight for extra income opportunities yourself. A photographer who leans more towards traditional family portraits may not be suitable for what you are looking for. The right person understands marketing and should work well with you as you relay your ideas of the look you are after. Do not rely on family members unless they are professionals. However, your photos may work too, only use pictures that look professional, well lit, and have the right balance.

A tremendous thank you gift for your clients may be a professionally printed portfolio with their photographs inside. Of course, you can include a handwritten note and perhaps a gift certificate for a local business that they would be interested in. You may even choose to personalize scented candles and other decorative items for thank you gifts.

The end of the project does not mean this is the end of the relationship with your client. Of course, you want that final payment in your hand. There is an art form to following up within two weeks to a month, asking your clients how they are enjoying the house and if there have been any questions or concerns that popped up. Take care of your clients, even after you are no longer paid to. Let them know you are still available, and they have help with any issues that arise. The more you nurture these relationships, the more likely they will recommend you to their friends, family and acquaintances, or return for further projects themselves.

In The Next Chapter...

In the next and final chapter, we will discuss how to build and market your business. You have all the knowledge on analyzing your approach with design, clients and contractors, but how about your fundamental business skills? We look at what you will need to do to promote your business, tips on marketing and creating a solid plan to generate ongoing business with a viable client base.

CHAPTER SIX - GETTING OUT THERE

In This Chapter, You Will Learn...

- The essentials of writing a business plan and its benefits
- Marketing techniques to build contacts and your client base
- How professional photography builds your portfolio and gains customer confidence

We will explore what you need to craft a viable, thriving and in-demand interior design business. Why? Because there is more to this industry than just picking out all the latest and greatest items in home décor and fashion. There is a little matter of organizing and promoting your business to keep the bills paid.

Get that notebook and pen handy. You will want to take notes and then do some research with the upcoming information.

The Business Plan

I hope this isn't the first time you have heard of a business plan. In case it is, a business plan is a curation of information related to the "real-life plan" and operation strategy of your business. It includes: your business's description, the operation practices, marketing plans, sales projections, cash flow and expense sheets, analysis of the market, your competitors and your backup plan should you run into obstacles.

That does not sound so bad. If you balked at it, I had the same reaction the first time I realized the enormity of research and work I had to do to prepare a business plan. So why would you bother with such a thing?

By researching and gathering all the information related to your business, you gain real insight into what it will take to run your business. You will not just be a designer; you will be a business owner. To do that, you must have a businessperson mindset and be ready to tackle opportunities and obstacles with your sharp problem-solving skills. You will become the expert on your industry, your marketing strategy, your competition, your contingency plans, your target market and most of all, your company.

The work is intimidating, yes. The benefits are hugely rewarding, though. Trust me. It is worth it in the end.

A little side note of great importance, if you require business financing of any kind, you will be asked for a business plan from the bank or finance company. Financial institutions want to see how equipped you are to repay their loan, how well you know your company and are viable. They also look at risk.

Even if you have no requirements for lending currently, a business plan is still a good idea. The strategies you create will be your guide to track sales projections, what you will charge and how many clients you need per month to break even and make a profit. You will know when and how to implement various marketing strategies.

After I calmed down a bit, I realized that I would have to tackle one element at a time not to get overwhelmed. By breaking it down into sections, the tasks seemed less daunting, and I got to work. Getting the information and writing my business plan became an adventure where I gained more confidence in myself and my abilities.

Now that I have got you convinced let's look at what a business plan entails. It is not difficult to do a Google search and find business plan templates. I have included a link to a site that provides a template and useful information on writing simple or more complex business plans.

I have borrowed the simple business plan outline from the following link but have elaborated further in the descriptions: https://articles.bplans.com/a-standard-business-plan-outline/

The following outline gives you the elements you will need to research and complete to create a complete and comprehensive business plan. Keep in mind that the order you complete them is not necessarily in the same order as the outline. The business plan starts with the Executive Summary, but it is completed last. Finish writing the other sections first.

Executive Summary – a one to two-page summary of the entire business plan. It is a quick snapshot of each section that highlights the main aspects of your business. The reader gets an overview of your business and is either intrigued enough to continue reading or stop. It includes a summary of the problem you are solving for your customers along with the solution. Who your target market is, who the founding member or owners are and the financial forecast. Remember that this is a summary, so keep it simple while encouraging the reader to learn more.

Opportunity – fully describe the problem or need you to resolve for your customers and the solution you are selling to solve them. It is more effective to define the needs and benefits from the customer's viewpoint, not just from the company's. Include how much the product or service costs, how you will deliver them to your customer and how you arrived at those numbers. Include cost and price sheets; however, more information is provided in the financial forecast.

Market Analysis – providing information and research on your target market, the types of customers you are looking for, including age, income, and how the target market may change. Discuss in more detail the target customer's needs, how you will reach them, where they live and how you will deliver your product/service to them. Describe your competitors and their location, what they charge for the same or similar services or products and how you will compete with them. Show that there is still room or opportunity for your business in the market.

Execution – outlines how you plan to market your business. Including: a marketing schedule with costs involved, sales projections (which will have more detail in the Financial Plan) and the logistics of running your business on a daily, monthly and yearly basis. Describe any technology or special equipment you will be using, such as Minutes Matter programs or specific camera equipment. Your place of business and facilities and what you need to get your business running. Also, it includes your contingency plan and how you will monitor your business to ensure it is on track and how you will handle obstacles.

Company and Management Summary: describe your company's structure. Includes: registration information as a sole proprietor or incorporated business, who the owner(s) and manager are, where the business is registered and where you do business. It is where you summarize your experience and education. Attach your resume to the business plan as well.

<u>Financial Plan</u>: all the financial data for the company. Including: the projected sales forecast for a year (two is even better), a P & L (profit and loss) and cash flow statement, a balance sheet and a brief description of the assumptions you made to come up with the numbers. Remember to include real-life data based on research to have a clear and realistic picture for the reader and your knowledge. Include information on what you will need to break even and at what point you will begin to make a profit. It is also where you will discuss any lending needs you have, your funds, and your repayment plan.

Please include any other pertinent documents relevant to your business plan.

As you can see, it is no joke. To consider yourself a serious business person, writing a well thought out and comprehensive business plan will prove to others that you have the 'chops' to run a successful company.

Marketing

Everyone in business is looking for the most effective marketing for the least amount of money. You will likely have learned a thing or two while researching your business plan, but if you are like me, you may have decided to come back to that section and read on. Hopefully, by giving you marketing tips and ideas now, it will help you form your business plan's marketing strategy.

Marketing methods had changed drastically from the time when I started my business to now. Newspaper advertisements have dropped drastically, as have telephone book directory ads. Radio advertising is also a struggle as more people opt for subscribed music apps and satellite radio in their vehicles. So how does a company reach their target market audience when some of these old tried and true methods are not getting the reach they once did?

Yes, social media is a considerable element of successful marketing strategies nowadays. We will discuss more of that in a moment. There are still many ways to market your business without breaking the bank.

Somewhere along the road, I learned that the most expensive advertising methods are often the ones with the least ROA (return on investment). That is disconcerting, especially when you have a minimal budget to work with. You are counting on those dollars to generate interest from your target market and turn into lucrative sales.

On the flip side, the least expensive marketing tools were the ones that tended to be the most successful. I will discuss social media campaigns and networking soon, but I want to go over more marketing fundamentals before we branch off.

Your most expensive forms of advertising are television, radio. Then they go down from there to magazine advertisements, newspaper, direct mail, email and social media campaigns, training seminars, webinars and podcasts down to word of mouth.

Guess which one is the most successful? Yep, you guessed it. Word of mouth. And while it cost you valuable dollars to get them through the preverbal door, that expense is spread out and lessened the more times that paying customers spreads the good word. It leads to viable leads and more business for you. That needs and deserves most of your attention when it comes to marketing.

It means that you need to have exceptional customer service skills. Empathizing with the customer's needs, wants and desires and meeting them preferably before realizing they had an issue requiring resolution. It entails service at the beginning of the interaction, during the process and following up not just after completion of the job but into the future. Customers/clients want to feel like they are part of your business family, even becoming loyal to your brand and concept. The more they feel nurtured and cared for, the more quickly they find value in you and your services/products. Then they can't stop talking about you to everyone they come across with a similar issue.

You become the expert in your field, the one in demand and the trusted advisor. It is the goal. You are spending more time and less money addressing your target market's needs and keeping the business machine turning out profitable word-of-mouth customers.

That isn't to say that you don't need a solid and appealing marketing presence on various platforms. I guarantee that those potential clients will look you up on your website, social media sites, and any Google reviews you may have before they reach out. It is a multi-layered approach that will bring these people across the finish line with their pocketbooks open.

Do not get me wrong here. Getting those initial clients will take experimentation of many different avenues to know what indeed works for you and what does not. The goal is to capitalize on those clients and encourage them to share their stellar experience with others. A great way to encourage this is by providing them with the link for a Google Review. Offer a referral program with a gift card to a restaurant or a fun activity for every paying referral they bring you. Be consistent in tracking these leads and referrals, though, as you need to follow through on your promise or risk your reputation.

> *Tip: Do not offer to give gift cards or payment for positive Google Reviews. It shows a lack of confidence in your business and genuine intentions with your clients.*

People tend to purchase with confidence more often when they have had a person or business referred to them. Even just seeing several positive reviews online gives them more confidence in the business's ability to help solve their need in a professional manner.

Be sure to respond to all reviews, no matter your feedback, quickly and positively. Offer to resolve any issues that show up, be classy and polite too. Other potential clients will see how you fix problems and determine whether they want to work with you. *Never* reply to negative feedback in a defensive or unprofessional manner. There is always a way to resolve the issue without appearing like you are scrapping it out with someone.

As I mentioned, television and radio advertisements are expensive for limited return. Still, the appeal is that they have access to large audiences. All the radio salespeople will tell you that it is crucial to be in front of your customers frequently and continuously for that marketing strategy to pay off. Businesses are paying monthly for daily ads (I am talking thousands of dollars a month per radio station) to promote their products or services. Having managed a multi-million-dollar business that opted for this route, I analyzed this marketing campaign very closely for ROA.

As years passed, I found we were becoming unsuccessful with various sales or promotions on the radio. Fewer people were willing to listen to the radio advertisements, preferring to listen to just the music or news. Heck, I was one of them. We spent upwards of six thousand dollars a month and did not get much return for the effort and expense. But the radio sales people were happy!

What did work for us? Aside from repeat customers, word of mouth and snazzy product offering, we layered our marketing strategy between direct mail, paid advertising on social media, trade shows, rebranding and merchandising our company. Our absolute best marketing tool was our location and the street signage that posted our specials and promotions.

The solution? Instead of spending over six thousand dollars a month on radio, I reduced our advertising budget to one thousand dollars except for scheduled months. We wanted a specific radio ad to go along with national campaigns. We spent less money for more awareness and an increase in our customer base.

It is one example of how challenging and expensive marketing can be. Especially when pointed at the wrong target audience or your message is not received. In terms of marketing for an interior design company, you will likely employ various methods to be seen as much as possible.

I have spoken before about writing for my local newspaper. Not only did my clients find me, believe me, to be an expert in my field and seek me out, but the newspaper *paid me* for my advertising. I did not promote my business within the article but instead gave tips and advice that people found valuable. They mentioned my business along with my contact information, but that was all.

People do the same through blog posts on their website. It includes guest posts on other social media platforms—any place where their audience may be interested in your products or services. Because there are so many people doing this, it may become challenging to reach people in the same way my newspaper articles did. We are getting to social media, I promise.

Several marketing elements include presenting who you are as an individual designer and your business in a recognizable way. It is your brand, and it is not limited to your logo. It is the typography you choose, the way you design your marketing materials and with what colors. It is *the foundation* of your marketing presence. Every piece of letterhead, every email, every ad, business card, pen and invoice will have this consistently presented and branded. Your brand will be stated repeatedly and must consistently reach across your website, printed materials and social media platforms.

Along with this, there are other tried and true marketing tools that you should think about for your interior design business. Of course, I may miss something that proves to be a worthwhile opportunity, so keep your eyes and mind open to new ideas. The idea is to be inventive and versatile because you never know what will prove to have stellar results or something no one else is doing.

Consider promoting your business by:
- Designing your unique brand, logo and color scheme to suit your business
- Build a branded dynamic, inspiring and

informative website
- Create a business presence on social media platforms such as Facebook, Instagram, Pinterest and LinkedIn
- Join industry-related groups and organizations both online and in-person
- Volunteer for causes close to your heart where you can also network
- Display your business and industry related trade show
- Publish articles, blogs, podcasts, webinars and how-to videos
- Distribute marketing brochures, promotional items and business cards to local businesses and suppliers in your trade area relative to interior design
- Join networking groups that give you the opportunity to present your business and trade leads for potential clients and projects
- Always have your business card on you, even at kids' sporting events, trips to the grocery store or running errands
- Use a graphic display of your logo, business name and phone number on your vehicle
- Display branded signage on clients' lawn while the project is underway
- Use promotional items as thank you gifts and incentives at trade shows
- Partner with realtors, home builders, trades and salespeople, and contractors when possible

- Direct mail campaigns targeting homeowners looking to sell their homes or renovate, perhaps when you are about to showcase your work or are in a tradeshow
- Use paid promotions on Facebook and Instagram to drive people to your various pages and website
- Dress for success everywhere you go as you are the 'face' of your company.
- Sponsor a local cause that provides good exposure for your business rather than just a mention
- Google Ads and Analytics to optimize your website and its content
- Free information event nights at one of your partnering suppliers to provide industry design tips etc. and showcasing your know how
- Joining your local Chamber of Commerce
- Utilizing all business programs aimed at growing, highlighting and supporting local business
- Customer referrals - gift card program
- Unsolicited client testimonials, with their permission, promoted in print or on social media
- Cultivate subscribers to your email list and promote yourself through email campaigns
- Hire students to drop fliers in home owners' mailboxes in select target areas.
- Creating a weekly, monthly and yearly mar-

keting strategy calendar
- Most importantly, *ASK FOR THEIR BUSINESS*

Marketing strategies to avoid:

- Paid realtor advertising folders
- Getting speeding tickets or breaking traffic laws while driving the vehicle with your advertising on it (including rude behavior while driving)
- Any marketing gimmick or scheme that requires you to pay monthly fees without options to cancel at any time
- The higher the price of advertising, the more you should triple think the worthiness of the expense
- Lending your brand or name to any project or business that does not have a good reputation
- Giving too much of your time away to clients, freebies and causes, especially when you are spending more time doing this than making money
- Donations to every request you receive, especially unofficial donation requests
- Emailing clients or subscribers excessively
- Not analyzing the success of marketing campaigns
- Not following and adjusting the marketing strategy calendar to accommodate for what is working and what is not

These are just some ideas of what you can do, and what you

should not, for your marketing campaigns. You will need an idea of what you can afford to spend monthly on marketing and stay within that budget. When researching your business plan, you will find the costs of all the marketing methods you intend to use. It will help you plan for both the expense and how you will accomplish sales to make it lucrative.

Make sure to analyze and document which campaigns are working for you by asking your clients or customers how they discovered your business. The more information you can get from them, the better. Ask what it was that brought them to you? Did the marketing material or online platforms appeal to them? Try to ask open-ended questions to get an in-depth understanding of their buying process. Only, be casual and light-hearted about it. I have stated, "We are analyzing our marketing strategies and would appreciate your feedback on how you dis-covered our business."

Marketing Schedule

Like having a schedule to track the design project, it is vital to have a planned-out plan for your marketing. You will have researched the costs involved for various forms of advertising and decided which of them were the best fit for your budget and business. You budgeted a monthly amount towards advertising in your cash flow plan as well. What do you need a marketing schedule for then?

A marketing schedule not only plans how much you spend where but highlights what the campaign will be, how many posts per day/week and how you will manage the content. For that matter, a well planned out marketing schedule will include the content you plan to use.

Large corporations plan their marketing for the entire year ahead, along with the campaigns they have designed for them. The benefit of this is you have a clear picture of how you drive your business's exposure. Still, being a smaller or independent company, you have more flexibility to react to events in the marketplace.

For instance, perhaps you foresee a trend emerging after attending a trade event or design show. You can integrate this into your marketing schedule with the relevant content without adjusting the rest of your marketing plan.

I suggest you look at the dates around trade shows, interior design events or shows, local annual charity functions, etc. See how you can craft your marketing around key interest points and then fit them into a calendar for the year.

Planning your marketing plan in advance gives you the time to design, print and deliver any materials and signage by the appropriate deadlines. In my experience, it creates a lot of panic when you discover a deadline is approaching and you are still in the middle of the graphic design. It can mean rushing and missing editing errors and paying more money for faster shipping options.

It can also save you from marketing too heavily in certain months and not at all in others. Not only will you be more consistent when marketing yourself, but you can plan out your spending for busy or slow months.

How To Make A Marketing Schedule:

- Start with a January to December calendar that allows you to fill in a decent amount of information each week of the month. If you are technologically inclined, create a calendar with Microsoft Office and edit it to your preferences
- Create a space to document monthly budget, deadlines, notes and potential target market reach for each week
- Research the dates of trade-related events that you plan to advertise around and put

document them on the relevant dates

- Plan the types of marketing mediums you plan to use around these events
- Research who you will use for graphic design, printing, delivering and how much time each will take. Using a different color, insert the dates you need to begin preparing the materials and the date you need to start delivering. Include deadlines and notes, so you have them at your fingertips later.
- Analyze your plan to see if you are using various marketing methods throughout the year on your schedule, whether one month is too heavy or going over budget. Ensure you include details of the campaign (Like a 'Color of the Year' launch) and what marketing methods you plan to use
- Print this off and keep it handy to refer to quickly and often. Analyze your campaigns for successful reach, turnover and total cost, so you have the numbers for your cash flow sheet but also to look back at the end of the year when planning the following year's schedule

As you can tell, this marketing schedule becomes your planner. The more you plan, the better you are prepared. The more prepared you are, the more time and money you save. I know I would rather spend my time designing projects and finding fabulous décor pieces.

It can be just as beneficial to plan your social media posts with a similar schedule. There are social media planners you can purchase for that very purpose. I would recommend using a monthly/daily calendar that allows you to schedule different posts and what the content will be, at various times throughout the day, and on what platforms. Being consistent keeps you front of mind with clients and potential customers. Still, it also keeps you from being repetitive or overdoing with a social media marketing planner.

Social Media

Here we are... as promised. I am going to discuss how social media is essential to your business in this modern age. Not only is it relatively inexpensive, but it is your all-access pass to your brand, style, experience and skills as a designer.

Anyone who hears your name, including your competition, will check you out on Instagram, Facebook, LinkedIn, and other available platforms. Including Google Reviews. They are likely to check you online if they are interested in your services, so it is a good idea to have your IP address for your website on everything.

It is also crucial to brand all your platforms throughout with the same feel, style, quality, fonts, colors, photography, descriptors, and language. Every time you create a post or blog, you use the same photo and 'blurb' across the board every time you make a post or blog. Instead, it means that a client will experience the same look and feel of your business, a flow if you will, as they travel between one platform to the next.

Navigating the world of social media may be a breeze to you, or it may seem like a maze without a map. There are many courses or blogs to teach you how to optimize your website and advertisements. Most of them will entice you with a freebie, begin with, and then attempt to sell you their program for success. Suppose you feel comfortable creating your ads and promoting them on your various social media accounts. In that case, this may not be worth the time or money. If you are genuinely lost, you may want a step-by-step guide through the process. I would start with the 'help' sections on advertising under each platform and then decide how much more instruction you need. There are lots of YouTube videos to guide you as well.

Content is the communication and information you provide to instruct your clients on contacting you and why you are the perfect person for their project. You want to use keywords and phrases that take you to the top of search engine lists. Keywords and phrases need to be used throughout articles, headings, titles, blogs, posts and business descriptions, but not overused to the point that the search engine blocks you. Don't make it awkward for your audience to read.

How do you know what keywords or phrases to use? Google Keyword Planner with Google Ads will help you discover what words or phrases are the most searched for in your industry. Even targeting top searches for specific geographical areas. It can save you a lot of time and blunders with ineffective content with your target market. The right keywords will have a wider reach and likely a better result with people in the target market you are aiming for.

Yes, you must sign up for Google Ads and be using 'Expert mode' to access this feature. Yes, you must pay to subscribe, but you will want this feature anyway. You will be able to properly optimize your website and advertisements according to any budget you set for yourself. It may seem like yet another form of a monthly payment. Still, I can assure you that you want to be showing up at the top of your target market's search list rather than page four, and your competitors will be using this tool too.

Google Ads has many tools to optimize your website, including providing analytics for your website, email and online marketing campaigns.

And... for a new businessperson who has never set up anything like this before, it can be overwhelming. Even more, experienced people can find the idea of setting up all their online profiles daunting. I would highly recommend checking out www.hubspot.com for any information on their free blogs that you can implement for yourself. If it interests you further and you need help, they have different packages to help you. Another good site is www.revlocal.ca.

One thing though, while I have discovered the ability and passion for writing, you may not have that talent up your sleeve. If you need help in that regard, you will need a copywriter and likely a graphic designer to help you put your platforms and campaigns together. It will be a worthwhile investment as you will be relying on your online presence for most of your marketing. You cannot afford to give the wrong impression or miss opportunities for clumsy headlines or content that your potential clients have trouble connecting with.

A professional copywriter can help you brand consistently between all mediums of your advertising. Each will communicate differently or have a different look. Still, all connect to your business smoothly with the same underlying message that converts lookers into paying clients.

The cost for a copywriter and graphic designer will vary depending on the scope of work you require and how much you can accomplish yourself. The more professionals you have on board, budget allowing, the more professional you appear. That is a monumental element to your success in the interior design business.

Paid advertising can go hand in hand between Facebook and Instagram as the same company owns them. You can opt to advertise your post on both. However, watch for the little slider button at the bottom of the Facebook advertising set-up page. Switch it off if you don't intend to advertise on Instagram as well. If you are promoting on both platforms, take your ad and double the price, which catches people off guard.

Facebook and Instagram advertising are as inexpensive or expensive as you wish them to be. When setting up the ad, you can refine key search topics such as home renovation, blinds and drapery or design, as well as the target area you are aiming for. It will show you the potential reach, which is the number of people that fit that criteria in the area and the cost for that promotion over your selected time. You may decide you are happy with the budget and location covered or choose to narrow it down.

Tip: You can begin your campaign with Facebook or Insta-
gram and allow it to run for a day or two while you are getting
the most traffic to your ad, and then cancel the promotion
before it completes the full schedule. You only get charged for
the time the ad is running, and you get the best exposure dur-
ing the beginning.
Monitor the number of people reached, and when you notice it
declining, that is the time to cancel or
pause the ad. It saves you money and still gives you optimal
exposure.

Social media is inundated with posts and advertisements. Without paid advertising, you rely on your friends and family following your site and hoping that other people navigate their way to you. But by promoting yourself, you can track down your target market, gear your content, relevancy and photography to their interests and gain more followers. That is where you have a legitimate following that helps your business.

You will undoubtedly find several options to get 'thousands of followers by...' from marketing schemes that promise you your business's exposure and success. Honestly, I find this disingenuous and for show. People who have not chosen to follow you for no other reason than to win something or trade shows waste your time. You want to be garnering dedicated clients and an interested audience in your business, not exposing your followers to a barrage of follow requests.

LinkedIn is a social networking platform geared towards professionals and business people to showcase your business and talents. How you market or post on this site will be vastly different than how you approach more entertainment-based platforms like Facebook or Instagram. Here you will be catering to colleagues, companies you want to partner with and less about customers. Of course, you may garner business from this approach. However, on LinkedIn, you are better to promote your education, projects you have completed and the successful results you achieved by working with other trades or builders.

On all social media platforms, the more you interact and make comments on others' pages and sites, the better. Showing genuine interest, not just suggestions or critiques, mind you, gives you a personal presence that is often lacking online. Give your followers praise and attention, respond to their comments or concerns with professional listening skills, and an open approach. These people are gold to you. If there is a concern that needs addressing, move the conversation to private messaging rather than respond on the public feed. You can manage the issue privately without additional comments coming from other followers. People are braver online than they are in person. You want to keep your platforms as positive and professional as possible. That said, your communications and responses need to be timely, cheerful, appreciative and relevant to your followers. Your posts included.

The success of a social media marketing strategy will come down to planning, consistency and exciting content. It will also take some finesse in the timing of and how often you post.

Tip: According to Revlocal.ca, here is the frequency you should post on each social media platform for optimal results: (for their blog on the reasoning, see "How Often Should Your Business Post on Social Media")

Facebook:	*1 per day, up to 5 times a week*
Twitter:	*3-5 times per day*
LinkedIn:	*1-2 per day, business related posts*
Instagram:	*1-2 per day*

When you begin developing your social media platforms, keep consistent messaging and branding in the forefront of your mind, then dig in and have some fun with it! You are a designer, after all, and you can use your creative talents daily through social media along with your interior design projects. If you get to the point where you are too busy to post according to the suggestions above, you can hire out your social media management. You want to ensure that you are using a person or company to maintain your standards and help you plan your messaging and promotions properly. It may take some initial meetings and communication while they handle this for you, but they should save you time, not take more of it.

Overall, social media is no longer just a frivolous waste of time for people with nothing better to do. It is how people entertain themselves, shop, communicate and promote their business. You do not want to be left behind. Connecting with your clients... past, potential, current and future, will be through the various avenues of social media, not just email or your website.

While giving your clients the ease of finding you on various platforms, there is nothing important as your website's online presence.

Website

You will need a website for your business. All of your online marketing leads to your website, and it acts as your digital business card.

Marketing is always about promoting yourself, attracting the people who need your services and are most likely to use your services or buy your products. Your website is a way for them to check you out without having to speak to you directly. Yes, people prefer to do some research on businesses before they commit to a physical conversation.

Your website holds all the vital information about your company, past, current and future projects, who you partner with and promote. It is where you not only tell your visitors about your company but also about yourself. Even better, present testimonials of clients who tell other people about their experience with you and your company for you.

According to Hubspot.com, ninety-two percent of consumers hesitate to make a purchase (or "convert" from looking to buying/book-

ing) if there are no customer reviews. Ninety-seven percent say customer reviews factor into their buying decision.

They call this 'social proof.' Those statistics are strong indicators that your visitors are more likely to believe your past clients than all the marketing and promotions you do for yourself.

You better believe it. You need to have the whole package between visually pleasing photography, relevant and exciting content, ease of use within your website and social media platforms. Oh, and you need to provide value for your products and services too.

Creating your website from scratch might send you over the edge if creating your social media platforms was not already daunting enough. Unless you have a side gig as a website designer, that is. Thankfully, there are some great sites out there that will take care of this for you.

Websites like www.wix.com or www.godaddy.com will not only provide easy to use templates that you can use to customize your website, but you can purchase and manage your domain name here too.

On the other hand, should you wish to invest in a professionally designed website, it is worth paying a professional to format, organize and implement your webpage correctly. There are integrations for pop-ups and subscription opt-ins you may want to consider. Professional website designers can charge one thousand dollars and up. Still, when you believe this to be one of your primary marketing tools. It is a worthwhile expense, especially if it saves you the time to design it yourself.

I would recommend that the first thing you do is get busy purchasing your business name, if not your name. Purchase a '.com' or a '.ca' domain if you can. It is your first branding point that your clients will identify with you when they are online. The same goes for your social media usernames. Keep them consistent and easy to locate.

The first page that your visitor finds, whether they did an online search or typed in your URL, is called the main landing page.

It acts as an introduction to your business, and first impressions are crucial. The main page's information should include: a welcome message, a headline and subhead that portrays your motto and statement for your company, a short description of your business that entices the visitor to investigate the other pages, and beautiful professional photography.

Other pages on your website can include: an 'About Us' page, 'Projects,' 'Trades & Partners', and 'Blog.' Of course, you can customize these to your company, and you will want to brand them as well.

As you create content for each page, make sure you use the same keywords and phrases you used in your social media platforms. And, especially, your marketing campaigns. It helps your rankings with Google Ads and lowers the cost of bidding on the words and phrases, making your business more relevant to search engine queries. But you want to use the Google Ads tools to analyze which keywords and phrases are the most popular and relevant to you, or Google will advertise outside of your target market. Therefore, your ads become less successful. Again, consider www.hubspot.com or www.revlocal.ca for information on optimizing your advertising and website, as well as a professional copywriter.

A successful website will incorporate various means of communication too. Consider including videos, tutorials, audio/podcasts, photography and written content. You want to appeal to all the senses, just like in sound design, as much as possible. I realize you cannot recreate smells through your website. You can procure the memory of scent through visuals... just a thought. If done correctly, your visitors get a more fulfilling experience on your website. It gives them more reason to stick around and explore all your pages, encouraging them to move from 'thinking about it' to 'I'm in!'

Having beautifully crafted content designed to engage your visitors and turn them into clients is one element. Include links embedded in the content that lead to blog posts, or even better, a call-to-action (CTA). Encourage them to subscribe with a freebie as an incentive. You do not want to overdo it, but the real magic happens when they not only follow you on social media but join your email list too.

You want to create free how-to's, checklists and blogs as incentive pieces that encourage your visitors to provide their email addresses to you. You offer the freebie on an automated 'Thank You' page as a download or a link that opens in a separate window on their browser. It lets them read over the information you provided without moving away from your website, as it is still open in the original tab.

As a designer, you must market your designs. The only way to accomplish this is to provide top-notch professional photography on your website and social media platforms, especially visual ones like Pinterest and Instagram. Having photos taken with your phone just will not cut it on your marketing mediums. You can get by with these photos for a regular post, but not on your website. You are trying to showcase your abilities and the finished result of projects.

Professional Photography

Have you ever been sucked into a photograph on the cover of a magazine or an Instagram page? One of the most recent photos I could not take my eyes off Vanity Fair's July/August 2020 cover of Viola Davis. It lit perfectly to hint at the color of her dress against a similar colored background. There was little contrast between her skin, the fabric and the backdrop. There was just a hint of her silhouette in the lighting. It was divine and striking, but still soft, and I could not stop going back to it.

That is the effect you are looking for with the photography of your projects, products and even your services. Your portrait should be a professional portrayal of who you are for your clients. I doubt you will need to hire the calibre of photographer that would come with magazine shoots, but if you can afford it, then fill your boots. And of course, I do not mean that you should stage your photography shoots to be as elaborate as a photo-shoot either.

When your potential clients fall upon your blissful website, I guarantee it will be the impact of your photographs that entices them to book a consultation with you.

You need a photographer in your back pocket, maybe two, who understand how to set up angles, lighting, and filters that best highlight interior design projects and understand marketing to some degree. You are not just looking for a quick picture. You are looking to create interest points and highlight specific design elements unique to your skills and brand.

You will likely have seen some photographers on social media posts or through some of your networking channels. We will discuss that more in a moment. It is vital to see their work and investigate the comments and reviews from their customers. Check out their website. When you are ready, have an in-person meeting to see how you click.

The photographer who fits your needs the most can provide the goods and be a team member you can rely on with strong communication skills between the two of you. You will be re-laying what you are trying to accomplish with a photoshoot. They need to bring their creative skills to the table to meet your expectations. Yes, you are their client, but I guarantee you, this person will become part of your essential team that you cannot live without. The right photographer will make it easy to work with them and have ideas you had not even thought of. They are your design guru who showcases you to potential clients and who also gives you a tangible and marketable product for your services.

When you begin looking for this person, remember that they need to eat too. Many people think they can just trade services or want a photographer to undercut their listed prices. This is not honoring or valuing what they do. When you get going as a de-signer, you will know how that feels when you get texts or mes-sages asking for 'quick free advice.'

Remember, you can include the costs of photography within

your pricing for your clients and then work out an agreement between you and the photographer. They will want constant work and the chance to work with someone who is providing it to them.

What about when you are just starting? That is okay. Do some trial runs with prospective photographers to see how you like their work and pay them for their time. Let them know you are willing to pay their regular price now but would like to renegotiate as you get busier. The other lovely thing is that you use the photography on your website and your social media posts. You can credit them, which is also marketing their work. It is a valuable element for the photographer. Like you, the more times they can get their name to show up on something, the more potential business contacts you can reach.

You can credit trades, suppliers, brands and others who have collaborated on your project too. As you share your contacts and partners, consider that it is not just potential clients seeing your posts. Your competition will be paying attention to the projects you are doing. Some of them may have lost out to you on a job. They are only too happy to use any information you provide to copy what you are doing. Clients could also try to go directly to the source as well. These are things to think about as you market yourself. You want to protect your contacts at the same time.

Photos will come to you in specific file sizes. Compress digital files for mobile phone users on your site, which may be a different format for desktop users. Otherwise, you want high definition (HD) shots for your website and social media campaigns. Smartphone photos are not optimal for websites. You need digital camera photos.

In the age of selfies, this is not where you want to promote yourself with them. Get a professional photo of yourself, preferably with you in a casual conversation with someone just off-screen. The formal portrait speaks of a dated time, and while they are professional, you want a modern feel to them. Your photographer will have a better idea of how to accomplish this with you. Consider a professional photo for your 'About Me' page on your website. Casual but classy pictures may create interest throughout your website and social media platforms. The formal shot will be more suitable for your LinkedIn profile, for instance.

What if I cannot afford to hire a professional photographer for my design projects? Sometimes when you are just starting, it is hard to pay considerable fees, including photography expenses. I would suggest using a good quality digital camera that takes wide-angle shots and educate yourself on the basics of its settings. Without purchasing extra flashes and lighting rigs, you will have to rely on the room's lighting and what the camera provides.

At the bare minimum, have your portrait photography done professionally and wait until you have a design project worth hiring a pro to create marketing material and shots for you. Once you have a portfolio going, you will have the ball rolling towards having all your photography being of that calibre. When that time comes, make sure that older, remove unappealing shots from your platforms and website.

Networking

Easily one of the most intimidating marketing methods is networking. Networking involves meeting people, sometimes in large groups, intending to talk about your business and generate interest.

Where do you network with other people?

It happens every day at the local coffee shop or our kids' soccer game. Networking is a social gathering with two or more people who connect and share information. In some cases, it is a more formal gathering like a fundraiser or a business party. Other times it is running into an acquaintance while you are running an errand. Often, your local Chamber of Commerce hosts monthly networking events to introduce new businesses to their current membership.

Networking can include paid membership groups with a focused agenda of promoting the members to prospects they acquire through their day-to-day operations. They track leads, follow-ups, and conversions and provide training material and moral support in each other's business endeavors. They can also offer mentoring or give creative ideas to each other. The members rotate on presentations of their company to the group. They attend one-on-one meetings at each other's physical business and even bring potential members as guests to expose them to the networking possibilities. Some groups cost a pretty penny to join, and there is an application process proving the viability of your company. Still, there have been some solid success stories that come from them. I know some who stayed in business during slumps in the economy because of referrals from their fellow members alone.

Networking is a vital tool to have in your marketing methods. The more you can physically put yourself out there, the more likely people are to remember you. Posts get lost in the multitude of mass daily social media input. People will not know you are still actively in business unless you are showing up in the community.

Okay, but how does one talk to strangers?

For some people, they have a gift of starting conversations with strangers and rolling into a full-blown exchange where they become buddies after that. I have known one or two of them, and it takes real charisma. Others struggle with knowing what to say, who they should approach or avoid and how to promote themselves without coming off as pushy.

I was always the quiet observer in my life, so I found that it took a lot of practice and several years before becoming more comfortable with it. But while you feel a little unsure of yourself, I guarantee others in the room feel the same way. And the 'ice breakers' will find you too.

First, you must appear confident in yourself. If you show up biting your nails, looking like you are about to run for the bathroom, or like the only reason you came was for the food, people will be less inclined to talk to you. It defeats the purpose of you being there.

Second, you need to smile and have an open expression. If you do not look pleasant, again, people will avoid you. It is okay to make eye contact and smile at people as you enter the room. Say hello to people, offer your business card and ask for theirs.

Third, stand up tall and be seen. Get into the center of the room. Check out display tables and engage in conversation with presenters. Show people that you are the professional and trusted advisor in your field. Wear clothing with some color to it, even if it is an accessory like a scarf or a handbag. It gives something for people to comment on. Also, use the coat check and keep your hands free as much as possible. Refrain from fidgeting and having to empty your hands to shake someone else's.

And lastly, talk. After introducing myself, I found that if I asked the other person about their business and how they got into it, it carried the conversation a little longer. Then, usually, they would eventually get around to asking the same thing of me.

These conversations give you valuable clues as to whether this person has the potential to become a partner, collaborator, client or someone who can refer your business to others. And visa versa. You never know who will become a beneficial ally, so be careful not to write anyone off after a networking event.

I met people through a Chamber of Commerce, 'Business After Hours' event. I did business with them through my home staging company and then again later when managing the decorating center. These relationships can last for years, and often, they become friendships of sorts.

Do some research on networking opportunities in your area and make a list of them. Make a point of joining home builder associations, the Chamber of Commerce, trade organizations and even volunteer for causes close to your heart, but that relate well with your company. Offer to be a guest speaker at one of their events.

Networking may seem a bit nerve-wracking to begin with. Eventually, you will get the hang of it and appreciate the value of this relatively inexpensive tool. The more you attend, the more comfortable these networking events will feel. When you can pull off one of these events with ease, it will feel like nothing to manage less formal networking situations.

Conclusion

It is not the time to be shy. Promoting your company does not always happen with a clever advertisement. You are *always* promoting yourself, whether you know it or not. Do not leave the house or your office without an adequate supply of business cards stocked in your purse or wallet. Leaving them in the car will not do. You must have them on you when the moment to exchange information presents itself.

Marketing your business will be your second full-time job, but there will be no primary full-time job without it. Do it wisely, efficiently and consistently. Marketing will feel less complicated, and you will see a solid return on your investment. If you are not, then you have missed the mark in reaching and converting your target market.

Remember to analyze and analyze some more. Update your website, refresh your feeds and keep your brand in front of your target market. Tweak what needs tweaking and observe what is working. Revisit past clients and keep those relationships alive. Host appreciation events that tie launches a new product or service. Be brave, bold and creative in your marketing that speaks to your target audience and lures them in.

Time To Fly The Nest

Here we are. You have powered your way through all the knowledge I could think of to share with you. I am humbled to say thank you. It is one thing to share tips and information, and it is another to have someone read it and, hopefully, find it useful.

Now you understand yourself as a designer and a business-person. You have a grasp on relationships with clients, trades and salespeople. You know the steps of selecting a product and design elements. You understand the nitty-gritty of how they all work, and finally, how you become the trusted advisor and mar-keting guru to be the best interior designer you can be.

If there is one thing I know, it takes a tremendous amount of guts to follow your dreams. Many nay-sayers out there gave up on their dreams. They decided to become professional critics of anyone trying to achieve theirs.

I'm telling you, follow your heart. When something feels truly exciting, you are on the right path. Whether that is your design career, finding the right area rug or nailing the best Instagram post *ever.* Your gut instinct is your best and the only tool you will ever need, and I hope that my book has given you more confi-dence to follow it.

Again, thank you for trusting me with your time. Thank you for bringing beauty and pleasure to people's lives. We all need more of that. Thank you for challenging yourself, uplifting others and inspiring them to dream too.

What better than to be a facilitator of someone's dream com-ing true?

Good luck to you in your interior design endeavors. May suc-cess come to you in reputation, creativity, health, wellbeing and abundance. I hope you shine bright and bring people into your light with you so the world can be a better place. And last but not least, I hope you find real joy on your path personally, profes-sionally and with your family. We never travel alone.

Until next time,

Jenny Kennedy

Printed in Great Britain
by Amazon

13170980R00151